Dancing
with the
Witchdoctor

*One Woman's Stories of Mystery
and Adventure in Africa*

KELLY JAMES

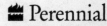 Perennial

An Imprint of HarperCollinsPublishers

First Perennial edition published 2002.

Designed by Jessica Shatan

Maps by Jeffrey L. Ward

The Library of Congress has catalogued the hardcover edition as follows:
James, Kelly.
   Dancing with the witchdoctor/Kelly James.
     p. cm.
   ISBN 0-06-018627-5
     1. James, Kelly. 2. Women private investigators—California—San Francisco—
   Biography. 3. Criminal investigation—Africa—Case studies. I. Title.
   HV8083.J35 A3 2001
   363.28'9'092—dc21
   [B]   00-54621

ISBN 0-06-093390-9 (pbk.)

02 03 04 05 06 ❖/RRD 10 9 8 7 6 5 4 3 2 1

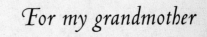
For my grandmother

*As a woman I have no country. As a woman
my country is the whole world.*

—VIRGINIA WOOLF

About the Author

KELLY JAMES is an international investigator. She also gives seminars on international business culture and, when time allows, lectures to third-world university women on the international job market. Aside from English, James speaks Swahili, Zulu, Spanish, and Greek. She lives mostly in Mexico.

CONTENTS

Many of the names and physical characteristics of various characters who appear in this book have been changed to protect their privacy.

Dancing
with the
Witchdoctor

INTRODUCTION

The women in this book are real; their stories are true. These heroic odysseys happened to me, but they are not about me. I am the teller, the conveyor of messages from cultures far away but as real as your own. I feel I could begin these tales with the words "Call me Kelly," echoing the first line of my second favorite book. The events of Herman Melville's *Moby-Dick* happened to Ishmael, but the book was not about Ishmael. However, if Ishmael hadn't told the story, we would not have known Moby-Dick or Captain Ahab and the rest of the crew.

My name is Kelly James. What you need to know about me, I'll tell you now. I am an international private investigator. For twenty years, I've been paid to investigate on five continents and in more countries than I can remember, but it was in Africa that I realized my greatest adventures and most memorable insights into the human experience. A few of my friends who've talked me into sharing an escapade with them will tell you that I'm an "addict of dancing on the edge." Addict, dancer, maybe, but I am certainly a gypsy, a sleuth, and an adventurer. I do tort work, investigating safari, ship, and plane accidents for plaintiffs' attorneys. I also search for missing persons and investigate murders and thefts, sometimes in concert with or at crossways of international law. Also, I take on tangled assignments for multinational corporations, many more in the last ten years as the corporate search for cheap labor and new markets extends to third- and fourth-world countries. In addition to a couple of fairly useless degrees, the credentials for what I do consist of languages, cultural studies, a great deal of travel, and skills in living without luxury.

My work in third- and fourth-world countries is far from glamorous. It isn't easy and it isn't conducive to long-term institutional relationships, such as religion and marriage. I'm the tired, stray woman in jeans you see on the plane or train ordering a cognac and a pillow, the runny-nosed woman in the drugstore late at night buying cough syrup, or the woman eating alone at the counter admiring someone's grandchildren. If you look close, you might see me on a dusty airstrip waiting for a ride or on the bow of a cargo ship entering or leaving some grimy port.

In reality, I'm an explorer. My first favorite book is *The Search for the Source of the Nile,* the intrepid adventures of the nineteenth-century explorer Sir Richard Francis Burton. I read it when I was twelve and knew then and there that I was destined to emulate Sir Richard. That one book held everything and everywhere I wanted to be, and it still does on the days I dream. From that one book, I began a lifetime love affair with Africa.

I lay the credit and blame for who and what I am on Sir Richard Burton, but that's my short, curt answer to the often-asked "Why?" The truth is, when I was first introduced to that big, beautiful book, I was most certainly primed and most probably genetically programmed. It happened on a Sunday near my twelfth birthday.

Our ranch had been crowded for several days. It was late summer and harvest time in the wilds of the northwest a few miles from Canada, and the other ranchers in the area had come to help. It was the custom. The women stayed in the house, cooking and sewing, working on the recipes and quilts they would enter into next week's county fair. I worked with Papa on the thresher, running errands, feeling important. Two years older than my sister, I was my father's son. He taught me to ride before mother took off my booties. He taught me to shoot—kill game and dress it. He taught me that fear was something to be looked in the face and challenged. I was just five when he taught me direction by blindfolding me, slapping the quirt to my horse, and sending us at a lope into the perilous forest. I could read a U.S. Government Survey map before I could read a book and a compass before I could tell time. One of my rewards, when I was very good, was to sit atop one of Papa's prized Clydesdales, he atop the other, and we would ride for two days in search of stray cattle. Big events were auctions, horse shows, and buying new cowboy boots. Life couldn't have been better. That is, until that day of harvest when I came to an inevitable impasse and was rescued, in the nick of time, by the dauntless Sir Richard.

Of the ranchers' children, there were only girls, my sister and I and four others, a fact that was always, at sometime during these cooperative occasions, noted by the women in private, hushed confessions. My own mother blamed the doctor for botching the delivery of my sister, rendering her incapable of another birth, which would surely have been the son Papa wanted. Betsy, the woman who made the county's best headcheese, insisted it was the water on their ranch that had left her barren, with the exception of only a daughter. All the women had their alibi for breeding failure and ongoing exoneration seemed to be a necessary part of their community.

The four girls from the other ranches were older than me by several years, and they had always tossed older-girl smiles to my sister and me, like decorated cookies. I'd watched these girls go from kittens to dogs, dogs to horses, and jeans to dresses. On this occasion of harvest, they came wearing dresses sewn with darts pointing toward their pert bosoms and shoes with short narrow heels that stuck in the cracks of the floor. They stayed inside, cloistered in affected whispers about boys and movies. These were ranch girls, not girls from town! Girls from town, the ones at school an hour and a half bus ride away, were expected to be girls, ruffled and prissy. But these ranch girls represented, unless there was a miracle, which I prayed for, what I would become: a girl with bumps on my chest and exposed legs extending out of patent leather shoes. The threat these girls presented put the same knot in my stomach that Old Man Brooks did when he turned from farmer to preacher, ranting fire, brimstone, and death to the sinner, which he did during harvest, coinciding with his yearly batch of corn liquor.

And so it was on that Sunday, near my twelfth birthday, that the only two things that I had feared in my life—and until then had convinced myself were as far away as China and old age—had combined forces like a two-headed snake. I was going to turn into a girl, and I was going to burn eternally for convincing my father that I was a boy. Both were probably going to happen sooner rather than later.

It happened at tea time, this astounding realization. The house was a plethora of colored aprons, quilts, and table linen, and combined with the smells of pies, cakes, and the evening meal roasting in the oven, it was intoxicating. The men and I sat together around the big table, tired, hungry, and quiet. The women and other girls sat around the smaller table giddy with conversation. I watched them, those nearly nubile girls with their pinkies up, cheeks rouged, left hands politely in their laps, speaking in their mothers' voices. Suddenly, the fear that had been creeping like a leopard at midnight pounced. Jumping out of my chair to the sounds of breaking glass and women's gasps, I hit the door running.

Bolting to the barn, choking on the cloud of new hay that hung there, I began throwing blankets and bridles out of the tack room, preparing to saddle my horse, Jerry. It was difficult to see with the haze of hay so thick, my eyes streaming, the sun in blinding streaks creating empty shadows. I was on Jerry, riding out of the corral, before I realized that I had Papa's saddlebag. I wasn't allowed to ride without my saddlebag, which contained a thirty-eight revolver, a snake kit, a compass, and dry rations. I didn't care. I wasn't going back. Papa's would do; it contained the same stuff and more, and he wouldn't be riding that day. In a thundering lope, Jerry and I streaked toward the pond on the south forty, with my dog, Red, womanhood, and fire and brimstone all breathing down my neck in hot pursuit.

I sat for a long time in the high grass around the pond looking at my reflection, as I often did. It was Papa's face, Papa's curly Irish red hair. "Spitting image," I was often told, an expression my grandmother said was Southern and began as a bastardization of "spirit and image." I took off my shirt and stood up to see the mirror of my chest, throwing back my shoulders and breathing deep to mimic Papa's barrel chest. There were no lady bumps, just ribs, the bony ribs of a skinny kid who would be metamorphosed into a woman and burn in hell for lying. I opened Papa's saddlebag, looking for his pistol. They would find me still a boy, a boy who could ride and hunt and bail hay and slaughter cows, a boy my Papa had been proud of.

Papa's pistol was snug against his burlap book pouch, which usually contained only a light paperback by Zane Grey or Louis L'Amour. But the pouch was heavy, its seams stressed. I opened it, curious. I found a big, broken-backed book with gold-edged pages. The only book I'd ever seen with gold-edged pages was my grandmother's Bible and Papa never read the Bible. The green gilt-stamped cloth of the cover was worn thin and the title faded: *The Search for the Source of the Nile.*

Intrigued, I sat back down in the high grass with the book, Papa's gun and Red by my side. Almost immediately, I felt the transformation in me begin. Reading voraciously the depictions of people and creatures alien and extraordinary, events lurid and wondrous, I felt consumed with a quest to explore the world expanding before me. The light had faded and I was squinting at the pages before I knew that several hours had passed. Jerry stood under a tree, snoozing. I moved closer to the pond to see my reflection again, sure that it had changed. And it had.

The pond was now stirring, a vast cinema reflecting the odysseys of the valiant Sir Richard and his cohorts John Hanning Speke, Sir Samuel Baker, Dr. Stanley Livingston—brave, brash, and brilliant! It was a preview, I decided, of the person I would become. I would be what I was in training to be, had practiced and honed the skills for: an explorer in a world where disparity was the order and whether I was male or female was inconsequential.

That was the day I began my trek, my love affair with Africa, right then and there at the pond on the south forty. But it would have been a course without a compass except for one other significant genetic factor: my maternal grandmother. It has been said that my grandmother and I have more in common than a name. Without question, she is a heroine to me—and a mentor.

By the time I knew my grandmother, she was in her fifties, had outlived three husbands and was somewhat of a legend, at least within the far reaches of her social life, which she devoted mostly to philanthropic organizations. But within the family, she was remembered for surviving the ravages of poverty and for the ornery stubbornness she used like a weapon. The oldest of six children, she was farmed out as a midwife's assistant until she was ten years old, then given a job assisting the local undertaker in embalming bodies. Her mother was dead by then, and she had assumed her role as well, teaching etiquette, cooking, and sewing to her sisters, and wrestling manners and self-esteem into her brothers. When the last sibling left the confines of the rambling family unit, my grandmother married. In only a few years, consumption had taken her husband and she was a widow raising four children without benefit of anything but her own well-honed iron will. My mother recalls being one of four towheaded siblings living in Arizona with their Amazonian mother and a tribe of Indians. For nearly four years my grandmother was crew boss over a band of Yaquis, who worked by government arrangement for a cotton plantation. She spoke the language and kept her crew working, out of Mexico, out of jail, and in their tepees, which kept her own children fed and housed and eventually enabled them to move on to a better life in California.

There were those who didn't like my grandmother, certainly the timid. She wasn't an affectionate woman, but within her presence one felt safe or at least on the side of power. By everyone's account, she was strong, brave, honest, and incredibly ornery when crossed. I always cheered on her orneriness, knowing in my heart that she was carrying the banner of good over evil. It was also said of her, especially by family, "She had a need to look under every rock." I always thought that looking under rocks, studying situations from every angle, contributed greatly to her wisdom and to her sensibility, a quality that I'd been brought up to believe was inherent to the Scots. I truly feel a little of her Scots blood pulsing in mine. Most of my family will tell you, while they roll their eyes, that there's more than a little and that it's more than the looking under rocks, which might be true. She taught me things, important things. She taught me to play baseball and chess and that they were the same as the game of life. And she taught me, "Do what you do well and there will always be a path."

As it turned out, what I did best was private investigation. My San Francisco business provided me with sufficient income to travel Africa, trekking the routes of Sir Richard; re-creating those images reflected in the pond; studying African cultures, politics, and languages. I had two well-developed paths, which were separate, until yet another memorable Sunday.

It was brunch at the Palace Garden Court, a formal gastronomical ritual at my favorite San Francisco restaurant. My services were being romanced by a well-known chubby lawyer who toasted me with mimosas. Under a turn-of-the-century glass canopy, he told me why. He was handling a buffalo-goring case that had taken place at a popular tent camp in the Maasi Mara of Kenya: one mean buffalo, two women gored, one dead. Over eggs piled with caviar, I told him that I knew of the safari incident. I had been in Kenya at the time; I knew the camp, the players, and, most importantly to his case, I knew the safari guard responsible for the women. His rusty World War II rifle hadn't been fired since the hunting moratorium in Kenya had removed meaning from his life and he chose a new one with Jack Daniel's. And yes, I spoke Swahili. "Would I investigate the case?" he asked me.

Would I investigate the case? Like a clap of thunder on a summer's day, the two paths of my life became one. My grandmother's advice was that everything until then had been training. Now, just like Sir Richard, I was responsible for writing it all down. A great writer of letters to her widespread family and enormous circle of friends, a storyteller and historian, my grandmother encouraged me. The four stories in this book first appeared in letters I wrote from Africa to my grandmother.

I have now told you all you need to know to "Call me Kelly." And so it is, with the spirit and image of Sir Richard, my Papa, and my grandmother, that I bring to you these four odysseys, all unrelated, all taking place in the 1980s, when my love affair with Africa was in full bloom. These four are first, in honor of my grandmother. Always one to rally round indomitable women, she loved these stories. There will be more. I've promised.

Detour

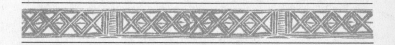

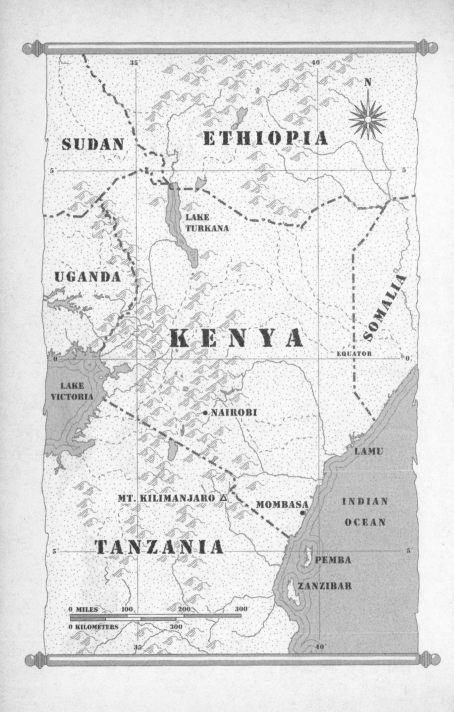

The zebra-striped buses crammed with the Norfolk Hotel's camera-armed tourists were still in the bush. This was the time of day when the locals crowded the patio bar to drink quinine with gin and savor the late edition of Nairobi's social and political dirt. Today, I didn't need any. What I needed was to be on a plane home. Instead, I was keeping an eye out for a brown leather jacket, black beret, ponytail, and sandals. His name was Frank Wagner Jr., German, arriving from Frankfurt. I'd never met him, but on the basis of his description, the time I'd been waiting, and the two beers I'd consumed, I wasn't going to like him. Worse, he was keeping me from my flight to San Francisco. Home. I didn't tire easily of Africa, but I'd been in three countries in as many months, missed celebrating my fortieth birthday, and had returned to Kenya only two days before. And it was September. September in San Francisco makes April in Paris a wholesome stepsister. I lusted for home.

The call had come the day before from a London barrister named Charles Childress. He'd interrupted my happy packing. "It's a jolly lot of money for a few days at best, Kelly dear. A simple matter of confirming the police report." His drollness be damned. Confirming a Kenyan police report could trap me there until Halloween, particularly if murder was suspected. But Childress had me by the wallet.

I sat with the dregs of my beer, visualizing a wide-brimmed cup of frothy cappuccino at Puccini's. My North Beach neighborhood friends would be there: warm smiles, fuzzy dogs, sexy neon stories, and, if I got lucky, maybe a little neon for me. I could see the glassy bay, taste the salty air. "Ms. Kelly?" The German was standing at my table, beret in hand.

In ten minutes I knew all I wanted to know about the German. Some of it he told me. He wasn't particularly interested in whether his stepmother, Freda Wagner, had killed herself, or been killed and by whom. Frank Wagner Jr. was only interested in settling her affairs, that is, her personal effects: bank accounts, money. Freda had married Frank Sr. when Junior was eighteen. That was sixteen years ago, when he was just getting his rock and roll career started. He'd been pretty busy since then, never really getting to know her. His own mother died when he was ten. His father died only two and a half years ago, of malaria, just before their Kenyan coffee farm was sold. Freda collected money from that sale, money that must still be in Kenya. Junior was squirming in his leather jacket, confident he was making a bad impression.

I confirmed it for him. "So then, you've come with authority to inherit whatever she left. Finding out how your stepmother died was the lawyer's idea?"

"Well, yes." He was rubbing his thin lips together, tugging at his stubby ponytail. "I am her only heir."

"And if she was murdered?" I asked. "Your lawyer seemed to believe she may have been murdered."

He shuffled his sandals, examining them until he thought of what to say. "Our lawyer knew her for years, said she had malaria, but doesn't believe she would kill herself. She was one of those strong, educated women who . . ." Contorting his puffy posture, he gave me a glance and didn't finish. I waited. After a few moments he seemed to resolve his hesitation, shot me a dagger, and went on. "Maybe she was murdered. But that's a police matter, is it not, Ms. Kelly? Shouldn't we concentrate our efforts on finding the money? Her accounts in Frankfurt are empty." Still shuffling his sandals, he whined, "I should have been here long before now. The trail might be cold. She should have had at least two hundred and fifty thousand dollars, her share of the sale of the coffee business. She wouldn't have been carrying that around with her. It must be somewhere in a Kenyan bank."

His demeanor suggested desperation. I needed to know about the sale of the coffee farm. I also needed to see the paperwork, particularly the police report. We couldn't do it there. I'd booked him a room at the Norfolk. I took him upstairs.

While I raked through the papers in Frank Wagner's briefcase, Frank called room service for beer and rummaged in his jacket for a joint. Lit up, hyperventilating, pinky up like a pro, he transformed himself into a rocker: babbling, painting images of bitchin' gigs, bitchin' women, bitchin' drugs. His English was American; he'd lived in New York for ten years. He said he played in an American band, but when I asked which one, he changed the subject. When I asked him again, he raised his several chins defensively and said that it was all coming together, he was almost there. As if to punctuate the fact that his star was rising, he pulled a harmonica out of his pocket and played a little something that sounded like bad bagpipes.

After a few bars he put his harp away and I directed his energy toward enlightening me. Flinging his tattooed arms carelessly over the back of the sofa, exposing the sweat stains of his Rolling Stones T-shirt, he toked and began a rote dissertation of the Wagner family history, which he admitted had been related to him by the family lawyer several days before.

His grandfather bought the coffee farm when Kenya belonged to England. He was killed in the bloody Mau Mau, the uprising that brought about Kenya's revolution and eventually its independence. The coffee farm was mostly burned. His father and mother built it up again, putting in a lot of hard work, which contributed to his mother's death in 1959. After independence in 1963, there was new Kenyan law. The only way his father could keep the farm was to sell it, then lease it back. When he no longer owned the land, though, he took less interest in running the coffee business and spent more time in Germany. In 1967 he married Freda.

Frank stopped his droning account of the Wagners long enough to let the bellman in with the beer. Then he swilled, toked again, and said, "This is where our heroine, Frau Freda, comes in, whoever she was. You'll like this part." Impatient, I motioned for him to finish.

Freda loved the farm and spent more time in Kenya than his father. But after Jomo Kenyatta was assassinated and Daniel Moi became president, there was continuous civil unrest—constant controversy over labor reform—and it took both of them to run the farm full-time. When Frank's father contracted malaria, Freda assumed full responsibility. She took a special interest in the workers, improved their living conditions and raised their wages. She began a nursery for them, then a school. And when the farm began losing money, she launched a marketing campaign for Kenyan coffee, raised the price, and put the farm back in the black.

Apparently that was all Frank knew. He waddled his head, stoned, grinning stupidly. "My beloved stepmom, she must have been something!"

Anxious as hell to escape Junior, I had pertinent papers in one hand, the door handle in the other, before I finally recognized Freda, Freda Wagner. I'd heard about, even read about, her model coffee farm and her work promoting Kenyan coffee. I rummaged through the papers for her pictures again, an eight-by-ten glossy business portrait and an enlarged snapshot of her picking coffee. A handsome woman, with a gentle, intelligent face; a large, strong frame; long gray hair pulled back loosely. Holding the pictures to the light, I saw she was definitely the woman I'd read about, and I'd met her—at her coffee farm, in fact. I was there with a friend buying some horses Freda had for sale, maybe five years ago. She had impressed me. We had tea and talked about any number of things. Freda Wagner, for Christ's sake, dead.

"You really didn't know your stepmother?" I asked, a bit incredulous.

"No!" he answered, emphatic, lifting his limp head off the back of the sofa, looking at me as though I'd asked a dumb question.

So I tried another. "Didn't you ever come to Kenya, to the farm, spend any time with your dad?"

"No!" He was still emphatic. "My mother dragged me there a few times when I was a kid. It was dirty, dusty, cows everywhere, chickens in the house. I remember guns at the door, angry black faces, shouting." He rested his ponytail on the back of the sofa again. "My life as a kid was boarding school. Memories of my parents, other than nightmares of Africa, are a few pictures. I inherited the family home in Frankfurt, in the suburbs. I can't find my way around it, or to it!" He forced a laugh. "It's on the market. I'm an urban boy. A musician, always been a musician." For a moment, standing there with my hand on the doorknob, I felt a spark of empathy for a scared little kid, a stranger to his parents. Then he scoffed, "And now my fate's in the hands of a bitchin' redheaded private dick."

I told the sweaty, stoned, fat, thirty-five-year-old rock and roller whose band I'd probably never heard of that I'd rap on his door about nine the next morning and give him my take on the situation. He nodded.

I ordered dinner in, not prepared to undo all the good-byes done yesterday. I pored over the pile of Wagner papers and then washed the pot smoke out of my bitchin' red hair, wondering why Frank Junior's fate was in my hands. In addition to the house in the suburbs of Frankfurt left to him in Freda's will, two years ago he'd received a sum equal to $500,000 from the sale of the coffee business. According to Dad's will, Junior was only to have received one-third of the proceeds of the sale, but Freda had made it two-thirds, keeping one-third, or $250,000, for herself. The terms of the contract of sale required Freda to stay on for three years as CEO for the new owners, for which she was paid a wage of $50,000 per year plus her residence at the farm. Her contract wouldn't have expired for six months.

The police report was from Mombasa, not Nairobi; San Francisco was getting farther away. The report said that Freda Wagner, fifty-three years old, was shot through the back of the head with a thirty-eight revolver at close range in her room at the Pwani Hotel, Southshore, Mombasa, Kenya. The revolver was found next to her body, a suicide note on the dresser. A copy of the note, blurred and in German, translated, "I'm sorry it's over, it was an incredible . . ." I couldn't read or didn't know the last word. It was signed, and the signature surely resembled the signature on the contracts. The police apparently had some suspicions of murder but only because she was shot in the back of the head. They concluded that it was suicide for lack of a motive. She wasn't robbed. Her personal belongings, including her passport, wallet, and fifty or so dollars' worth of shillings, were in her room. No mention of large sums of money, credit cards, bank accounts, or personal effects beyond a list of items one would carry in an overnight suitcase. There were statements from several guests in adjoining rooms, some of whom may have heard the shot the night before, but the body wasn't discovered until nine o'clock the next morning by the housekeeper. The police were unable to locate anyone at the hotel or in Mombasa who knew her. The coroner's report was three weeks old. I'd checked over Junior's passport at the front desk. The only Kenya stamp was his entry that day, and his passport was four years old. He probably wasn't a suspect.

Junior looked as I'd hoped he would at nine in the morning: not ready for anything. With his shirt off, pants hanging beneath the shadow of a beastly belly, he flung open the door, nearly toppling in the draft he created. I told him we'd have tea instead, four o'clock. He grunted. I traipsed off, glad not to have his company.

I remembered the way to the coffee farm, guiding the taxi driver along the myriad of dusty roads that dissected fields of pineapple, bananas, papayas, and coffee. The gate guard glanced at my identification and waved us through. I asked the cabby to wait and began wandering among a complex of low stucco buildings. A white-haired man with ink-black skin and a bright red shirt came along. I asked him directions, and he took me to a small office where everyone was wearing matching flowered shirts and smiles. I showed them my letter of introduction, translating it into Swahili for them. Their faces turned sad, their words melancholy. They gave me a pass to pin on my lapel and said I should follow the red-shirted man.

We walked along a path banked on either side by a picket fence sagging under profuse yellow climbing roses. The smell wafting toward the perfect Nairobi sun put me in my grandmother's garden of twenty years past. For the length of the path, I felt better about not going home. We passed by a pond with tropical fish, several beautiful iron sculptures of coffee workers, an aviary with bright, noisy birds, and several women in straw hats sitting on a bench smoking near a grave with a small, black granite headstone. The grave was littered with cut flowers and surrounded by new plantings, their blooms half open. The stone read, "Our beloved Freda." Smaller letters spelled out "Freda Wagner" and the dates of her birth and death.

The path ended at the steps to a sprawling bungalow fronted by a wide porch. Thatch hanging from the roof was trimmed neatly at head level. On the porch there were rattan swings and furniture with fuchsia-colored pillows. On a glass table there were vases filled with ruby-colored dahlias. I remembered having tea at that table with Freda Wagner.

My red-shirted escort knocked on the sliding glass door and called out, *"Jambo, nisemehe!"* In a moment a lovely, lithe, bay-skinned woman was letting us in. Her smile was wide and bright white. She greeted us with, *"Hujambo, habari ya siku nying?"* Greetings, how have you been lately?

When she and the man had chatted a moment, I introduced myself and told her why I was there. Her countenance changed. Tapping her tongue several times on her rosy upper lip, she said, *"Karibu,"* indicating that I should follow her and my escort could be excused. We passed through an enormous room adorned with furniture covered in indigenous wild skins. The walls were decorated with colorful paintings and batiks. Bronze sculptures of African tribesmen stood at the doors as sentries.

In a small sitting room with a formal tea table and four chairs, my hostess said, *"Kaa kitako."* Sit down. We both did, and then we just sat there for what seemed like several minutes, silent. I had the feeling she needed to control her emotions before she spoke. I wasn't in a hurry. There was a tranquilizing air about the place, a soft fragrance and a comfortable calm, the antithesis of little Franky Wagner's recollections. I waited, happily anesthetized. In her time, and with a polite smile and a deep breath, she took a tea bell off the table, jingled it, and told me *memsahib* Freda always said that "difficult subjects are made easy over tea."

The woman's name was Unyoya, a name given her by Freda Wagner fifteen years before, when they picked coffee together. It meant feather. Unyoya had worked in that house, Freda's house, since 1975. *Memsahib* was still there, but she couldn't be seen now, except in the gardens, late evenings and early mornings. She is here now, sitting there by the window, Unyoya told me. She likes to sit there and think. She calls that garden her thinking garden. Unyoya turned to look at an empty overstuffed chair for several quiet minutes. I felt compelled to look at it too and at the lovely garden of purple iris, yellow zinnias, and white lilacs.

A woman in a small white apron carrying a large tea service was a welcome sight. In the next hour, Unyoya and I emptied the teapot and ate every biscuit. She talked, unhurried, choosing her smooth Swahili words carefully, about life with her *memsahib*, her friend, her heroine—heroine to all coffee workers, mother to all children. Wonderful stories, legends already to some, I supposed. The new owners had told her that someone else might be living there soon, but Unyoya knew that wouldn't be possible. Everything in the house was Freda, not belonging to Freda but actually was Freda. She was everything on the farm, and she was in every person who worked there. My cynical self briefly envisioned all the workers being fed cocoa leaves for maintaining tranquility, but physically and spiritually I felt at peace and needed Freda's magic all to be true.

After we looked at scrapbooks, Unyoya wanted to show me around the house. She took me into Freda's bedroom, opened her closets, her drawers. Everything was there, everything except the stuff women need all the time. There were no cosmetics, fragrances, jewelry; no underwear, gown, or slippers. There were also no bedside pictures or notepaper and books. More missing, I thought, than would fit in a weekend case going to Mombasa. I asked Unyoya about these personal things. She said proudly, honestly, that all of *memsahib's* things were exactly as she'd left them, but each time she returned from Mombasa she'd had fewer things. I asked her when she had last seen Freda, other than mornings and evenings in the garden. She took me to a calendar in the tearoom and showed me the circled date, two months and three weeks before. Freda had taken the train to Mombasa. She went there often, always on the train. She had malaria, like her husband. He had gone there, too, but not after he became terribly ill. I asked her if they'd gone there together, if they had friends there. She didn't know. She only knew that the mister went there often before he had malaria, and *memsahib* went there often after she had malaria. She liked to be on the sea. In the last year, her weekend trips had extended into a week, sometimes two weeks. On her final trip she had called several times, saying she needed to stay longer. Unyoya pointed to the black X on the calendar, the day the police came to tell them. I went back to look at the scrapbooks again. The pictures were dated, the last ones of Freda taken over a year ago. She was thin, gaunt, and tired looking, unlike her pictures from the year before. Unyoya said that the malaria had spoiled her appetite and her energy, but not her heart.

I rode back into Nairobi with the window down. Freda Wagner had left a part of herself on that farm, her essence like a web, capturing Unyoya and the other workers and probably anyone placing a foot on her grounds—certainly me. I shook myself and asked the cabby if he had malaria. He said he did sometimes, everybody had it sometimes. I knew some things about malaria. I'd contracted it two years before, in Mombasa. I went home. I got better. If one is lucky enough not to get the mosquito with the deadly variety, one has a good chance of learning to live with it, eventually getting rid of it. Freda had been ill, maybe too ill to carry on in Kenya, but why didn't she return to Germany for good medical care? What was in Mombasa for her? Mombasa, the malaria capital of the world.

The coffee farm's main office was downtown on a noisy street of poorly maintained two-story office buildings, their fronts mostly obscured by vendors and crippled beggars. I bought a samosa from a relatively sanitary-looking vendor with no teeth. He made us each one, and while we ate, we talked, watching the aggressive hawkers and panhandlers. It was impossible to understand most of what he was saying, but he seemed a kind man with adamant ideas about how things should be.

The sign over the door was being repainted, but the brilliant coffee posters in the windows confirmed that it was the right place. The guard was all smiles in his clean navy-blue uniform and rusty thirty-caliber rifle. A man at the front desk, wearing a tie and an ill-fitting European suit, escorted me to the office of Mr. H. W. Janjo, executive vice president of Coffee Kenya Corporation.

A picture of Freda Wagner hung over Mr. Janjo's desk, surrounded by bright red and green coffee posters. Mr. Janjo, a short, round-faced man with garters on his sleeves, loved Freda Wagner. When I thought he might cry, he did. I waited. He ordered tea. I waited. When the tea was gone and the authorizations from Frankfurt read, Mr. Janjo used both Swahili and English to tell me about his wonderful friend Freda Wagner, a woman who knew how to overcome adversity, how to get things done without sacrificing anyone's integrity. His accolades were as lofty as Unyoya's. I listened, again feeling caught up in Freda's presence. Mr. Janjo nearly broke down a second time when he talked of her dreadful illness. He felt guilty; the corporation was partly to blame. She had continued to work long after she should have sought serious help for the malaria. It was impossible to replace her, which was the reason she wouldn't quit and go back to Frankfurt for good medical care. He didn't know what they were going to do without her; things were already a mess.

It was obvious to me that Mr. Janjo's personal grief and company concerns came from his heart; but nonetheless, I asked him to show me Freda's pay records. He did, without hesitation, even the canceled checks. He wrote down her account number, assuring me that Coffee Kenya could not and would not touch her account. Freda had cashed all her checks; she was paid quarterly in advance of the pay period. He also gave me a copy of her will, a simple one-page document addressed to Coffee Kenya Corporation. She had made it about one year before. There was nothing in it addressing the disposition of her personal bank account. All personal property left on the farm was to remain there for perpetuity, with the exception of a few articles that were to go to a museum. He showed me the receipt from the museum. Her clothes were to go to the household help. Shaking his head sadly, he said that the help would not take her clothes because they believed she was still wearing them.

In the cab back to the Norfolk I mulled over motive. A suicide motive, bought by the Mombasa police and sold to Janjo, didn't fit my growing image of Freda. The report had concluded suicide for lack of motive, case closed. A tidy report to fit neatly in a file. And murder was highly unlikely by Coffee Kenya Corporation. They were obviously in the web of Freda's saintly essence; she had been the backbone and ribs of the business and was sorely missed. The sale had been closed over two years before and the money dispersed. No motive there. I expected to find Freda's money, at least the $250,000, in her bank account. Her stepson may have had a murder motive, but he hadn't been in Kenya, and I doubted that he could get it together to find and hire an assassin. Still, Frank Junior seemed a desperate man.

Junior was elated. Freda's bank account had been found! He didn't flinch over her will and disposition of art. "African art, big deal," he jeered. "Let's go to the bank!" And so we did. The next morning we were first in line when they opened the doors to Freda's bank, a sparse concrete tomb in the center of town. Frank, his sagging eyes reminding me of one of my grandmother's hounds, admitted it was the earliest he'd been up since boarding school. As we waited, he stood on one sandal, then the other, the strained buttons of his shirt pressed against the counter. A bank official with dirty white cuffs and very long fingers, black on top and white underneath, leafed through Frank's papers. Occasionally he glanced at Frank and muttered, causing Frank to stroke his ponytail and groan. This refrain went on until my ankles began to swell and I nudged Frank aside. The man and I spoke in Swahili and decided the job should go to the bank president, who wasn't yet sitting at the big desk in the corner. We went there to wait.

While Frank sat in the straight, hardbacked chair, two buttons on his shirt surrendered, and beads of sweat gave him a glistening mustache. He seemed vulnerable enough. I said, "You look like a desperate man, Frank Junior, like a man who went through five hundred thousand dollars in two years and it wasn't enough. You obviously don't have expensive taste, so I'm guessing you have bad habits."

Without looking at me, he responded in a low, calm voice. "I'm a musician. By definition I have bad habits."

"How is more money, Freda's money, going to affect your fate?" I asked, dogged. "The fate you said was in my hands?"

"None of your goddamn business," he murmured, still not looking at me. "I'm about to get what I came for. Then I'm through with you and this cesspool country." His smirk sent sweat cascading down his chins.

I scooted my chair next to his and punched back with my best sinister smile. "I was hired to solve the mystery of Freda's death. You're a suspect. I can have you detained in this cesspool as long as necessary. Now humor me and tell me why you're so desperate for Freda's two fifty."

His eyes crossed mine and then went to the man walking toward us, shoes clicking sharply on the bare floor. Frank whispered, "You're a redheaded witch dick," then smiled at the bank president seating himself at the desk.

Frank's papers, together with mine, shuffled and reshuffled across the huge splintered desk, were becoming dog-eared when the president adjusted his limp tie and declared everything was in order. We followed him back to the man with the dirty cuffs, where we waited for his long fingers to finish flipping through a stack of filthy money and registering it on a ten-key calculator. Finished, he looked up at the president and received his instructions in Swahili. He was to close Freda Wagner's account, convert the shillings to American dollars, and give Mr. Frank Wagner Jr. a bank draft for the amount. With a nod of compliance, the man left his counter. The president shook our hands, and we were left to wait again.

It was only five minutes later that the long-fingered man was back at his counter, accompanied by a woman in wide spectacles and corn-rowed hair. She appeared ready for confrontation. She presented us with an account on thick ledger paper headed "Freda Wagner," and placed a red lacquered finger on the final entry. "This account was closed on June fifteenth, almost three months ago, as you can see." She spoke in a high-pitched, perfect Kenyan-English dialect. "I closed the account myself and gave Frau Wagner a bank draft for the amount." Eyes enlarged by thick lenses, she stared at Frank, waiting for a response. Frank didn't have one. He was blinking his darting eyes as though he'd just stepped into a dark theater. I nudged him aside and asked the woman to convert the amount that had been in Freda's account to dollars. She did some rapid tapping on the ten key and announced that the draft, converted to American dollars, was $110,000. Frank groaned loudly. I asked to see the complete record of her account. She was happy to show it to me. Two years and three months ago, Frau Wagner had withdrawn the equivalent of $270,000. Since then, there had been regular deposits at three-month intervals, but only the two large withdrawals that totaled $380,000. I asked if she could tell me whether Freda had opened an account in their bank branch in Mombasa. She couldn't, but if that were the case, Frau Wagner surely would have done so by transfer. I asked if she could call Mombasa, just to be certain. She forced a smile and said she would do so if we cared to wait. I thanked Mrs. Doinyo, the name on her lapel pin, and told her we would be back for that information right after lunch. I knew how long it could take to get a call through to Mombasa in peak hours.

I dragged Frank into the Hilton Hotel, where the café served up high-calorie pizzas, American style. He ordered three beers and drank two of them in silence before the pizza arrived. Armed with the third beer, he gasped, "Goddamn women!"

The waiter was rearranging the table to make room for the pizza when I asked, "Are you damning women in general or just Freda?"

"Women! All of them I know." He slammed his bottle down, picked out a slice of pizza, and pushed a large portion of it into his mouth.

"But you didn't know Freda," I said defensively, trying not to watch the food tumbling about the chasm in his face.

"What do you think she did with the money?" he demanded, grabbing another slice, stringing cheese across the table. "Why do you think she put it in a bank in Mombasa?"

"Why are you so anxious to get your hands on money that was clearly not marked for you?"

"It's rightfully my money!" he exclaimed, spewing pizza and pointing his beer bottle at me. I couldn't watch anymore.

While I was sitting in the lobby waiting for Junior to finish stuffing himself, two friends of mine spotted me and dragged me off to the bar to find out why I wasn't in San Francisco, where I had been headed the last time they'd seen me. They were white Kenyans, married to white Kenyan women. I asked them about the Wagners. They knew them well and chattered on. They had a long history with Freda and Frank at the Methega Club, at the polo fields, countless parties, all fond memories. Their wives had been close to Freda, until Frank died and Freda simply stopped being social. They knew she'd been very sick with malaria. They always asked about her when they ran into Constance. I must know Constance: a nurse, German, good friend of Freda's who works at the clinic, the black clinic. Constance always told them Freda was very sick but still running the farm. Even Constance probably never dreamed Freda was sick enough to be suicidal. However, since her death, they'd heard rumors of how she'd looked the last year. They were sorry they hadn't been more concerned. They couldn't understand why she hadn't returned to Germany for help with the malaria, but for that matter, look at old Frank; he'd died here as well. He'd gone to Frankfurt for a few weeks to take the cure, but he came back, got sicker than ever, and died. Stubborn Germans, they both agreed.

When I returned to the café, Junior was sitting at an empty table looking fretful, cheese hanging from one of his chins. He didn't wait for me to sit down. "I blew the five hundred thousand making videos." His proclamation was loud. "Okay, some of it went up my nose, but mostly videos. If you don't have a video, you can't make it in my business. They cost like hell. You have to have good writers, good musicians, stage crews, special effects. They're expensive, big bucks." He flagged the waiter and ordered another beer. "One for you?" he asked me, trying a smile. I shook my head at the waiter, and the new and improved Frank went on. "I thought the first one was going to be a hit, and it would have been if . . ." He looked around for a napkin, grabbed one from another table, wiped the cheese I'd been staring at from his chin, and continued. "The second one was better but didn't fly. They told me I needed a female lead." He looked at me, the first time I'd seen his eyes wide open. "Now I have a female lead! She's bitchin'! I'm bitchin'! Great writers, great music! This is it, finally!" He slumped back on the padded plastic seat, the dark hair of his mounded belly protruding through the gap in his shirt. "But I'm out of money," he whined. "I've got that monster house for sale in Frankfurt, but they tell me it could take five years to sell. If I don't get to New York with two hundred grand in my pocket by the end of September, the bitch lead walks to another band." The beer came and he swilled. "Freda plugging herself . . ." Cowering, he rephrased. "Freda's unfortunate death is, well it's fortunate for me, in fact it's going to save me, if we can find her money." He started to say something else but decided to let things settle while he finished his beer. I waited. He had taken the stand, and I wanted to hear it all.

Finally, he said, "I know I'm not a suspect, but who is?" He wiped his mouth and became fidgety, glancing first at me and then at everything else in the room. "Do you really think she was murdered? If she was murdered, do you think someone has her money? She was sick, you know. The lawyer said she had bad malaria. She could have killed herself. People do that, lots of them." He paused a moment before he asked, "Well, what do you think, detective woman?"

It sounded better than redheaded witch dick. I said, "I'm thinking all of the above. Let's get back to the bank."

The bank was now jammed with customers on their lunch break, their black feet and faces pinched in English shoes and rules. I left Frank there. He protested until I was out of earshot, but he could stand in line for Mrs. Doinyo's response as well as I could. I would meet him back at the Norfolk.

The cabby dropped me in front of the clinic and a herd of people waiting for God knows what. The clinic was for blacks only. Inside, everyone in a white uniform was white. Everyone in a green uniform was black. I followed the receptionist's directions through the crowded halls and up to the second floor, where I found a woman fitting the description of Constance frowning over a chart. Strands of gray hair had leaked out from under her starched white hat, and her uniform was stained with orange, brown, and blood. When I spoke her name, she gave a reflexive "Yes?" without looking up. I introduced myself over the sounds of a child somewhere, screaming at the top of its lungs. She finished checking the chart before she looked at me. Studying me curiously, then smiling in recognition, she said she remembered me from a party at someone's house that I'd forgotten. She described the hat I'd worn. I apologized for not remembering her and told her why I'd come to the clinic. She led me to a couple of plastic chairs at the end of the hall.

Constance was a tired-looking woman with heavy, dark lines between her eyes, possibly from breathing the disinfectants that failed to mask the stench of the place. I asked her straight out, "Did Freda Wagner kill herself?" Tears welled in her eyes as she ground at her teeth and flexed the muscle of her jaw. Sighing heavily, she didn't answer. I asked again, "Do you believe Freda killed herself?"

She looked at me, desperation in her glistening blue eyes. Tears spilled down her face. "I cannot answer that question." I asked her if she couldn't or wouldn't. She repeated herself. "I cannot answer that question." I asked her, then, if she could tell me why Freda went to Mombasa every week and why she died there. She put her face in her hands and began to sob. Feeling like a brute, I put my hand on her heaving back and tried to think of something comforting to say. From behind a closed door near us, the screams of a hysterical woman bounced around the corridor.

Finally, Constance looked up. Her eyes red and her nose running, she said, "Freda was my best friend. We understood each other . . . we trusted each other's confidences. We both believed in what we do, my work here, her work." She had her head back in her hands. I waited. She tried again. "I cannot tell you anything about Freda. She lives in my heart, still. I will always honor her. She will always trust me." She frowned, furrowing the lines ever deeper between her eyes. "Whether you understand it or not, the results are the same." She stood up and dug into the pocket of her dirty uniform and pulled out a tissue. When she'd finished wiping her eyes and blowing her nose, she tried smiling at me. A door opened and a gurney burst through followed by several masked figures all talking at once. Constance said, "You'll have to excuse me. It's a busy day today." Someone called her name, and she added, "Every day." She started off and then turned to say, "Freda will always be the best person I know. If you get to know her, you'll understand."

I watched the worn heels of her white shoes hurrying into the room where the gurney had disappeared. I understood two things. Constance probably knew what happened to Freda, and Constance was a noble woman, probably with a noble reason for not telling. The rest I'd have to brood over.

Frank was sitting at the Norfolk patio bar when I returned, still looking pathetic. He hadn't had time to get drunk, but he was working on it. I paused at his table just long enough for him to confirm that Mrs. Doinyo found nothing in the Mombasa branch. I told him "Later," and headed for my room. I needed a bath, I needed to pack and I needed to call Uli.

Uli, my consummate pilot, actually answered his phone. It was his usual German grunt, the sort of coughing grunt made by a restless lion. "Good, Uli, you're in and rested, I hope. I need a ride."

He made a few more indecipherable noises before responding in his thick accent. "We have only just returned, darling, and no, I am not rested. Why are you not on your way to the States?"

"Change in plans. I'm still in Nairobi, and I need to get where you are, Mombasa, Southshore." I waited for more lion noises, then added, "Tonight, or first thing in the morning."

"What is your hurry, darling? Important?"

"Yeah, I'm in a hurry to get this done and go home as planned. It's not code one, well, not even urgent, but I sure as hell want to get to Southshore ASAP, and I'd like to fly there direct, avoid the ferry, at least initially."

"Good," he said flatly, followed by silence. I could see him sitting there in his starched shirt, rubbing the tip of his cigarette holder across his pencil-thin black mustache.

Finally, I asked, "Good what? Good, you're coming?"

"No. Good that it is not urgent. I am . . . indisposed." His well-enunciated *indisposed* was followed by a female giggle in close proximity. Uli, like all the bush pilots that I've known, had peculiar personal propensities. His was an insatiable black-whore fetish. He was well known in white circles for flaunting them at socially stiff English events. The whores knew him as a well-paying rogue who would take them home at night but leave them locked in his house the next day until he returned from flying his missions; it was a compromise, he rationalized, allowing them to sleep in but not rob him blind.

"Uli, you're my goddamn pilot. Your whores now have you indisposed?"

"It is not the whores, Kelly darling, it is that airplane. I have been in it for days, as you know, and now the government has hired me to track down and map all of the Maasi engangs in the Maasi Mara, part of their effort to move some of them away from tourist camps, make them wear trousers." He grunted a laugh. "Detribalize! That is the Kenyan government's word and their mission, to get rid of all their primitive people, convert them to proper behavioral types like myself."

"You're going to map Maasi villages for the Kenyan government? They're getting serious about this detribalizing!"

"Serious enough to make it very clear that I could not say no. Take the train tonight, darling; you like the train."

He was right. And Freda always took the train. Maybe I'd learn something. Uli and I talked a few minutes more about Freda. He knew of her, had heard of her death, nothing more, but he'd ask around. I told him where I'd be, hung up, called the train station, and grabbed my bag. I'd leave a note in Frank's box and call him in a few days when I had some information. Frank was too heavy to carry around Mombasa.

The train still ran on an English schedule, leaving the station promptly at 7 P.M. It was my practice to stand on the platform as long as possible, enjoying the bits of theater produced by boarding. People with their baggage scurried to their proper class amid emotional farewells, happy bon voyages, slaps on the back for luck, shouts and kisses from open windows. Finally the chief steward in his dark coat, hand cupped to his mouth, yelled, "All aboard!" The overnight train to Mombasa: a turn-of-the-century English triumph over lions and renegade tribes, a subject in African history. My favorite train in the world, it was always a good ride for me: a five-course dinner with starched waiters and linen served by an open window with an occasional glimpse of a giraffe or zebra, clean porters and sheets, compartment service. And a hypnotic track rhythm capable of producing virtual-reality dreams.

Then there was breakfast, a time to prepare for entry into one of the steamiest ports in the world. Holding my cup to keep it from bouncing, the steward poured more coffee. Breakfast was long over. He wanted me to leave. He said, "Ten minutes Mombasa, madam." I knew it was thirty. I needed another cup. What an incredible night. Freda had followed me on the train, filled my compartment with her mystery. The woman had some kind of power, and I seemed to be vulnerable. Maybe it was the second after-dinner brandy, I don't know, but I talked to her. I asked her questions and her answers came in dream images, about the farm, the workers, her school. But she didn't answer when I asked why she bailed out, if she bailed out, and about her malaria. I told her, "WASPs have to go home, Freda; we have to go home to get well! You could have taken a few months, straightened up the mess when you returned. Why did you empty your bank account and go to Mombasa, the malaria capital of the world, to die of malaria?" Now I was talking to her again and the train was bouncing badly, spilling my coffee. I signaled the waiter for more and apologized with a large tip. He told me not to hurry.

Freda was courageous, intelligent, and compassionate. The articles I'd read, the Norfolk gossip, Mr. Janjo, Unyoya, and Constance all agreed. Janjo had said she could not be replaced, but she could have had a substitute for a month or two. She knew that. Women like Freda take care of themselves. Freda Wagner had to have known there was a better solution. The reason she didn't go home was bigger than the coffee farm. Constance knew the reason, the reason that apparently could only be shared by noble women. The steward was calling, "Mombasa! Mombasa, madam!"

Every form of humanity swims in the humidity of Mombasa. Veiled women, turbaned men, tribal people, beggars, prostitutes, English and German expatriates, tourists, and the likes of myself—persons on business of one kind or another. I pushed my way through the throngs rushing to and from the station and grabbed a cab to the Castle Hotel.

Pia, an Indian girl whose life I'd crossed, always made the phone at the Castle convenient to me. She was there with a big smile. The phones hadn't worked yet that morning, but I should wait. Eight o'clock was always a bad time for phones.

I waited in the patio café and watched the prostitutes work the morning train arrivals. The Castle whores were vicious, just off or still on the street, young, dumb, hungry, staying alive and spreading disease. At the moment they where hassling two young white women having breakfast, who were being ogled by a table of very young French sailors in tasseled hats and short pants. First one of the whores and then another would get up from the table they occupied in force and yell out, "White women have pussies like watermelon!" It was a favorite chant of theirs. It would be followed by ashtray throwing. Pia saved me the bad theater. The phones were working.

I called the Pwani Hotel on Southshore, where Freda stayed the night she died. The manager was overly eager to see me. We agreed on that afternoon. My next call was to the police. Miraculously I got through, and miraculously they, too, would see me.

The police were difficult, suspicious of my documents of authorization, and wary. I was white and female, and I was speaking Swahili. They had been expecting someone from the family for weeks, but not an investigator and not a woman. The rumpled detective who had prepared the report shoved a shoebox tied with string at me, along with a form to sign. He said that everything else had been left with the manager at the Pwani. As far as they were concerned, the case was closed. I asked if they had been able to locate anyone in Mombasa who knew Frau Wagner. Disgruntled, he tapped the shoebox I was opening, containing her passport and fifty dollars' worth of shillings, and said that she was a tourist; she had no friends in Mombasa as far as they knew. I told him that she lived near Nairobi and had been coming to Mombasa every week for over two years. He adjusted his dirty police hat and gave me a sarcastic look before saying he knew she was a white authority in Nairobi, that's why they had to keep the case open, but now that I was here, the case was mine. I asked if he'd ever seen anyone shoot him- or herself through the back of the head. He said that Africans didn't kill themselves; they were too busy trying to stay alive. When I asked if he'd checked for local bank accounts in her name, he slapped the police report I was holding and said that it was all there, nothing to add. I tried a few more questions, reasoning that cooperation was important—after all, we both sort of had the same job. That really pissed him off. He had dozens of deaths a day to deal with—murders, disease, accidents—and he was sure that I couldn't live on his salary.

The taxi smoked, belched, and backfired through the narrow wind-
ing streets of Old Town, scattering donkey carts and veiled women
with bundles on their heads. East Indians, who came with the trade
winds before the English had a map of Africa, settled Old Town and it
hadn't changed much in several hundred years. The door to Kumlesh's
shop was open. I tipped the cabby heavily and told him to get his car
fixed.

Kumlesh was in, glad to see me, and right away he knew I had
something for him to do. "Your smile is different when you are working, Kelly."

Melted from the heat, I flopped in one of the chairs nearest the
door. "I just came from the police. Until then I was Mary Tyler
Moore."

He called out in Hindi to someone in the back to bring tea and
then came and sat beside me. "Who is Mary . . ."

"Bad joke, Kumlesh, never mind." I dabbed at my face with a
handkerchief, asking him if he had some time for me.

"Yes, I have time, for you I always have time." He pushed his thick
glasses up and leaned his face toward mine. "Unless it is not legal, then
I have to make time." He laughed, patting himself on his jiggling
tummy.

We drank iced tea and talked unhurriedly about his real business,
selling imported jewelry, and about the current skulduggery in
Kenyan politics. I had known Kumlesh for several years before I
began working in Africa. Attempting to study the influence of the
Indian culture and Hindu religion in Kenya, I had been fascinated by
his brother, Hitesh, a very young Hindu guru with a following.
Hitesh and I became fast friends, religion aside, and sometime later I
met Kumlesh, the older brother, wizard of the family finances, inside
track to anything one needed to know in Kenya; eventually, he
became my Kenya office. Informant, confidant, extended family,
Kumlesh was my alchemist, a term he liked to be associated with.

Kumlesh's sisters came out from the back and around the counters of
displayed jewelry to say hello and giggle. Then his mother, a scary, ugly
woman who had always made it clear that she didn't approve of me,
came to take a bow. When the salutations were over, Kumlesh ordered
more tea and dismissed everyone. I told him of Freda Wagner and the
help I needed. He said it would take two days for him to find out if

Freda had a bank account anywhere in Mombasa. I had authorization to get that information, but it would take me a week, and he'd get the real report, in case someone other than Freda had closed an account. I also wanted him to tap into his sources on Southshore, in particular the Pwani Hotel, to find out who knew what about Freda Wagner.

Our business was over. I gave him an envelope containing cash; he gave me one containing my phone messages over the last few months. Signaling his personal taxi for me, he asked, "You will be going to the temple to see Hitesh?" When I assured him that was my next stop, he laughed happily. "He is never surprised to see you, but he has a surprise for you."

The street in front of the temple was crowded with children and mothers, apparently waiting for the temple doors to open. I excused Kumlesh's driver and then pardoned my way through the unruly, uniformed children. Their mothers, in silk saris, bunches of keys tied at their flabby midriffs, were busy scolding their tykes, warning them to be careful with the colorfully wrapped packages they carried, gifts for their guru.

I found the side door unlocked and made my way through the room with the white plastic cow and on to the door I knew to be Hitesh's office. My light knock was answered immediately in Hindi. Opening the door I found Hitesh sitting cross-legged on his floor mat, his back to me. He asked who it was but didn't wait for an answer before he exclaimed, "Kelly!"

"How do you do that, Hitesh? I can't surprise you, even when I surprise you." I walked around to face him and then sat down on his mat. He was laughing and bobbing his head from side to side. I said, "You have two dozen kids out there ready to storm the place."

"I know," he said, opening his eyes and letting them wander. "This is their patience lesson for today. Should I get up, or are you comfortable?"

"I'm always comfortable sitting with you, Hitesh. You have air conditioning."

He did his silly giggle and reached for my hand. "You are working. You are tired." He put both his hands around mine. "And you are not having enough sex."

"Right on all three. I'm supposed to be home taking the cure for all those maladies, but alas, like the rest of the world, I'm a slave to money." I put my arm around him and kissed his forehead. "Kumlesh said you have a surprise."

"I do. I was hoping you would come this day. I have been practicing. But first, let me feel your face." He put his hands on my face, then felt my hair and neck. "You are older than when you were here last, only three months past."

"Lack of sex ages people rapidly," I quipped.

"This is very true, that is why I am so old. But you are learning some things, some new things about yourself." He took his hands away and put them on mine again. "Tell me what it is that has you thinking so hard."

"I don't know, I'm certainly thinking hard, but I'm not learning much yet. It's this woman that I'm here about. She's dead, I don't know why yet, but people I've talked to . . . who knew her . . . seem to be under some kind of spell, as though she were still here."

"And you?" he asked. "Are you, too, under her spell now?"

"Probably. It feels that way. I went to her home. There was certainly a spell about that place, a beautiful space, for her, her workers. She gave them wages enough to live on, a school. She did things that otherwise wouldn't have been done." I looked around and laughed nervously. "She was with me on the train last night. I talked to her. I think she's here now."

"And now, since you've spoken to her, what have you learned?"

"I think she's using me."

"She is using you. Kelly, this woman is obviously a heroine to you; now you must be a heroine to her. You must find out what she died for. It is the thing she died for that she wants you to know."

"And when I know?" I asked, feeling a bit put upon.

"When you know, then you will decide."

"Okay, Hitesh, that's enough spooky guru stuff. Tell me your surprise."

"It is not to tell." He began getting to his feet. "It is to show." He made his way behind his desk, opened a drawer, and took out a small cassette player. Feeling around on it, he found the play button and pushed it so hard he wavered, nearly toppling over. The room filled with blaring music, and in seconds I recognized Creedence Clearwater Revival rocking out "Proud Mary." Hitesh calmly made his way around to the center of the room, kicked his mat to the side, and began gyrating to the sound, his white robe flowing and flopping, his head bobbing as though on a spindle. He wiggled his finger for me to join him. I couldn't resist. We danced, until Creedence faded away.

"Well, what do you think, Kelly?" he asked, collapsing on the floor.

"I feel better, and I think you're amazing! How do you do that without falling down? You're blind, you crazy guru!"

"Is it not a wonderful accomplishment?" he asked, laughing and panting. "I have come to terms with a part of my brain I have argued with since I was ten years old, when I could no longer see. But I think it is these musicians, these Clearwater people, that I must thank. Their music is a bridge to balance that I could not get to before, and this woman Proud Mary that they sing of, and their way of life with no money, it is truly inspirational." He crossed his legs and looked shy. "Kelly, you wouldn't know how I could go about thanking them, would you?"

"I think you already have. And Proud Mary—I think she's a river-boat."

Everyone going to the Southshore takes the ferry. It's the only way from Mombasa. Sweating, waiting for the ferry to unload, and the mass of humanity to swarm up the hill pushed along by bleating cars of every vintage and from every country, I thought about Freda doing the same thing, weekend after weekend, and then longer weekends, and finally one last time. I opened my briefcase and slipped out her pictures, showing them to the cabby. He said what the porters and waiters on the train had said, that she looked like a lot of white women.

Finally, the swarm began in the other direction as the ferry began to load. The moment we were aboard, I was out of the cab to inhale the sea breeze and dry my clothes. I bought cashews in a paper cone from a ragged child and stood at the rail eating them, thinking of Freda doing the same thing.

A tap on my shoulder startled me. I turned around and nearly jumped out of my skin. A woman with gray hair tied back loosely was asking me how much she should pay the runny-nosed girl holding out the cone of cashews. Maybe the cabby and the porters were right about Freda looking like lots of white women, but Freda wouldn't have had to ask how much to pay a ragged child. After advising the woman, I turned back to the rail and began putting questions to Freda again. "Did you have a boyfriend out here, Freda? Or a girlfriend? Maybe a doctor promising a cure? What was your motive for making this trek every weekend?"

The Pwani: a gleaming white three-story hotel laced with red bougainvillea and fronted by a salt-white beach. The language, the food, the beds, and the prostitutes—all made for Germans. The front desk called the house manager. He hurried in, belly bouncing, shaking his head and rattling off in German, some of which I understood. It had been more than three weeks. The police had told him that he had to hold everything for the family. Didn't anyone care about that poor woman? I introduced myself, and he switched easily to English. His name was Hans Kruger. Proudly, he told me that he had been there that morning; he was the second person to see the body. The maid had called him at precisely 9 A.M. I didn't ask, but he wanted to show me the room. He didn't ask, but I insisted on showing him my letters of authorization. We took the elevator to the third floor, and I followed him down a long corridor to room 335.

As Kruger fumbled with keys, I asked if 335 was the room that Freda always stayed in. He looked up, surprised, pushing his glasses up on the hook of his nose. "Frau Wagner occupied this room for three days, less than three days, her first time at the Pwani, at least this year. I checked the records for the police. Her passport was German, of course," he shrugged, "but her address was Nairobi."

He went back to his key fumbling, found the right one, and opened the door slowly. I'm sure I gasped. The room hadn't been touched. Freda's overnight case lay open on the caddy, her slippers near a blood-stained chair, which sat over a large area of bloodstained carpet. The bed was unmade, and toilet articles and used towels cluttered the bathroom. I stood there a moment, surprised at my gut reaction. Strangely, Freda had become a friend. This room had been her final scene. There were her things: a book, a hat, sandals still caked with sand; and, there was her blood. Kruger was dancing around, his voice tuned for a large audience. "Not a single member of my staff knew her, and I checked with every guest of the hotel, all one hundred and fifty rooms. Well"—he rolled his eyes—"I questioned every room that was occupied, and that answered their telephone, about seventy. Not an easy task." He put his hand on his pudgy hip and pointed at Freda's case. "You see, there is her case.

That is all she came with, a weekend case. She made a reservation two days in advance for three days only." He cocked his hip in the other direction and pointed at the pool of dried blood. "Her body was there, found by the maid on the morning of the third day. The police said that we absolutely could not disturb anything, not anything! But then they never returned!" He threw up his hands and laughed.

Kruger was giving me the creeps. He'd probably given tours. I needed to go through the room, but not with him. I coaxed him back to the front desk, checked into room 336, and asked him for my own set of keys to 335.

After a shower, I sent for beer and sat on the balcony in a purple resin chair reading my phone messages from Kumlesh. There was nothing special: some social functions long missed, messages from Captain Mac each time he'd been in port, a couple of calls from friends trying to track me down on my birthday, and several messages from clients regarding subjects long since handled.

Bare feet on the rail, swilling my beer, I watched the figures on the long white beach. I couldn't quite see the string bikinis of the German women, nor their arms around their black vacation lovers, but I knew that's who they were. I knew that's why they came, just as the German men came for the beautiful black women with European features inherited from their German fathers. There were families, too, windsurfing, parasailing, and fishing, but the principal industry of Mombasa was prostitution. But Freda, why did she come? I was sure it wasn't for any of the above. And where had she been before checking into the room next door? Unyoya said that she had been gone two months before the police came. I got up, and leaning over the rail, I could see around the concrete divider into the balcony next door. It looked the same as mine, except for a pair of white sandals and a beach towel. She must have sat on that balcony, as I sitting here, just thinking. What was she thinking about? Was it about shooting herself in the back of the head? I wasn't ready to go over there. I took a nap instead. I dreamed of Freda parasailing over her coffee farm, the sail a brilliant coffee poster, then changing to the red, green, and black of the Kenyan flag with its ominous primitive shield.

The phone jolted me awake. It was Uli. "Frances Von Heilm lives in the hotel you are in, darling. Is that not where the Wagner woman was murdered?"

"Yes, yes, of course. I remember her. Did she know Freda?"

"Frances Von Heilm knows everyone, darling, and certainly I cannot find anyone else who knew Frau Wagner."

"Thanks, Uli." I hung up and called Kruger to ask him if Frances Von Heilm was indeed registered in the hotel. He confirmed that she was, a permanent suite. She had arrived back from Germany a few days ago and was in the dining room as we spoke.

The dining room was full, and I had to wait for a table. Scanning the room, I spotted the woman I remembered meeting several years before, Frances Von Heilm, the wealthy widow of a German scientist who had developed a strategic part for a strategic missile used to blow things up at long distances. I'd met her at one of the parties aboard the *Osprey*, Captain Daniel MacKinnon's ship. The captain gave regular "by invitation only" parties in port for the purpose of promoting political goodwill for his politically forbidden South African cargo ship. Invitations were extended only to persons with sufficient money and clout to understand the importance of uninterrupted trade between the countries of East Africa, and to Captain Mac's personal friends. I fit into the latter category.

Frances, in a flimsy, long silk dress, and her black escort, in a white linen suit, were just leaving their table as I was being seated. Frances walked with a slight limp, hanging onto her very young man's arm with one hand and holding the hem of her dress away from her shoes with the other. She looked as I'd seen her last, bright orange hair and lipstick, lots of jewelry, but a trifle older, maybe seventy now. As the couple walked past my table, I stopped them, introducing myself in English, reminding Frances we'd met before aboard the *Osprey*. She studied me a moment, remembering me finally. She introduced her escort as Jono. I asked her if we could have a drink later. She smiled at Jono wickedly. The pleasure would be hers, if I came to her suite, 305.

Before going to Frau Von Heilm's suite, I respectfully changed from my slacks into a white gauze dress and tried something *up* with my hair. Jono met me at the door, wearing a Don Juan demeanor. He'd removed his jacket, revealing his shirt open to the middle of his ebony chest. Frances held out a frail hand and beckoned me to her well-stocked bar. I chose a cognac and settled into a bright blue sofa, facing my hosts in two large white chairs. Frances, looking amused, wanted to know how it was that I, an American woman, a detective she had been told, knew Captain MacKinnon and a few more of her friends. While I did my best to pacify her curiosity without too much explanation, Jono was moving in on me. He had transferred himself from chair to sofa and had his well-developed arm around my bare shoulders. Frances continued to ask questions. Jono moved his spare hand to my waist. Frances smiled approvingly.

I hurried to the reason I was there. "Frances, do you know Freda Wagner?"

"How could I know Freda Wagner?" She took a long drag off her ivory cigarette holder, exhaling as she added, "She is dead."

"Death doesn't seem to end people's relationships with Freda," I said, mostly to myself. I added, "So, I would guess then that you never knew her?"

"That is correct. I knew her husband, when he used to come to Mombasa. He always stayed here at the Pwani; she never accompanied him. Apparently he became ill with malaria, stopped coming. I heard that he died a couple of years ago." She put the cigarette holder to her lips, readying it before she said, "I was surprised to learn that she died here in this hotel, suicide apparently, or was it?" She took the awaited drag, watching me intently.

"That's what the police concluded." I removed Jono's hand from my thigh, directing a polite smile into his twenty-year-old eyes. "The family sent me to confirm the report."

Frances began making her way out of the chair as she said, "So that is why you are here—Freda Wagner." She limped to the bar and refilled her snifter. "I cannot help you, Kelly. I was in Germany when it happened. They put the newspapers in my suite when I am gone; I read about it only a few days ago when I returned." She smiled at Jono, wiggling a finger for him to come to her. He did, wrapping her up in his arms. She nuzzled into him and said, "Kelly isn't going to play with us, darling."

Considering that my cue, I stood up and thanked them for the drink. On the way to the door, I asked, "Did either of you hear anything from other hotel guests regarding her death?"

"Only that there had been a suicide in one of the rooms," Frances answered. "On this floor, 335."

"How about friends? Did she have any friends that you know of here or in Mombasa?"

Frances had followed me, leaning on Jono. "The only thing I knew about Freda Wagner was what I read in the paper. Apparently she was an incredible woman, admired by everyone, with possibly the exception of her husband." She laughed, waving the cigarette holder like a hanky. "Good-bye, Kelly," she purred. "I am sorry I could not help." Jono opened the door for me, and Frances chided, "If you become bored with being a detective, stop by." She cackled, and Jono shut the door behind me.

I couldn't sleep worth a damn. Maybe I shouldn't have taken the room next to Freda's. I still hadn't gone through it, and it was there, right beyond the wall of my bed, haunting me. And Frances's parting shot, Freda's husband not admiring her, bugged me, for no good reason other than it was insulting to Freda. He was long out of the picture and couldn't possibly figure in Freda's death. And I certainly shouldn't have had bratwurst for dinner. I got up, fixed a bicarbonate, and took it to the balcony, groping my way in the dark to one of the purple chairs.

It was a clear night, no moon, the tinted ground lights of the hotel filtering a green hue up the three stories of balconies. There were still people in the pool and a few spotlighted couples around the patio bar dancing: black against white, clinging, caressing in foreplay. I sat watching the tiny figures, listening to the rock music, too far away to identify a song, thinking about Hitesh bopping around. What a guy, my blind guru, dancing to "Proud Mary." Christ, I needed to dance more. I was thinking about doing just that, heading for the music, when a noise startled the hell out of me. A loud noise. A chair leg scooted over a floor, a concrete floor, a balcony floor—Freda's balcony floor. I froze a moment, listening to every sound. Had I imagined it? No, but perhaps it came from the balcony above or below. It hadn't come from the balcony to the left of mine, I was quite sure, but I leaned over the rail and looked anyway. There was no one there. If I were to look into Freda's balcony and someone were there, I'd frighten them away. There was only one thing to do. I got the keys to 335.

Barefoot in pajamas, armed with my handy child's baseball bat, leaded, I crept out my door and very carefully, very quietly, placed the key to 335 in the lock. It turned easily. I pushed the door open a crack, listening. There was no sound. Tiptoeing in, leaving the door open a bit, I felt my way along the foyer wall, stopping where it opened into the room. It was mostly dark, only that eerie green hue filtering up and in like a cello at a funeral. I resisted switching on a light until I had a better sense of things. The drapes were mostly open to the balcony, just as they were that morning with Kruger. I moved a bit farther into the room. The sliding door was open. It hadn't been that morning. Anxiously, I traced the room with my eyes, identifying objects. No one here. I had to assume someone was on the balcony.

Gripping the bat, I moved toward the sliding door, placing my feet carefully, unsure of what was on the floor. Where the end of the drape met the wall, I cracked it the width of my eye. There was no one in either of the two chairs, but the hammock moved. Yes, there was someone in the hammock! I leaned against the wall to catch my breath and to decide if I wanted the confrontation to be on the balcony. Maybe it would be better to wait outside the room or simply knock on the door.

After a minute or so, I took another peek. The figure had moved from the hammock to the rail. It was a small figure, a woman in a long, loose dress, a galabiya maybe. While I squinted at her image, she turned around, resting her bottom against the rail and looking into the room. She was a black woman, very short hair, nearly bald. Perhaps she was a maid. Maids had keys to the rooms, and they would certainly know this room was vacant. While I pondered the maid theory, the woman walked into the room, fell onto the bed and began to weep. Now I felt guilty! A voyeur to her grief, I had invaded her privacy. How could I confront her without terrifying her? When I was about to make my move, the woman got up, still sobbing and walked into the bathroom as though she were exhausted. She blew her nose and ran some water, then reappeared in the foyer. The fragment of light leaking through the door from the hall silhouetted her alarm; the door was not shut as she'd left it. She was out the door like a sliver. I bolted, tripping over Freda's sandy beach shoes, staggering into the foyer. Flinging open the door, I looked down the hall both ways. Not a trace, not a sound. The elevator was quiet. She was gone.

I found the woman's escape: the stairs adjacent to the elevator and two doors from 335. Was she a maid with a broken heart needing a place to cry? Or had she murdered Freda and was now remorseful? I had felt her grief; it paralyzed me. "Christ," I moaned. I'd sure as hell blown that one. I doubted that she'd be back.

The next morning it was mango and coffee on the balcony. I was brooding, a bit bent, wishing I'd handled last night differently, all of it. I should have met Frau Von Heilm alone, for breakfast or tea, when she didn't have other things on her mind. But then, maybe she gave me all she had. Certainly Freda's visitor was a mystery that could have been solved.

I was getting in the shower to soothe my ego with the Pwani's lavender soap when I heard a knock at the door. The peephole showed a distorted black face, too close to identify. In three languages I called out, "Who's there?" but the face didn't respond. Irritated, I threw on my beach cover-up and yelled in English, "Leave or I'm calling the desk!" As I picked up the phone, the voice at the door said, "I am Jono. I know about Freda Wagner."

Jono was a kid in jeans, white T-shirt, and tennis shoes. I said, "You're much younger in the morning." He said that it was the clothes. Frances liked him in fancy clothes that made him look her age. We both laughed. I took him onto the balcony. "So, you do know Freda Wagner," I said, motioning for him to sit.

"No, not really." He scooted his purple chair near mine, making the same noise that had alarmed me last night. "My sister knows her," he said, taking a seat and reaching for my hand. I pulled it away. "You don't like dark skin?" he asked seriously.

"I like dark skin just fine," I said sharply. "And like everything I like, I like it when it suits me."

Jono looked puzzled only a second before he put his index finger on my knee, moving it in a figure eight. "I can suit you, Kelly, I can suit you perfectly." His coarse voice was well rehearsed.

"Look, Jono," I said, flicking his finger like a crumb, "I'm simply not interested in twenty-year-olds, of any shade, not for a few years." Feeling a need to preserve his professional ego, his means to a living, I added with a smile, "If I'd known you, say, ten years ago, I would have thought you perfect." I got up and stood over him with my hand on my hip. "Now, do you have something to tell me about Freda Wagner?"

"Okay." He put his hands behind his head and looked up at me, his eyes bright in the morning sun. "I have information to sell you. How much will you pay?"

We haggled. Finally, I bought what he was selling. His sister worked at a special school. "It is so special," he said sarcastically, "she will not tell me why it is special, more like top secret, I think. It is probably guarded with guns!" He chuckled and went on to say that his sister would be fired if she talked about the place or took anyone there, and she loved her job like a religion. He took her to work every morning, dropping her off at the end of a road. She took a trail from there. He picked her up in the same place every night.

He stopped talking, got up, and stood beside me at the rail. "Yes?" I asked, impatient. "This is a school, a children's school?"

"I am not sure about that part," he said casually, before beginning a smug smile. "But Freda Wagner works there. I think she is the boss, was the boss."

I sat down. "How do you know that?"

"Because . . ." He waved a finger, looking up into his brain as though he were Sherlock Holmes about to make a deduction. "One evening, when I picked up my sister, she was crying. She said her boss died. Two days later she was reading the paper, the article about Freda Wagner, and she was crying again. When I take her to work now, she is always sad, not happy like she was before." He shrugged his muscular shoulders, grinning, "But still it is, how do you say, sacred, this job of hers."

"Can you take me there?"

"I can take you to the end of the road." He rubbed his fingers together, indicating that it would cost more money, then added emphatically, "My sister would kill me if I went farther."

"When?"

"Anytime, but you cannot tell my sister how you found the place, if you find the place. It is somewhere in the jungle, the jungle that is used by people who leave their tribes."

"Tribal people, renegade tribal people are living there, where this school is?" I was beginning to doubt everything he was saying. Maybe I was being set up.

Jono could tell he was suspect. "Kelly, I tell you the truth. I do not believe they are renegade, but people from tribes whose land is taken by the government." He screwed his face in confusion. "The government is moving some tribes, making them live where they tell them to live. De . . . detribalize. I think that is what it is called. My sister walks there every day. She tells me it is safe."

Twenty minutes later I met Jono in the lobby. I gave him a letter to read addressed to myself. It stated where I was going, generally, with whom and why. When Jono finished reading it, I asked the desk manager to put it in my box and told Jono that he would get paid when I returned to retrieve the letter. He rolled his eyes, shook his head, and pointed the way to his shiny German motorcycle, a gift from Frances, he bragged.

We rode about fifteen miles south of the Pwani before we turned onto a rutted road meandering off into a thick jungle. I tightened my grip around Jono's firm middle and we bumped along, the road more narrow, the jungle more dense. After several miles, Jono stopped the bike at an intersection with a nearly indiscernible track. "This is where I leave my sister," he said without turning around. "I will take you on, as far as I can, but I must have your word not to tell her, and . . ." He raised a hand, rubbing his fingers together, indicating it would cost extra. A grunt in his ear, I agreed, knowing he probably took his sister farther every day. Squeezing the throttle gingerly, he followed the track, which wound around a natural reservoir of fresh water and came to an abrupt end at a tall barbed wire fence. Jono parked the bike, we dismounted, and he asked, "How long do I wait?"

"You wait until I return!" I said, sufficiently incredulous for him to know that he'd better.

He leaned against a bank of tree roots and grinned. "What if you do not return?"

I pulled the wire loop off the pole, opened the barbed wire gate, and started up a wide, sandy white trail, yelling over my shoulder, "If I haven't returned in three hours, come after me!"

The trail meandered as the road had. The humidity was intense. I'd walked less than a quarter mile when I began seeing tents of plastic, huts of mud and sticks, a goat here, a naked child there. It was another quarter mile before I saw an adult, and I wished I hadn't. He was standing in the middle of the trail urinating. His hair was ochered red, and he carried a long spear, like a Maasi, but he wore long pants and tennis shoes, or what was left of them. Obviously a displaced Maasi warrior with an identity crisis, he didn't look pleased to see me walking toward him. When I was twenty feet away, I said, *"Jambo!"* a Swahili greeting, in a happy voice accompanied by an exaggerated smile. He scowled even more but stepped off the trail. As I passed by, he said something, a few words I recognized as Maasi but didn't understand. Pulling strands of his ochered hair away from his head, he said it again. I stopped and held out some of my own red hair and said, "Irish!" He cocked his head to hear it again. "Irish!" I repeated, still holding my hair, still smiling. He mimicked me, then we said it together and both laughed. I walked on. There were others in sparse and sketchy costumes, some gathering wood, some building shelters, some wearing smiles, some not.

Around a wide bend in the trail, I came upon several substantial structures pieced together with jungle wood. The trail forked there. Three or four women adorned in tribal jewelry sat in front of the structures on spotted skins with their infant children. I paused for a smile. One of the women, a child on her stringy breast, got up and pointed toward the trail to the right. Nodding gratefully, I followed her direction.

The trail grew narrow and swampy; the jungle closed in. I rolled up the hems of my khakis and tread carefully on boards that had been laid over large roots in muddy pools. Noisy birds of every color flitted around, a warning of my intrusion. Soaked with sweat, wishing for a lung of oxygen, I was delighted when the sun suddenly came blasting through and the jungle receded. In front of me was a pond surrounded by brilliant orange, yellow, and red hibiscus. Beyond the pond there was a compound of stucco buildings, each painted a different pastel color. Their roofs were thatched, neatly trimmed, and half tucked into the jungle. I could feel Freda's presence.

The trail around the pond, laid with stones, led to a high wire fence and locked gate in front of the compound. Two large German shepherd dogs came bounding toward the gate, barking, the hair on their backs erect. I waited. In a moment a girl appeared. She wore a long apron over her shorts and was carrying a bucket. I wondered if she was Jono's sister. She hushed the dogs and said, *"Jambo. Unatoka wapi?"* Hello. Where do you come from?

With the dogs quiet, I could hear children playing, some crying. I told the girl that I was sent by the family of Freda Wagner. She looked me over suspiciously from head to toe, put down the bucket, and disappeared into a blue building. The dogs came back to the fence and took up their barking. In a few minutes an older woman with chestnut skin, a gray dusting on her close-cropped hair, came out of the building, followed by two more shepherds. These dogs didn't bark, they growled, all of their teeth exposed, and the woman made no attempt to stop them. Above the canine commotion, she spoke in German. *"Wie heissen sie?"* What is your name? I answered her in English, explaining that I was American but sent by Freda's barrister. She gave me a wary look and switched to English, "There is no one here who can speak with you. You must leave now."

I protested. "It is most important that I speak with persons close to Freda concerning her death. Please, I am a friend of Freda's." I felt that I could say that in honesty.

The woman gave me a sardonic smile and said, "If you were a friend of Freda's, there would be no need for you to speak of her." She picked up the bucket the girl had left and repeated, "You will go now." Then she turned around and went back into the blue building, leaving me alone with the snarling compound dogs.

Back at the Pwani, I tore up the letter from my box and paid Jono off. The only thing I told him was that I couldn't get past the guards, no one could. He wasn't surprised. He walked me to my room, wanting to know if there was anything else he could do for me. Maybe I wanted to go dancing. Other women would see him dancing with me and want his time. I asked how much he would pay me for that kind of exposure. He laughed. I told him good-bye, closed the door, and made my way to the shower—a cold one.

I was eating the lunch I'd had sent up and struggling with answers to my failed trip into the jungle when Kumlesh called. He had the information I'd requested. "That was fast," I said, "even for an alchemist."

He giggled and said, "Yes, and good news, I think. I will see you today?"

"Yes, of course. At your shop, between four and five?"

"That is good, Kelly. Good-bye then. Oh, Kelly, there has also been two calls for you. One seemed urgent." I could hear him fumbling with paper. "From London, a barrister, regarding a person you are interested in. And the second message is from your captain."

"Okay, thanks, Kumlesh." I knew he wouldn't give any more information over the phone than necessary. The phones of Kenya, particularly Mombasa, were easy to tap and frequently were. I was sure that Frank had called Charles Childress in London, complaining that I'd abandoned him. I put in a call to the Norfolk. He wasn't in. I left my number.

The afternoon rains coincided with the ride into town. It was miserably hot and the taxi was in bad need of shocks. The ferry was so jammed that I couldn't get a door open. The pedestrian traffic was just as tight, all headed for Mombasa nightlife, all soaked, the makeup running off the faces of the prostitutes. I sat in the sweltering taxi, anxious about what Kumlesh had learned. I certainly needed a break if I was going to bring Freda's demise to a proper closure.

Kumlesh was standing in his door watching the rain. He sent for tea and handed me the written telephone messages: Charles Childress was upset that I'd left his client sitting in Nairobi and expected an explanation from me immediately. The message from Captain Mac was the one he always sent when he was in port: "If you are in town, your pass is at the gate."

"Nothing to worry you, I hope," Kumlesh said, handing me a hot cup of strong tea boiled with milk. I confirmed it was nothing and asked him what he'd found. He filtered through his leather case looking for the right file. "The first thing I should tell you, Kelly, is that no one on Southshore knows your Freda Wagner." Somehow I wasn't surprised.

He took two copies of ledger paper from a folder and put one of them in front of me, the print so small I could barely see it. "Here is the account," he said proudly. "Frau Wagner made two deposits." I strained to see that he was pointing to an amount in shillings shown beside a date. "This figure, deposited two years and three months ago, computes to," he looked upward for the answer, "approximately two hundred and seventy thousand in dollars." He glanced at me for my nodding response and went on. "On June 16 of this year, three months ago, she made the second deposit of"—he was pointing and calculating again—"approximately one hundred and ten thousand dollars."

"Well!" I exclaimed. "A perfect match to her withdrawals from the Nairobi bank! Three hundred eighty thousand. But why would . . . "

"There is more, Kelly," he eagerly interrupted, putting the second page on my lap. "One year after she opened the account, three other names were added. Here they are: Hariri Mwimbaji, Shamba La Mwimbaji, and Tumba La Ua Kaunda." Kumlesh looked amused. "These are unusual names."

"Yes," I nodded. "Hariri, that means silk, and Shamba La, that's a songster, isn't it? And, Tumba La Ua is flower bud. I suspect these are names given by Freda. And Hariri and Shamba La must be related, sisters or mother and daughter, agreed?"

"Yes, most likely." He rubbed his nose under his glasses. "These women with the exotic names, they now own this account. Four weeks ago, Frau Wagner removed her name. She signed off personally; a teller verified it for me." Taking off his glasses, he sipped at his tea. I thought about Frank's disappointment. He no longer had an inheritance from Freda. "The name on the account," Kumlesh said, tapping the top of the paper with the stem of his glasses, "is *Kipengee*. Does that make any sense to you?"

"*Kipengee* . . . no. That means detour in Swahili, doesn't it? What a strange title for an account, *detour*. Do you know if it's registered as a business?"

Kumlesh shook his head. "I checked and it is not, but that is not surprising, Kelly. It gets more interesting. There are no checks written on this account, only cash withdrawals, almost all by Frau Wagner. The balance of the account today is"—he put his glasses back on to read the numbers—"in dollars, about two hundred and twenty-five thousand. But the strangest thing of all is the address." He was pointing. "Look at this address. Do you recognize it?"

"Kumlesh, I can't see the address, my eyes are old, and without you, I need glasses. What is the address?" I asked impatiently, thinking I was ready for the punch line. I wasn't.

"The Marabou!" Kumlesh exclaimed. "The address is the Club Marabou."

"No! Why? What possible connection could Freda have to the Marabou?" I was sure this was a mistake. The Marabou was the neon of Mombasa, a casino, a nightclub, a whorehouse, a drug bastion, the last place in the world to look for Freda Wagner. I took Kumlesh's glasses off his nose and looked for myself. "Kumlesh, do you have a single clue what this is about?"

"No, Kelly, but I suspect that it must be some kind of money laundering. They do a large drug trade at the Marabou, and although the officials look the other way, the books have to balance. This woman might be a partner of the Marabou's . . ."

"No!" I interrupted. "That can't be possible." I shook myself.

"Sorry, Kumlesh, but I know that money came from Freda Wagner's coffee farm. It was her money. The deposits and withdrawals in Nairobi match these in Mombasa perfectly. If the address on the account is the Marabou, then perhaps one of these women works there, perhaps an accountant, maybe a dealer." I picked up the paper and looked at it again. "No checks means they paid cash for everything, no paper trail." Kumlesh nodded. "And," I added, "the Marabou is pretty much off limits to the police, and probably anyone else asking questions."

"I agree, Kelly," Kumlesh said, taking back his glasses. "Do you have a thought?"

"No." I moaned and slumped back in my chair. "No, not a thought, but I have a feeling, Kumlesh. These women are doing a lot to cover themselves, to not be discovered. Listen to what I did today." I righted myself, sipped the now cold tea, and told him about the compound in the middle of a jungle in the middle of a tribal reservation. When I finished, I asked him if he could think of any reason for such secrecy around a school, a compound for children, if indeed that was the case. He couldn't. We sat for a moment sipping, studying the situation. I said, "They spent a hundred and fifty-five thousand dollars. I can imagine that's about what it cost to build that compound." Again we sat, silent, wondering. "The Marabou, for Christ's sake," I murmured. "They actually mail the statements to the Marabou?"

"Kelly, you know how the mail is here. The statements are picked up by someone from the Marabou, usually the accountant, I was told. The accountant's name is Bhatnagar, Robert Bhatnagar, Indian. I know who he is, but I resisted asking him without consulting you first. I know that you have contacts at the Marabou that may be more useful, more knowledgeable on the inside track."

"My inside track," I snickered, "as you know is Captain Mac, who knows all the whores because his lady was the head madam, until he made a semi-honest woman of her."

"Captain MacKinnon may be your best bet, Kelly. You need to find out who these women are. Someone at the Marabou knows."

"Well," I laughed, "it's Captain Mac to the rescue again. I guess I'm headed for the port." We said our good-byes, the sisters came out, and the mother came out, thankfully in her veil. I was at the door when I remembered something. "Kumlesh," I said, opening my briefcase again. "Look at this note, Freda's note, the suicide note. It's in German. What is this word?" I pointed. "It says, '. . . it has been an incredible . . .' An incredible what?"

Kumlesh pushed up his glasses. "Detour, that is German for detour, *kipengee* in Swahili, the name of the account."

I read the entire note again, translating it from the German. "I'm sorry it's over, it was an incredible detour." That was her clue, I supposed, her only clue.

The port was busy, a line of cars in the rain waiting to be processed one at a time. Finally, the guard handed me the pass left by Captain Mac and waved the taxi through. Nearly dark, the *Osprey* was lit like Christmas, a jolly-looking bucket of bolts—Captain Mac's name for it. A 400-foot cargo ship, one of the last of its like, it boasted seven officers above, with uniforms if called for, and seven crewman below. The officers were first- or second-generation South Africans transplanted from the British Isles, with the exception of the ensign, who came from an island of the Seychelles. The crew were all Mauritian: strong, cheap, ship-savvy labor, rarely allowed off ship in any port. The South African cargo line, a small fleet of poorly equipped antiquated ships, trespassed the forbidden ports and dangerous waters of East Africa to bring trade to many countries where it was otherwise cut off by warring factions on land.

I told the taxi driver not to wait, saluted the Mauritian crewman doing deck watch, whom I knew, then carefully trod the wet gangplank. Captain Mac was sitting alone in the *Osprey's* bar, which boasted the sign "Zan-Z-Bar," aptly named for one of its ports of call. "Kelly! Bloody hell, you're in town! Sit yourself down. You look in need of some of my prize rum—and a towel." He was up, ducking his square frame and wavy head of brown hair under the bar. He tossed me a towel, boasting, "And I just happen to have mango, Kelly my dear." He held up a pitcher. "I had a feeling in my bones you were in town. Ah, but I can see you're working, not here for the fun of it."

"I doubt that I've ever been to Mombasa for the fun of it, Captain," I quipped, drying my hair. "You're the only fun I have in Mombasa, and God knows I can't count on you! Your schedule is as unpredictable as mine."

"Not so," he said, handing me a beautiful, flesh-colored drink of mango juice and his prize rum, a wonderful dark grog from India. "I'm in this port on a regular schedule, barring hurricanes, warring factions in Somalia, bombs in Mozambique, insufficient parts for the bucket here"—he slapped the bar—"and of course, sometimes we have to wait for a new shipment of penicillin, particularly in this port." He laughed heartily and said, "Cheers, Kelly! 'Tis always good to have you aboard." We drank and he added, "Unless, that is, you're looking again for a ride into Beira." He shook his finger in my face. "Then we're going to argue like bloody hell."

"No, Captain, I'm looking for a ride to somewhere much more dangerous than Mozambique. I was hoping to accompany you to the Marabou tonight. I assume you'll be going?"

Sid, the engineer, waltzed into the Zan-Z-Bar unshaven and scratching. "'Tis a dark night in hell when the captain and meself don't make it to the Marabou, Kelly me lass." He came around and gave me a rough buss on the cheek, then ducked under the bar for a short glass and a bottle of Irish whiskey. "Know'n you be going with us, lassie, will be turn'n this wet night into a summer's day." He held up his glass. "Cheers!"

In a few minutes the young, tall, dark-skinned, blonde-haired, blue-eyed Ensign Basso joined us, shirt off—such a tease. Then Duncan, the redheaded, mustached navigator, crept in, looking as though the only thing that could save him was a drink. We all tossed a few, listening to each other's stories, the captain's repertoire befitting his life of risk, which he led with his square chin and a great sense of timing and wit. I'd done him a favor once, a personal favor that we never discussed again, and he had returned it many times over, a good friend and comrade on the Indian Ocean.

At about nine, Ensign Basso brought around the ship's Mombasa jalopy, and we were off to the Marabou, starched and ironed. I'd changed into one of Duncan's white merchant marine uniforms, orders of the captain, for my own safety. The officer's uniform ruled at the Marabou and, I'd had occasion to learn, was a single woman's best defense with the whores; it would keep me from being mugged, mickeyed, or worse.

The Marabou, the audacious source of Mombasa's principal revenue, sat at the edge of the bay lit like a beacon from hell. Inside, the tables were full. Men in black turbans and uniformed sailors spat on dice and thew them, speaking their mother's names. Women adorned in sequins wore stress on their faces and held cigarettes over their cards. We left Sid and Duncan there rubbing their hands together and descended the stairs.

The captain found his woman, Rose, then his waiter, making the financial arrangements for a table. The entertainment hadn't begun, and the stage was crowded with prostitutes, their bodies oblivious to the beat of the music, swaying only for eyes in the audience who would buy. Some French sailors, in their summer short pants, tasseled hats, and scrubbed faces, got up to dance. They formed a circle, protecting themselves as long as possible. Working girls crowded around Basso, two on his lap like black widow spiders, their arms and legs wrapped around him, their mouths biting his ears and neck. He squirmed uncomfortably, pleading with Rose for help. She sent them away.

The noise level prevented conversation across the table. The captain and Rose were snuggled together. He'd promised to find out what he could from her about the women named Hariri and Shamba La Mwimbaji and Tumba La Ua Kaunda—Silk, Songster, and Flower Bud.

Sid and Duncan soon joined us. Sid said he couldn't be late for his motorcycle-driving lesson. The prostitutes left the stage, torches were brought out, and a thunderous drumroll announced the beginning of the show. An incredibly beautiful girl, wearing only a motorcycle helmet and boots, came out and climbed on a fantasy cycle. She gave a few sidekicks with her shiny boots, the sound of an engine roared, and she imaginatively settled into a straddle and began gyrating her small, firm tits and ass. That was the show, at least her part of it.

The next act belonged to the nearly naked, well-toned body of Rose's brother, Mandi. The smell of kerosene was strong as he held a huge flaming torch over his head, preparing to swallow it. I didn't watch. Rose once told me that Mandi coughed blood every morning.

Basso had moved closer and put his arm around my shoulders, attempting conversation. I never objected to his attention, but I couldn't hear what he was saying and thought it just as well, until I realized that he was relaying a message from the captain. I put my ear to his mouth. The woman about to take the stage was Shamba La Mwimbaji—Songster.

I sat there enveloped in Basso, listening to Shamba La sing a beautiful French song. She was lovely, her voice satin, her dress green sequins, but what possible connection could she have with Freda Wagner, her money, and the compound I'd found in the jungle surrounded by displaced tribal people? At this point I could not ignore the ugly shape of the puzzle pieces fitting together in my head. I untangled myself from Basso and moved close enough to cup my hand and whisper to Rose.

The torches were carried off, and the whores, the ones not yet employed for the night, resumed their enticement on the stage. Rose had gone to deliver my message to Shamba La. Basso wanted to dance a slow one, and it seemed a good idea to me. They were playing "I Left My Heart in San Francisco." We swayed, melancholy, both wishing we were home. Basso—strong, straight arrow, always the hero—was often my answer to lust and love in a stormy port, and the night was feeling stormy. I watched for Rose to return.

A tap on the shoulder and Rose indicated the veranda; Shamba La was waiting for me. Basso went with me, past the draped bodies in final negotiations, past the silver-haired bouncer who saluted our uniforms, past the drug dealers, and beyond the swimming pool to the seawall. Even with the salt air, there was a smell of slime. Shamba La in her green sequins appeared out of the dark, her stage makeup glowing mistily.

"You are Kelly?" she asked in English, not waiting for an answer. "And you are a ship's officer, a white woman." She put her hand on her hip and demanded, "What do you want with me?"

"I am a friend of Freda Wagner," I said, now feeling that I had every right to say so. "I want to know how and why she died."

Songster wasn't prepared, in fact was obviously taken aback. She leaned against the dank seawall and didn't say anything for a minute or so; then she said, "You are the woman who came to Kipengee, the woman with red hair. How do you know Frau Wagner?"

"I met her five years ago, and since her family learned of her death, I've been following her trail. Yes, I am the woman who was at Kipengee—*Detour*—and I know of Hariri and Tumba La Ua Kaunda. I've seen your bank account. And now I expect you to tell me the rest of the story."

Even in the dark it was easy to see that Shamba La was fighting tears, but she stuck her chin out at Basso and demanded, "Who is this man, this officer?"

"My escort to this incredibly slimy . . ." I looked around and chose different words. "He is a fellow officer, my escort. Would you feel more comfortable if he waited for me inside?"

She nodded, and Basso walked as far as the pool, placing himself in a lounge chair. She lit a cigarette, took a long drag, and exhaled with a moan. "There is nothing at all I can tell you. If you are a friend of Frau Wagner's, as you claim, there is nothing you do not already know."

"Frau Wagner had many friends," I said too loudly, "and none of them know what happened to her here in Mombasa. And the truth is, Shamba La, if I don't learn how she died, there will be a full-scale investigation into her death. Would you ladies prefer dealing with me, a woman, a friend to Freda, or would you prefer dealing with her stepson and male investigators from London or Germany?"

Her eyes glistened, a tear tracking through her makeup and into her red mouth. Lips trembling, she took a deep breath and chose her words. "The only person who can make that decision is Hariri." I waited. She asked, "What is the name of your ship?"

"I'm staying at the Pwani," I said, "room 336, next to Freda's room. When can I expect Hariri?"

She took another drag off the cigarette, scowling. "I cannot promise she will see you. I can only tell her what you have told me." And with that, the sequined songster threw down the cigarette and walked away.

I treated myself to a night on the ship with Basso, a late morning, and a good English breakfast prepared by the Mauritian cook. The captain, Sid, and Duncan arrived by taxi just in time. They tossed their hats and crumpled jackets on the rack and took their places around the officers' table, unshaven and reeking of stale smoke. The captain glanced around. "Bloody hell, men!" he bellowed. "I may soon become too old for this port!" No one believed him, and no one responded. He piled his plate with eggs and asked, "Is the ship accounted for, no casualties, enough penicillin to go around?"

There were three messages for me at the Pwani, all from Frank at the Norfolk. I called him, wondering what I'd say. He wasn't in. I put on my bathing suit and went to the beach for a swim. It was hot, the water too warm to refresh, my skin too white to expose, my brain too tired of living with Freda and her mystery.

Back in my room, I ordered a beer, sat on the balcony, and put it to Freda. She was using me. Hitesh had agreed. But he also said that I needed to come through for her. He said it was the thing she died for that she wanted me to know. If she wanted me to know, why didn't she leave a better trail? Did she die for the secret things she was doing here? She built a compound, a school for children, maybe, hidden in the jungle, protected by mean German shepherd dogs and tribal people. Why would children need to be protected? Because they were not wanted—maybe by their fathers, maybe by their mothers—particularly if they were children of prostitutes. Abortions were hard to come by, and dangerous, and birth control was expensive, unavailable to most whores. But I knew there was another puzzle piece. I knew it was ugly. I ordered another beer.

At six o'clock I took a shower, dressed, and picked up the keys to 335. It was time I looked at Freda's room up close. I turned the key, switched on the lights, and grimaced, with the same feeling in my gut as when Kruger opened the door. Freda's sandals were where I'd stumbled over them, the sand scattered on the carpet. I picked them up. A European size 36. How could Freda fit into a 36? She was a big woman, five feet nine or ten. She probably weighed a hundred and fifty pounds, or did until she became ill. The sandals were not Freda's. I remembered the other sandals, the white ones on the balcony with the beach towel. I went there. Those were Freda's, size 41. The slippers near the bloodstained chair were also Freda's. Freda did not die alone.

I rummaged through her case. There was a set of underclothes, a pair of sneakers, a pair of socks, a bathing suit, and toilet articles. There was room for her nightgown and robe, but that's what she wore to the morgue. "Freda!" I exclaimed aloud, releasing a bit of grief, or just the anxiety that comes with rifling through a dead woman's personal things. "Unyoya said you were gone nearly two months before you died. Where the hell is all the stuff missing from your house?" I knew it was at Kipengee. I checked the closet: a pair of khaki slacks and a print shirt, nothing more.

A book, *Birds of East Africa*, was on the dresser next to Freda's hat. I tried on the hat, a straw floppy, well worn. I picked up her book and sat down in the chair where she died, the back of my shirt and the soles of my shoes resting on her dried blood. It was a severely uncomfortable chair. Freda would not have sat in that chair for long, certainly not by choice. She was a comfortable woman, her clothes, her hat, her hair, her face, all comfortable. She didn't sit in that chair reading while someone slipped in from the balcony and shot her. That chair was someone else's choice of Freda's place to die.

Feeling queasy, unable to look at the room anymore, I switched off the lights, went to the eerie green light of the balcony, and collapsed in the hammock. I was sure now that someone else had killed Freda. Freda had sat down in that chair and someone put a thirty-eight to her head and pulled the trigger. "Why, Freda?" I nearly shouted. "Why?"

I didn't hear the front door open. I didn't hear anything until the woman spoke to me. She was standing near the hammock. She said, "I am Hariri."

I scrambled to my feet and tried to make out who it was. It was the same small woman, the woman who had been there two nights before, nearly bald, maybe wearing the same loose dress. She sat down in one of the purple chairs. Very softly, she said, "I killed Freda."

I sat down, too. For a long time we both just sat there staring off over the balcony. We couldn't look at each other, not then. We both knew that would have been too much. So we waited.

Softly, very softly, she finally said, "I was the lover of her husband. I killed both of them."

After a few minutes she began to talk, a stronger voice. I glanced at her, just briefly. Tears were washing over the sharp bones of her thin face. "After he died, Freda came to Mombasa, to see me. She knew. And she was sick. She knew it was not the malaria sickness. She saw me, sick, our son—Frank's son—both of us sick."

Hariri was struggling. Allowing her dignity, I kept my eyes over the balcony and said, "This is so difficult. Please take your time. We have time." Then she looked at me, and I at her. In the green hue, her eyes, sunken, dark, wet, told me that she had little time. I asked her if she would like to be in the hammock. She shook her head and went on.

"Freda did not have children, no children of her own. She saw Bobi, Frank's son, my son, sick." There was a pause, a faulty breath. "Freda and I, it took us both. We were, how you say? Comrades. We were comrades in mothering. We were comrades in the disease, the disease that killed Frank. The disease I gave to him and he gave to her." She let her head drop between her shoulders. I moved my chair closer to her, put my arm around her, felt her skeletal structure. She began to sob, her ribs like a washboard on my hand. I put my face on the sharp ridges of her shoulder. This was the ugly puzzle piece I had dreaded to see.

After a few minutes, I asked, "Please, can you tell me about the school?"

She wiped her face on her sleeve before she spoke. "Freda, when she saw that Bobi is just one child, and they are many, the sick ones, she wants to make a place for them, a place where they are safe from those who fear the disease. The mothers, they cannot hide all the children, and there are those who would kill them because they have this sickness."

Hariri was becoming breathless. I remembered Unyoya and what Freda said about difficult subjects. I went to the phone and ordered a pot of tea and biscuits. Then I persuaded Hariri to move into the room, to lie on the bed. I brought her a cold washcloth and put it on her face. I took off her sandals, her size 36 sandals that hung loosely over the remaining flesh of her feet. I lay beside her and waited for the tea.

Propped up on pillows, Hariri and I drank the tea and ate the biscuits. She told me that Freda knew people in high places and gave the government money to let her build a school, a hospital and school, Kipengee, where it was safe. The tribal people helped her build it, in exchange for food and medical supplies, but she had to show them how. She bought medicine from Germany, for all the sicknesses, the malaria, the cholera, the yellow fever, but there was no medicine for the sickness they shared—Hariri, Freda, and Bobi—not even in Germany. Hariri looked at me, her deep eyes a big question. "Do you have this disease in America?"

"Yes," I told her. "I live in the city of San Francisco. Several of my friends have already died. We don't have medicine for it either." She frowned at me in disbelief. I asked her, "Why do you think that you gave Frank the disease? Were you already sick?"

"No. We are sick at the same time," she said.

"Then perhaps Frank gave it to you, and to Freda."

She was scowling. "But how can that be? The sickness come from Africa."

"Maybe, maybe not. But Frank came from Africa, and my friends in San Francisco have never been to Africa. Hariri, you cannot blame yourself. You did not kill Frank and Frank did not kill Freda. The disease did, a disease that no one knows anything about yet, except that it kills."

"Freda knew!" she said coarsely. "She ordered boxes, boxes that come on ships. Rubbers, colored ones." She grinned, amused. "Shamba La, my daughter, gives them to the women of the Marabou. Freda made the Marabou give her one of the rooms there. She taught the women. She gave them lessons. Now Shamba La teaches them."

"I heard your daughter sing. She is lovely."

Hariri beamed. "She never want to be a prostitute, and she is not. She is a singer, the songster. When I have disease, Bobi too, Shamba La wants to do something. She do whatever Freda say because she know Freda is the very best hope for all of us."

"Did Freda give you your names?"

"Yes." She smiled enough to expose her teeth, dark and yellow. "Freda gave everyone a name. She said we need a special name because we do a special thing. She give us all a beautiful name. She said we are all beautiful."

"Who is Tumba La Ua Kaunda, Flower Bud?"

"Tumba La Ua comes from Nairobi. The woman, Constance, brought her. You met Tumba La Ua at Kipengee. She is nurse, maybe doctor, but she not recognized at Nairobi. Her mother was prostitute; she died of syphilis. Tumba La Ua want to be a doctor to cure syphilis, but before Kenyatta no African can be doctor, and still it is too much money for school. Tumba La Ua says this is good work here at Kipengee, maybe she cure disease worse than syphilis."

It was time for me to ask Hariri about Freda's death, but I didn't have to. I took her hand and she knew the question. "Freda brought a gun from the coffee farm. It was small gun. It was Frank's gun. She did not want death to come in front of the children, where she is mostly living at Kipengee. She is too sick to go to Nairobi on the train, and she say no one at the coffee farm would know what to do. She come here to this room for death. I come with her. She was suffering, so much suffering." Hariri took a breath and swallowed hard. "I knew she wanted me to use the gun. She didn't have to tell me." She looked at me, her face streaked with tears. "I wish I had not left the gun for the police. Who will help me now?"

The tea was gone. The story was told. Hariri and I fell asleep.

When the sun came through the drapes, Hariri was gone. I had watched her leave. I knew that somehow she would make it back to Kipengee. She had paid for her crime and would continue to, for her few days remaining. On the dresser she left some photographs of a small, sickly black boy. On the back of each one was printed "Bobi."

On the train back to Nairobi, I talked to Freda again. I asked her why she wanted me to know the reason she died. Did she expect me to do something about it? Hitesh had said that when I knew the reason she died, I would decide what to do. Both of them expected too much. I'm not a heroine. All I could do is report her heroics, hers and Silk's and Songster's and Flower Bud's. "Is that what you want, Freda?" I screamed at her. "Will that please you?" Then I wept. For a long time, I wept.

Frank was still at the Norfolk, still stoned, still drunk. I told him to see me when he was sober, and he didn't have much time; I was leaving the next morning, going home to San Francisco. There were friends I needed to see, some while I still could.

In the cold light of morning, I gave a bleary-eyed Frank the bank records and the photographs of his half brother. Briefly, I recounted the story, concluding with the hard fact that he had no claim to Freda's money. He looked and listened like a stone. I walked out of his room, caught a taxi to the airport, and went home.

I never saw Frank again, but about a year and a half later I received a letter from him. He had sold the house in Frankfurt and made a video. I could see it, if I wanted, on MTV. He was giving a concert in New York the following month to benefit AIDS. Two tickets were enclosed.

This is for you Freda, finally, and for Hariri and for Shamba La and for Tumba La Ua and for Constance.

Gorillas
and
Banana
Beer

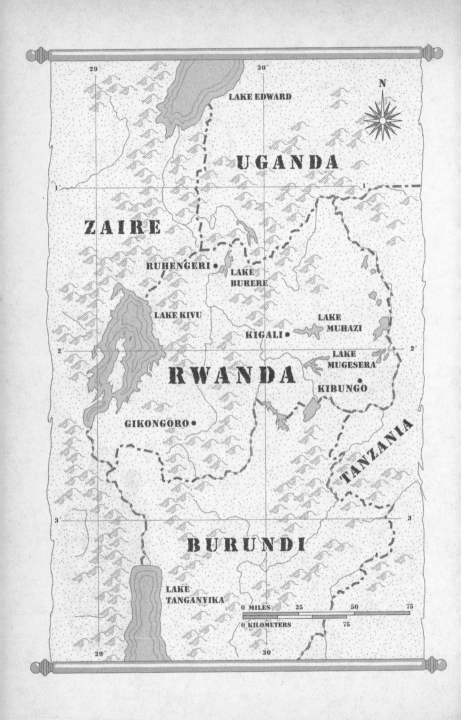

My body was chafed, my clothes were mildewed, and the rain on the low tin roof was a thundering headache. Streams of water washed under the back wall of the shack and over the slick mud floor, lapped at our feet, and then rushed out under a dripping blanket that had been hung as a front door. It was a shelter, and so far we were safe. Help wasn't coming, at least not that night.

The kid hadn't looked at me since I told him we weren't going to drink any of the banana beer. He'd slumped down on his end of the board bench and began cleaning the green gorilla dung out of the crevices of his canvas boots with a small stick. Methodically, he picked at his boots, squinting in the candlelight to get them just so, and when his boots seemed satisfactory, he began with the seams in his jeans.

Our hosts, three huge Watusis, sat on a bench opposite ours, just under the candles, jabbering. They were in a discussion that could have been a disagreement, but there would have been no way to hear them eight feet away over the rain even if I were able to understand Nyarwanda, and I wasn't. The oldest one, judging from his gnarled hands and graying hair—certainly the biggest and the only one with shoes—got up and, shrouding the shack in his shadow, dipped his tin can mug into the beer crock. Finding it empty, he sloshed over to the blanket door, stuck his head out, and bellowed.

The men were still in an animated discussion when two young girls struggled in under the blanket, a pole balanced between them slung with a fresh crock of banana beer. Soaking rags clinging to the bones of their ebony bodies, they set the large, earthen crock down awkwardly, knocking off the lid and slopping some of the beer on the fire. The fire, smoldering dung contained in a small bucket, spit and belched smoke that followed the glistening girls back out under the blanket carrying the empty crock. The kid, watching, shot me a dagger as the Watusis plunged their tin cups into the new brew.

The kid, Johnny—Jonathan, if he ever grew up—had been a pain in the ass. I couldn't imagine a worse companion. He had major problems, and his father had to have been drunk, or desperate, to ship him off to Africa, particularly to me. His father, a Boston trial lawyer with matching ego, was a client of mine. I investigated safari accident cases for him. I knew he had a son of about eighteen, an only child. I'd seen his portrait, heard the fatherly accolades, none of which fit the flaccid-faced kid at the end of the bench.

It had been a week since he landed at my hotel in Nairobi. He'd knocked on my door with a letter from Dad: "Please, Kelly, show him some lion kills, show him something that will shock him into becoming an adult." I wired Dad, telling him, "No! Baby-sitting isn't in the contract." But Dad didn't respond. The kid explained, apathetically, that Dad was in Las Vegas. I was making a list of all the Las Vegas hotels I could remember when the kid gave a yawn and told me that I was wasting my time. "Dad always registers under his current girlfriend's name, to throw Mom off course." The kid knew her only as Dolly.

Johnny was short, a doughboy who wore the expression of a basset hound, but he was eighteen and shaved and didn't need an escort in Nairobi if he stayed on the beaten path. I gave him the names of a few reputable safari companies, told him which part of the city to stay out of, and sent him packing. Three days later, he was back at my hotel door. He couldn't get a reservation. He had given my name, but everything was fully booked. I reminded him that his father sued these companies and I helped him win. How did he think my name would get him anything but thrown out of their offices? He rolled his eyes, an impassive "oh well," pulled a samosa from his pack, and wandered off. I didn't see him for a few more days and forgot about him. Alas, I should have changed hotels.

The Watusis were definitely in some kind of disagreement. They were taking turns giving dissertations summed up with finger wagging, their raspy voices occasionally rising above the thundering rain, causing the kid to squirm. A boy came in blinking water from his eyes, dripping, carrying more of the tallow candles that burned in the bottom half of broken bottles hung above the three men. He was probably the same boy who had lit the candles when we arrived, but it was difficult to tell. The children all had shaved heads, skeletal bodies, and they wore rags. The boy set about replacing the candles, the ricocheting shadows causing Johnny's dark eyes to flit and flicker. The men adjusted their posture in order to stay in each other's face during the argument while the boy squeezed between them. Leaning awkwardly over them, he lit the candles, then disappeared in the rain again without acknowledgment. The light in the kid's eyes settled back into languid, back into his solitary cinema. The kid was vacuous baggage, but I had to take the credit for being here. Whether he'd shown up at my hotel door or not, I would be in the same situation, but without responsibility for him, a responsibility that gnawed at me in the same place as my hunger.

The kid's timing, rather his father's audacity, couldn't have been worse. With a week to kill between jobs in Nairobi, I'd been contemplating another try at getting into Rwanda from Kenya—my third. For several years, I'd harbored a lust to see the mountain gorillas, the few that remained. My first attempt had been with Uli, my bush pilot, which resulted in his plane, with us in it, confiscated and held in Kibungo, an expensive predicament that took me three days to negotiate our way out of. The second try was with Kenya Air, a weekly flight from Nairobi to Kigali that only picked up passengers in Kigali and continued on to Brussels. Without prior government approval for official business, arrival into Rwanda was allowed only sporadically, and not from Kenya. I'd been turned back at Kigali, put on another plane and flown back to Nairobi. Rwanda only wanted tourists associated with the fully contained and very expensive mountain gorilla treks packaged in Belgium.

There were good reasons for keeping tourists few and on a short leash in Rwanda: no food, few accommodations, and dependably regular and extremely bloody uprisings between the Hutu and the Watusi. Nonetheless, I was motivated for another try with Uli. I'd been given the name of a tracker who supposedly worked with Dian Fossey, the woman who, against all odds, had studied the mountain gorillas. I was optimistic; maybe I would meet Fossey. I called Kumlesh in Mombasa. Kumlesh, the alchemist running my Kenya office-of-sorts, kept up with the kaleidoscope of African politics. I hoped he would have an improved political report on Rwanda.

"Based on the hunger problem that persists there, Kelly," Kumlesh's voice droned, "it is predictable that you will be harassed wherever you land. And an airplane, what a valuable property for their continuing civil war. My advice is the same as the last time you asked me. Go to Brussels and book . . ."

"And wait," I interrupted, "until the gorillas are gone and I'm too old to care!"

"You have so many virtues, Kelly, it is unfortunate that patience is not one of them."

I called Uli. Maybe he would have new and improved information. "You are one crazy woman, darling, with a pathetically short memory. Do you not recall lying on the ground with the end of a rifle at your head?" He hung up on me.

Dented but not daunted, I called Kenya Air to find out that the weekly flight to Brussels via Kigali left the next day. I was on the phone when, one more time, I heard the kid's timid knock at my door. He looked pathetic and I was hungry. I took him to dinner.

We had dinner in the Norfolk Hotel patio bar, a congenial setting for serious people-watching. The kid never looked up and didn't utter a word that wasn't torn from him. His one-sentence answers were as short as my energy for the subject: Dad made him come to Africa because he didn't want to go to Dad's Ivy League university. Dad wanted him to be like Dad, and Dad was miserable. If he could be anywhere he wanted, he'd be home in his room or back at his parochial school. And he made it very clear, the last place he wanted to be was riding around in a bus painted like a zebra with rich, fat people wearing khaki and gawking at the animals they'd rather be wearing. The kid was a mess. My grandmother would have said "empty as a preacher's pocket." I sat there looking at the top of his greasy dark head feeling a nasty attack of bleeding heart coming on.

About then, some friends of mine stopped by the table to chat and deliver the local gossip. The kid split during introductions, just walked off, the frayed hems of his trousers dragging, his short, pudgy frame bent under an unwieldy pack. Out loud, I said, "Maybe I'll bag the trip to Rwanda and take the poor little rich kid to the Abedaries fishing."

"Rwanda!" my friends said in unison. I had interrupted their chatter, reminding them of bigger news. Had I heard about Dian Fossey? She had been murdered, machete through the skull. They didn't know when. The news could be old, they said, as African news traveled around the world and back before it reached next door. I knew it had just happened or Kumlesh would have known.

Ten minutes later, I was in my room packing without another thought of poor little Johnny or the Abedaries. I'd been threatened with the end of something I hadn't seen yet. With Fossey out of the way, the poaching could be up for grabs and the gorillas gone by the next time I made it to Brussels with a year to spare. Or it could be the beginning of another bloody Watusi uprising with the mountain gorillas as a political target against the Hutu. I had to get to Rwanda.

At eight the next morning, I called the Rwandan embassy to hear the same story I'd heard the last time I was impulsive. They wouldn't sell me a visa. I couldn't leave the airport in Kigali. They cited civil unrest and didn't know or didn't want to talk about Fossey. At eight-thirty I was in a cab to the airport. At nine I purchased a ticket to Brussels via Kigali, all that was allowed. At ten I was on the plane buckling my seat belt, when little Johnny walked down the aisle and took the seat directly across from me. I couldn't believe it. He sat down and pulled out a comic book, as though he were on a school bus. I began the process of tearing answers from him again, but he only had one. If he didn't do something in Africa, his father would kill him, so he'd decided to go with me to Rwanda to see the mountain gorillas. The hotel had given him my itinerary. Confident that he'd be in Brussels, alone, before he figured out the situation, I took a nap.

In Kigali, everyone was ordered off the plane while it was inspected for the flight to Brussels. We were herded into a large holding area and queued up in front of a sign for passengers traveling to Belgium. There were signs and counters for other destinations, but they hadn't been used since Rwanda won its independence. A man in uniform was going through the queue checking people's documents before sending them on to the counter to have their papers stamped. The last time, I made it only as far as that counter, where I was told it was

Brussels or back to Kenya. For lack of a better idea, I decided to stand in front of a large customs sign for foreign passengers arriving in Rwanda.

No one noticed me for a while. I retied my money belt on the outside of my shirt and zipped up my documents neatly alongside the cash. Finally, the uniformed man was through the queue for Brussels and wandered my way asking questions in French. My French was lousy, but I guessed he was asking me if I had proper authorization to visit Rwanda. I gave him a confident "oui, oui," and he wandered off. I stood my ground, and in a few minutes a uniformed woman appeared, opened the chain between us, and snapped her fingers for my documents. That was when I noticed the kid standing tentatively, not far behind me. I ignored him and unzipped my money belt. Holding it open, I stepped closer to the woman, indicating it was all there for her to check. She pulled out my passport and airline ticket, giving them a glance. I continued to hold the belt open. In clear English, she asked, "Why do you come to Rwanda?" I answered, "Gorillas." She gave me the enlightened look inspired by money and smirked at the kid, who was now beside me saying, "I'm with her," which I was in no position to discuss. The woman returned my papers to my money belt and, with her index finger and the ease of a blackjack dealer, flipped out five twenties; with her other hand, she motioned for the kid and me to follow her to a counter. A few minutes later, we walked into Kigali with ten-day visas officially stamped. That was the beginning of the interminable nightmare in the shack.

The biggest Watusi was standing up again, a monstrous shadow against the candles. He had one hand on his hip, the other gesticulating to put a point across to his constituents. The argument was still going on. It was unnerving, considering the kid and I seemed to be a major factor, based on their constant referral to us by either gestures or nervous glances. Now, turned partially toward me, the outline of his muscled buttocks at my eye level, Goliath appeared to be snickering. He had an evil face, in any light, and his snickering was not a comforting feeling.

I thought about the prospects of anyone looking for us. We hadn't seen our trackers since before the gunshots. It was possible they were dead. If they were still alive and had made it back to headquarters, they might put together a search party, but that was unlikely. The road we came in on had to be a river by now. And they had our dollars in their pockets. If they admitted to superiors that they'd been moon-lighting, they would surely lose the money and probably their jobs. It was also disconcerting that the trackers were Hutus, a fierce tribe in political power in Rwanda and eternally at war with the Watusis. The giant Watusis, many over seven feet tall, were the bloodiest warriors in Africa, our hosts. The knife in my boot felt lame.

Neck veins now protruded on the oldest Watusi, the giant one with shoes; worse, he was waving his arms around toward me. Suddenly, the two men without shoes got up, gave me a few disgusted glances, and went out under the blanket. The elder one remained, holding his knees and rocking back and forth, nodding, obviously pleased with himself. He had the kid's attention; he'd put down his stick and begun, subconsciously I supposed, rocking in the same manner, his short legs curled under his chunky chin. One could have assumed they were contemplating the same thought, and it certainly could have been hunger. The Watusi had probably never had enough to eat, and the kid and I hadn't had much since we arrived in Rwanda, cer-tainly nothing that day since a shared loaf of bread at dawn. Our last loaf was in my pack, but food was difficult to come by, and I thought it best to leave it there until we wouldn't be obligated to pass it around. It was not likely that the Watusi had sent out for food that would be shared with us. Equally remote was the possibility of a dry place to sleep. Surely we were an imposition to the Watusis, if only by requiring them to keep dung and tallow burning through the night. Most certainly there would be a fee to negotiate when we finally were able to leave.

Looking back to the morning, I had to admit that my lust to see the gorillas might have clouded my judgment. On the other hand, the responsibility for that damn kid was the only reason I was questioning my judgment, and he may as well have been home in his room. We'd had only one brief conversation, if it could be called that: a brief exchange of words—his, semi-hysterical—regarding an incorrigible Belgian woman the trackers had thrown off the truck. The only other reactions he'd had to life or landscape had been in Ruhengeri when, on two occasions, we'd witnessed men practicing the right to sponta-neously beat their wives to the ground with a cane, fairly common in this violent culture. The kid had put his head on his knees and covered his ears with his hands, and he did that again later, when the Belgian woman landed in the mud. Africa was not doing for the kid what his father had hoped. It had taken two days to get from Kigali to the head-quarters of Parc National des Volcans, where the gorilla treks began. We found little food. We had to sleep in public shelters. We either walked or squeezed into buses. I was hungry, tired, and witchy; the kid wasn't any-thing! Seemingly, he saw nothing and felt nothing, and certainly he contributed nothing. He didn't speak a word of French, having studied only Latin, the perfect language not to use. He didn't laugh or cry. Nearly every question I asked him was answered with a shrug and an expression that said, "All of life is beneath me." Between clenched teeth, I practiced the tirade I would deliver at his father.

We had arrived at the headquarters of Parc National des Volcans that morning, before it officially opened. Unofficially, we were made to understand that the gorilla treks were scheduled long in advance and only accommodated people arriving in the tour vans from Brussels via Kigali, prepaid, preregistered, and prefed. Nonetheless, we waited around for a possibility. The vans arrived, depositing khaki-clad Europeans clutching white plastic Belgian boxed lunches. After a busy hour of paperwork and physical demonstrations on how not to piss off a gorilla, Parc National trackers loaded their charges back into the vans and rolled off toward the base of the high mountain volcanoes of the Virunga Forest. There, they would begin the serious trek on foot.

When the vans had gone and the staff settled down, I began nego-tiations, poorly. I'd hoped to persuade these hardworking people that it would be personally profitable to include us in one of the next day's treks. My lousy French sure as hell didn't impress them, and when I mentioned the name that I'd been given of the tracker who supposedly worked for Dian Fossey, everyone became nervous. They sent us to the back room, where an important and adamant-sounding man told us why our request was "absolutely impossible!" One of the gorilla families had a baby too young for tours, and another family had a virus; it had been necessary to cancel some of the reservations made a year in advance. It was difficult to argue with logic, particu-larly when we were being escorted to the door.

Concluding that our only chance was to return to Kigali and give a try with someone from the Belgian consulate, we began walking back toward the main road. We hadn't gone far when a government truck came from the direction of headquarters and stopped beside us. Two men got out and jabbered at us in a nearly indecipherable French dialect, indicating that we should get in the back of the truck. They were Hutus in ragged military uniforms, as the other park officials had been; nonetheless, I was wary. As precisely as my French allowed, I asked them if they spoke any language besides French and Nyarwanda. They shook their heads, but then the driver brightened and said, "Swahili."

"Vizuri sana!" Very good, I exclaimed. We could communicate.

The guy was believable. They were trackers for the family of gorillas with the baby. The baby was old enough for them to resume the treks; they would do it next week anyway. Because they had to do poacher patrols and because we had come all this way to see the gorillas, they would take us with them. We should pay them directly.

About then, a woman poked her head from behind the canvas that covered the rear of the truck. She looked about sixty, graying, weathered, and withered. She was Belgian but pleaded with us in bad English. If we didn't go along, they wouldn't take her. She had waited years to take this trip, and the cost had been her savings and all the stamina she had to get this far. She projected a scrawny arm to plead that the gorilla treks were booked a year ahead in Brussels, and she didn't have that long to live—maybe the gorillas didn't either. A deep, horsey cough followed as she slapped at her chest, gasping for air.

I asked the kid, sarcastically, what he thought we should do, knowing he'd give me his usual "I'd rather be home in my room" shrug. Gorilla lust had already convinced me that the baby gorilla was most certainly old enough not to be traumatized by our presence. I negotiated a fee, the same per head they were charging the Belgian woman. They would collect it later. We piled in the back of the truck and started off in the direction of the high volcanoes. A piece of real luck, I thought.

The Belgian woman had on brightly printed cotton pants that went to the ankles and a flimsy T-shirt. Her black high-top sneakers had seen better days and so had she, but she was wild with excitement to see the gorillas and mad as hell at the Belgian government for making it so difficult. Her enthusiastic carrying-on was limited only by the bouncing and noise of the truck. All those years emptying her husband's bedpan, she'd read, planned, and schemed this trip to Africa.

First, she would see the gorillas, then she would go to Kenya and see the lions and elephants, and last she would go to Egypt to see the pyramids and the Valley of the Kings. Her excitement was cheering, but when I repositioned myself at the rear to see at least where we'd been, her fervor faded into the noise of the truck.

The Rwandan countryside looked much like a patchwork quilt covering a lumpy bed. Every inch of land was farmed in a hand-to-mouth economy. The green, brown, and gold of the patchwork extended to where the volcanoes became steep and were consumed by jungle. It was easy to see from any distance the only place remaining for the gorillas to live, the only area not cleared and farmed—yet. It was visually obvious why Fossey was unpopular with Rwandans.

The sky darkened, preparing for the daily drizzle. The truck bumped along, slowly ascending, sliding where the road stayed very wet. I supposed we were about two-thirds of the way from beginning our climb on foot, when the truck came to a sudden stop. The trackers came around and told us it was time to settle the accounts. I dug out dollars, which they were delighted to get. The Belgian woman paid them in francs, moaning in English about the cost and hoping that the trackers would keep it all and give nothing to either government. She was particularly mad at the Rwandan government, absolutely certain that they were responsible for the death of Dian Fossey, her personal heroine. Hearing Fossey's name, the trackers gave the woman a dour warning, which I translated as: "It could be dangerous speaking of things you know nothing about."

We started off again but hadn't gone a mile when the truck slid to another stop. The uniforms again appeared at the back of the truck wanting money. They had forgotten to collect for transportation. This set the Belgian woman into a fit. She ranted and raved, mostly about how everyone tried to cheat her, interjecting her horsey cough and slapping at her chest. I cut in long enough to pay the ten dollars they wanted for the kid and me, and then she started all over again. It was the common aggressive behavior of an inexperienced traveler on a tight budget, her anger and loudness giving her security, like carrying a bigger gun. This incorrigible woman was obviously not reading the accelerating anger in the black faces with whom she negotiated. I watched her sadly, wanting to intervene, but fearful I might escalate the well-known Rwandan male tempers.

Suddenly, with no overt warning, the tracker who spoke Swahili hopped up into the back of the truck, grabbed the woman, and tossed her off into the mud. Before I could believe what had happened, the truck was roaring along again, leaving the woman sprawled. I yelled and pounded on the glass window to the cab, but the driver gave a show of his fist and gunned the truck on. The kid had his head down and his ears covered with his hands.

When the truck stopped next, we were still a distance of two patches, one green and one brown, from the edge of the quilt where the jungle began. It was obviously as far as we could go in the truck; the track had disappeared and the muddy brown field in front of us was steep. There were no dwellings or shelters to be seen, but people were working in the fields. The trackers came around and motioned for us to get out. This time they were carrying large machetes and pistols on their belts; the one who spoke Swahili had strapped on a rifle.

We left the truck and followed a foot trail of sorts, through the mud. It was raining by then. Women with babies tied to their bodies were digging potatoes with cane sticks. Small, muddy children, their stomachs bloated and noses running, were picking the potatoes out of the dirt and putting them in buckets. They stole glances at us without expression.

Johnny came alongside me; he wanted to ask me something. It felt like an event. In a rather demanding tone, he asked, "What was that woman doing?" I first assumed he was talking about one of the women in the field but then realized that he was oblivious to them. He was still thinking about the woman thrown off the truck. "Why would any woman in her right mind come to Africa, much less an old woman?" He was almost shrieking, but he hadn't taken his eyes off his muddy boots that became heavier with every step.

I began, "Listen, Johnny . . ."

"That lady, she was sick!" he interrupted. "About to die—she said she didn't have a year and she wanted to come here to this hell on earth, like you. Was she crazy? Is she dead, you think?"

I liked him better when he didn't talk. I assured him the woman wasn't dead and she would surely be picked up by night and taken someplace for care. But the kid stopped suddenly and actually looked at me. His voice cracked when he exclaimed, "But why would a woman, a woman even older than my mother, want to come here at all? She could see a gorilla in a zoo!"

The tracker behind us, impatient with our pace, held up his machete, motioning for us to move along. The kid stumbled forward, rubbing his nose with the back of his hand. He could have been weeping. It was impossible to tell in the drizzling rain, but the emotion of his outburst demanded a response. I tried. "The woman told us it was her fantasy, her dream to come here. She'd been caring for an invalid husband. This was her first opportunity to think of herself. And you're wrong! Mountain gorillas don't make it in zoos."

"I've seen them in zoos," he blubbered to himself.

"You've seen lowland gorillas, a smaller, less evolved ape, and they only make it sometimes, barely!" Adamant about this subject, I was loud. I lowered my voice. "These big guys are sometimes called 'sensitive giants' by people who give a damn. The emotional effects of being torn from family and locked away are devastating to them, but the zoos continue to try, continue to kill them." Hoping to thwart further eruptions and get back to silence, I added, "I would guess that the woman's references to how much time she has, and her coughing, is a ploy for getting her way, saving money."

It was a few minutes before he blubbered, "Women are so masochistic. She probably had a gorilla for a husband. When she got rid of him, she went looking for another gorilla, probably just like that Fossey woman did. Now *she* was really crazy! She was so masochistic she lived here with the gorillas and died here!" He flung an arm and added vehemently, "In the mud, with an axe through her head!"

"Jesus, Johnny, if you're comparing men to gorillas, I suspect gorillas are much kinder than the men of Rwanda."

Even before I'd finished the sentence, he mumbled, "Please don't use the Lord's name in vain."

Remembering he'd attended parochial schools, clearly with some kind of results, I apologized. He had me thinking about that pitiful woman. There certainly wouldn't be any retribution for her. The trackers had undoubtedly made a pact among themselves with a pat story, probably that the Belgian woman had stowed away in the truck. In case she made it back to headquarters with her story, it would be two against one, and one was obviously crazy—and a woman. I wished the spunky old gal had spent some time studying the cultures as well as the gorillas.

We were in the jungle soon and had to form a single file. Johnny walked behind me, silent the rest of the trek. I wondered about his mental health and why a father would send a kid so obviously disturbed alone to Africa. Dad must have been desperate or he wouldn't have risked being on good terms with me. The incident with the Belgian woman had finally upset the kid enough to speak, but not immediately. At the time he'd just covered his ears, and he was still not questioning the right of the driver to throw her off the truck; rather, he seemed to be more concerned with the right of the woman to come to Africa.

The pounding rain on the tin roof went on interminably, and the two younger, barefoot Watusi men were back carrying a plastic bag. Shaking themselves, wiping their eyes on the ragged collars of their shirts, they shuffled the bag between them and then reluctantly passed it to the elder Watusi, who jabbered loudly and indicated toward me. One of the men opened the bag and took out three very small pipes that looked to be made of bone. Reaching in the bag again, he pulled out a roughly carved wooden box. He presented the box in front of me and opened it, timidly holding it toward my nose. It looked and smelled like moldy alfalfa, but I assumed it was their form of ganga, something they smoked to give them hope and keep their minds off their bellies. I smiled and said, "Ganga?" They all mouthed something, Goliath nodding and laughing. This was obviously the conclusion of the argument that had been going on. Goliath had wanted to share their ganga stash, but the other two were opposed. Maybe the big bastard wasn't so bad. The kid, watching the man pack the three pipes, asked, "Ganga?"

The kid sucked on his pipe like a baby on a nipple. I'd warned him that it probably wouldn't kill him with dysentery, like banana beer, but it might make him sick. He didn't hesitate. He went back for seconds, eyes misty, lids drooping. The stuff tasted as bad as it smelled, but it soon delivered the relaxing, mildly hallucinogenic response I'd hoped might get us through the night more comfortably. Our host, Goliath, was obviously ecstatic that we had all smoked together. I supposed we had bonded in a way that made sitting in a flooded shack on the side of a volcano in Rwanda better somehow, certainly physiologically. I looked at my watch. It was midnight.

The next hour or so was better spent. I managed to lie with my head and back on the skinny board bench, my knees in the air and my feet nearly in Johnny's lap. He didn't seem to notice. He was leaning toward the fire, slapping his stick on the dung bucket. Maybe he was humming and tapping out a song, but I couldn't hear him, just the damn rain. My head was engaged in hypnagogic imagery from the day: the jungle, the birds, and those awesome mountain gorillas.

The baby gorilla, a male nearly three months old, had behaved like a two-year-old human. Curious, jabbering, he was often close enough to touch, several times grabbing at the tracker's rifle or the kid's camera. One gruff command from the mother would send the tyke scampering back to her lap, but only for a hug and kiss; then he was off again to tease and entertain us. I caught the kid talking to him a few times, looking younger himself. The five adult females, one with a two-year-old in her lap, watched us intently. They seemed calm, talking to each other in short sentences, probably about our being there, occasionally preening each other. The old silverback, clearly displeased with our presence, stomped around growling, barking instructions at the females to move farther away, which they did without hesitation. Several times he had us on our knees, as instructed by the trackers, subservient, grunting, and terrified. With a prehistoric beastly roar, he ran a couple of bluff charges by us, breaking off cane trees like toothpicks. If that wasn't enough of a show, he humped one of the females, shaking the ground, screaming pleasure.

Maybe as awesome as the gorillas was the trek through the rain forest looking for them: climbing like Tarzan up the vines that covered volcanic rock; seeing the trackers slash and hack at the fluorescent green jungle that seemed to repair itself behind us; hanging on tree limbs to find the next vista; wading through the trails of wet, green, pungent gorilla dung. And there was that knot in my stomach the first time we saw the silverback directly above us on a ledge, pounding his chest, showing all his teeth, sending his thundering warning echoing through the jungle like an approaching earthquake.

Deep into gorilla reverie, I fell off the bench, splattered into the water, and brought the Watusis to their feet laughing. The kid didn't move. He was in his sitting fetal position, head on his knees, snoozing. I didn't notice the Watusi woman until I got up. She was standing near the dripping blanket door, barefoot, the water rushing around her ankles. Smiling widely, she showed me her snaggletoothed mouth and then came and sat down on my bench, tapping it with the yellow claw of her index finger, indicating I should sit beside her. I supposed she had been waiting for me to wake up. It was impossible to tell her age. She was bald, wrinkled, leathered, and odoriferous. She got right in my face, yelled to be heard, and flung spittle with every syllable. I had no idea what she wanted, but she was adamant. I was fighting an urge to push her off the bench, when Goliath splashed two giant steps, grabbed her by her bony arm, and flung her over the dung fire onto the bare feet of the other two men. She scrambled up between them, wiggling onto the bench. Goliath splashed around a few more minutes, barking and wagging his finger at her, his threats muted by the relentless rain. The kid had his hands over his ears again.

The woman sat squished between the men, a harridan, her glinting eyes fixed on me like an evil spell. Claustrophobia was exacerbating my hunger and escalating my anxiety. The peaceful effects of the ganga had worn off, and I was grappling with just how concerned I should be regarding our situation. Conjuring up the events of the afternoon, I thought again about the last time we'd seen the trackers, the sharp cracking sounds of those two gunshots.

We had left the gorillas and started down the mountain when one of the trackers motioned for us to get down and stay there. We did and then watched while they crept off into the jungle, their pistols drawn. In a few minutes, the one who spoke Swahili returned. He pointed toward a protrusion of rocks and told us to get there as fast as we could. We should wait there for them, but not more than thirty minutes. If they didn't show, we should get off the mountain as best we could. Then, he was gone again.

We waited in the rocks, listening to the jungle wide-eyed. In about fifteen minutes we heard the two shots. It was impossible to tell from which way they came, but it felt too close. The kid actually took hold of my sleeve. I thought he was scared, but cool as a cucumber, he said, "It's probably poachers. I think we should go back and see if the baby gorilla is okay." I shut him up with a look; his first input of the trip was to get us killed! Stretching thirty minutes to forty-five, I wondered if the tracker with the rifle had tranquilizing bullets or real ones. They both had pistols, but the shots were from a rifle. I was not anxious to find my way out of that jungle without a machete, but when the rain stopped drizzling and started dumping, we started down.

Within a few minutes, we were swallowed by the rain forest so completely that it was difficult to know which way was down, much less which way we came from. For an hour or so I fought the constraints of the jungle—roots, limbs, rocks, and the rain, beating on my body like a club—while seemingly going in circles. The kid tripped along on my heels without a word. Darkness was imminent, and I was apoplectic, looking for a tree to spend the night in, when we came out on a large trail. I was so elated, I hugged the kid. He shuddered, repulsed, and then said, "I don't think we should have left the baby gorilla."

The trail took us out to the patchwork, but not where we'd gone in. It was all but dark and still raining hard. We couldn't see very far, but we managed to follow the trail along the edge of the jungle until we came upon some cows. There, the trail turned down the hill and stopped at the shack. No one was there when we arrived, but within a few minutes several women were fussing around in the rain, jabbering orders at each other. Very shortly, candles and dung were burning. Then, the two men without shoes came and put the blanket up for a door. When Goliath arrived, he brought a crock of beer and the tin can mugs. God knows where they all came from. The shack appeared to be used just for shelter, perhaps for the field workers. I assumed the Watusis lived nearby and felt obligated to keep us company, but without real communication it was impossible to know for sure what they were thinking. They knew we had been lost on a gorilla trip—that was obvious from their gestures—but I couldn't tell what else they knew, if anything.

The snaggletoothed woman continued to sit hunkered on the bench between the men, her unrelenting eyes remaining fixed on me. The elder man, Goliath, was beginning to nod off. My watch said 2 A.M. Their hospitality, if that's what it was, had tenacity. The kid looked to be snoozing again with his head in his lap. Shaking off the claustrophobia and anxiety, I got back into my horizontal position on the bench, carefully.

The sound of my own heart woke me. The rain had stopped. The kid had moved to the bench vacated by the Watusis. He lay on his belly, his arms draped to the ground, water lapping around his hands. The silence had woken him, too. His eyes wandered around the shack with mine. There was no one there. The candles and dung had been replaced recently. The crock was still there, the tin mugs washed up against a wall. I got up and went out under the blanket, peering into the night. It was black, no stars and nothing moving that I could see. When I stepped back into the shack, the water had already stopped flowing across the floor. Johnny was standing and stretching. As the last part of a yawn, he asked, "Now what?"

I said, "I don't know, what do you think? Maybe a short dissertation on gorilla poaching?" He rolled his lazy eyes, shrugged, and sat back down on the bench. I mimicked him and then began to laugh—it was a time when absurdity deserved a laugh—until the kid began to weep. Baffled by this newest neurotic behavior, I was considering consoling him, but the crone was back. She'd slipped under the blanket and onto my bench. Her voice, as jagged as her looks, made me wish for the rain again. There was no way of knowing what she was carrying on about, but she used the same words again and again, obdurately ranting her message. Occasionally she would rub the rags on her belly and make a face like a witch about to be fried. I decided she was terribly hungry. The loaf of bread was in my pack and I was ready to part with it, anything to stop her insufferable sermon!

I was digging in my pack, when the blanket was suddenly torn from its mooring and entangled in the arms and legs of someone staggering onto the muddy floor. It was one of our trackers. He groaned and rolled onto his back, writhing in the mud, holding on to a bloody, ragged pant leg with one hand, his pistol with the other. The kid and I got him up on one of the benches and the woman began tearing away at his trousers to find his wound. In a moment she was dipping banana beer out of the crock, pouring one tinful into a hole in his thigh, the next into his mouth. She did it several times and then handed the tin to me, indicating that I should continue. She then tore off her ragged shirttail and made a fresh tourniquet around his leg above the wound. The entire time she worked on him, she spoke in a sweet, solicitous voice, not the ragged shrieking she had used with me. Occasionally he said something to her, just a word or two. He was the tracker who spoke Swahili, but I waited until he'd settled down before I asked him what had happened. As he drifted off to sleep, his head in my lap, the pistol still clutched in his hand, he answered my question with just one word that translated to *poachers*.

The woman sat down next to the kid on the opposite bench. Within a few minutes, she was in his face with her redundant ranting. This time I covered *my* ears, prayed for the thundering rain again, and tried to guess at the source of panic in her face. She seemed mad and completely desperate. Perhaps, in her deranged mind was some kind of solution. That's how it was for at least another hour: the Hutu tracker, his head in my lap, a gaping hole in his leg, the kid and I listening to a woman railing on with a voice like a saw.

I admit to being glad to see Goliath stagger in again. He was rubbing his eyes and looking pretty sour. The woman jumped up and tried to escape, but he had her by her rags and literally threw her out of the shack. Her scream jarred my compassion, and hurriedly, I replaced my lap with my pack, propped up the tracker's head, and ducked out the door. The sky was lighter, and I could barely make out some of the patchwork borders, but there was no sign of the woman, or anyone. Only a promise of dawn.

When I went back inside, the kid still had his hands over his ears. The two men were talking quietly, the tracker still propped up on my pack, Goliath squatting beside him. I sat down next to the kid, gave him a pat on the shoulders, and asked him how hungry he was; maybe it was time to break out the bread, perhaps share it with the tracker. He took his hands down and was muttering something about beasts, when the tracker's voice suddenly escalated in anger, and Goliath staggered to his feet, shaking his head. The tracker raised up his pistol and growled something that ended in the tone of a threat, causing Goliath to begin shrugging defensively and back out of the shack.

When he was gone, I knelt down near the tracker to offer him bread and ask the questions I'd been asking myself since yesterday. He said that he was in too much pain to eat, only wanted more beer. I remembered some aspirin in my pack and dug it out for him. He swallowed it with beer and began to talk.

He said that poachers had been expected to make a try for the baby gorilla before the tours were resumed; babies, if they lived long enough to sell, were a hot commodity for the zoos they would soon die in. He and his partner had gone in every day to set up watch. That's where they were going when they met the Belgian woman, and then the kid and me. He paused, his face squeezed in regret. I doubted the regret was for the Belgian woman. I suspected he was dreading the explanation to authorities as to how the kid and I happened to be there and why he had dollars in his pockets. Instinctively, I knew that explanation wouldn't happen. He would do whatever was necessary to protect his job. Necessarily, the kid and I were expendable.

I still needed to know the situation and urged him on. Between gulps of beer, he told me that he wasn't sure the poachers saw the kid and me. They wouldn't have expected anyone except trackers, and they were ready and waiting for them with rifles. They shot twice, but only he was wounded. His partner helped him to a nearby cave, leaving a wide trail of blood that they wanted the poachers to follow. They knew the cave well and had hoped to set up an ambush there.

The poor bastard raised up to rub his leg, his face contorted in pain. He was sweating profusely. I refilled his cup and he went on.

His blood led the poachers to the cave, but, wary, they stopped short at the entry to discuss the situation. The trackers heard them say that they should get the gorilla before dark and come back and finish the trackers later; bleeding like that, they wouldn't go anywhere.

He paused to swill and handed me his empty cup. I told him that he should be drinking water, too, the way he was sweating, but he only wanted the beer. After taking a minute to catch his breath, he finished telling what he knew.

He had given the rifle with the tranquilizing bullets to his partner and told him to follow the poachers back to the gorillas. Then, he put together a tourniquet for his leg and began making his way to the shack, where they had agreed to meet later.

He rested a few minutes and then wanted to know our story. I told him, and it seemed to confirm his suspicions. If we had been made comfortable in the shack, it was to delay our returning to headquarters, giving the poachers more time to get the baby gorilla off the mountain. The people at the shack were Watusis who lived near the edge of the forest and migrated back and forth to Zaire with a few cows. There were several families and many were sick with a disease of some kind. They poached gorillas for food and were suspected of aiding other poachers for money.

The tracker's wound, the severity of his pain, and the potential for disaster gave cause for my vote to flee. I told him to point out the direction of the truck. I would give headquarters whatever story he wanted, but he needed to be rescued and taken to a hospital, and we all needed to be off the mountain and out of poacher range. He raised up, wagging his gun at me, wanting to make it clear that if the poachers were still in the area and we tried for an escape, they might kill us to buy more time. They may have taken the truck or disabled it so we couldn't leave. It would be better to wait for headquarters to find us. They would be looking as soon as it was dry enough to get up the mountain, probably about midday. By then, the other tracker might show up, if he was still alive.

"Jesus," I said in English. "I hope we're all still alive."

That got the kid's attention. I translated the story for him. His chubby cheeks went slack and his lip quivered, but he asked prosaically, "Do you think we are safe?"

I put the question to the tracker and he shrugged, sleepily, the banana beer having its effects. If the poachers were still on the mountain, they surely knew where we were; the Watusis would have kept them informed. But he thought that the poachers would want to avoid us, unless they needed hostages to get off the mountain or out of the country. The people who used the shack during the day were Hutu farmers. When they arrived to work, they would run the Watusis off. He held his gun up to indicate that getting rid of the Watusis was a good thing and the gun would help.

The tracker was nearly asleep again, but I had to ask him if he knew what the woman had been railing about. He answered as though it were a common thing. The woman wanted me to take some of the children out of the country. She believed that the land was sick, and if the children went somewhere else, they would be healed. She thought white people would take them, because white people pay to have men steal gorillas.

I walked outside, nauseated, wishing my stomach had something to throw up. The kid followed. I told him what the woman had been trying to say. The land was taking on color in the distance. In the shade of the mountain, we would be the last to have daylight. Steam was coming from our wet clothes, and I felt a chill when the kid said icily, "And they say I'm crazy when I tell them life sucks."

"Her life sure as hell sucks," I shuddered. "Every minute of her existence spent staying death from children." We just stood there together, a camaraderie in our steaming, like space travelers experiencing a realization together, like it or not.

The kid said, "That ugly old woman, another pathetic woman with no life."

"Excuse me, comrade, but I don't think you can compare that woman to anyone pathetic. She apparently has an incredible heart full of love for . . ."

"Women are all pathetic," he interrupted with a hiss, "just living their lives protecting their children, mostly from men."

"Not all of us are heroines," I snarled. "What about me? What about the Belgian woman today?"

"That Belgian woman," he moaned, pulling on his ears. "My mother keeps telling me when I go away to college, she'll do the things she's always wanted to do, but I don't think she's going to be quite as crazy as that Belgian woman, looking for another gorilla." He was spitting his words, now in disgust. "My mother's masochism is watching my father flaunt his bimbos. It makes her cry, *really, really* hard."

His satirical *really* caused his voice to crack, producing a cough. I asked, "What would your mother like to do?"

"How would I know?" he snapped.

"You've never asked her?" I was incredulous.

"No! She's only trying to get me to go to school because if I don't, my father will disinherit me!" The emotion in his last sentence apparently startling him, he returned to his prosaic monologue. "When I go to school, my father's going to leave her for one of his bimbos, and my mother will lie down and cry herself . . ." He didn't finish, just stuck his hands in his pocket and shrugged.

I was way beyond my expertise, so I went back to being a comrade, saying good-naturedly, "I'll bet your life will look pretty sweet after seeing this."

He flashed a deadly glance but grumbled nonchalantly, "Life is the same everywhere. Men are gorillas, worse. They both pound their chests, they're both ugly, but men lie, steal, murder, and beat their wives."

"Whew!" I expelled. "Damn, Johnny, you know, you could have a hell of an alliance with a few angry women I know, but if you really have no respect for men, or women, what can you expect of, or for, yourself?"

"Why should I expect any more than the kids that old woman wants us to take, or kids anywhere?" Completely fatalistic, again calm, he said, "All of us will either die, or grow up to be just like our parents. The baby gorilla will die or grow up to be a gorilla."

"Jesus, kid! Can't you conceive of possibly doing something that would bring you pleasure, maybe even something that would bring someone else pleasure? You're a pretty privileged kid in some ways. Maybe you could capitalize on the privileged part, maybe have some fun?"

"Fun?" He managed a smirk. "You mean like tramping around in the mud watching a baby gorilla play for the last time before the mother is killed and it's hauled off to die in a zoo, or watch another woman beg to keep kids alive?" Disgusted, shaking his head, he added, "I wish you wouldn't say Jesus."

I was stumped, completely unqualified even for a discussion with this kid, much less to counsel him. I stood there a few more minutes, still steaming, listening to my stomach complaining, then went back into the shack. The woman was there and before I sat down she had resumed her desperate sermon. The tracker opened his eyes, admonishing her as loudly as he could in his weakened condition. She retorted, and after a few exchanges, she was gone again.

The tracker rested his head back on my pack, but not before he took my sleeve. He had something more to tell me. He said the Watusi woman wanted to make a deal. She had told him that she knew about the poachers, and if I would take some children out of the country, she would tell everything. He was sure it was true and advised me to go along with her, say and do anything to make her talk. I asked what would happen to her if the giant with the shoes found out. It was an easy answer. He would kill her. But she would sell her soul to get even one sick child out of the country, and if she talked, they might be able to save the baby gorilla.

I went back outside. The kid was still standing there shrouded in his steamy doom. Far off the sun was shining, but the hills nearby were still in the gloom of murky, wet shade. A muddy trail led from the shack up toward the jungle, where I imagined the woman lived. I thought about her there, tending her sick children, feeding them breakfast, maybe gorilla meat, if they had any food at all. I wondered if she really knew about the poachers, or if she was saying what she felt she had to say. And then, I began pondering the heavy stuff. If one had a choice, whom should one save? Which was more important, a child, a mother, a gorilla? Wondering how the kid would answer that question, I presented it to him.

He didn't hesitate. "The baby gorilla."

We saw her coming. Down the muddy trail she plodded, and this time she wasn't alone. There were several children following her. I said, "Jesus Christ." The kid reprimanded me again, and I told him I wasn't sure but I might have been praying. We ducked back inside.

The woman came into the shack alone. She jabbered away to the poor, nearly incoherent tracker, who groaned and managed to open his eyes. She pointed at me and then at him and then at me, all the time cackling. The tracker motioned feebly for me to come closer. The woman was ready to show me the children, the ones who were sick but could still make the journey. I told him that I'd really like to help but I couldn't let her believe I could do what she wanted. He smiled pathetically and asked how I could convince her of anything she didn't want to believe.

The children came in. One at a time they entered the shack, walked around the cold bucket of dung ashes as though auditioning for a horror show, and went back out the door. The candles, like the dung, had burned out, and the light was poor, but more than I wanted. These kids were scared, and they were sick. Some had oozing sores. One had bleeding eyes. They all had bloated bellies and bald, skeletal heads. I had felt the pathos of children in Africa, but these were pathologically at the edge; this seemed the worst, or maybe it was the proximity. I remembered thinking how much fun it would be to hold the baby gorilla, play with it. I wanted to run and hide from these tortured faces. I kept squeezing my eyes closed, trying to improve them, something the haggard woman surely did every day of her life. From behind her eyelids, I must have been a glimmer of hope, a chance not to bury another child.

When I glanced at the kid, I was surprised to see that he didn't have his head down and ears covered. Instead, he was gaping at the children, his eyes and his mouth wide open. I continued to watch him, maybe because it gave my eyes a place to hide, but why was he able to watch them without hiding? I thought back about each time that I'd seen him with his face buried and ears covered. Perhaps he couldn't watch women in pain because he felt helpless to intervene and responsible by gender? But the children—didn't he feel responsible for them? Maybe he saw them as himself, as though they were better off dead. Maybe I was being audacious even trying to figure him out. In any case, I moved closer to him, as though being closer might give me a clue.

Goliath stormed in, bellowing. The child on parade scampered out and the woman tried to escape, but he had her, and this time he tossed her out with both hands. Her squeal brought me angrily to my feet, ridiculously facing his Herculean chest. The kid had his head down and ears covered.

Goliath completely ignored my stance. He had brought back the bag with the ganga and the pipes. He packed one of the pipes, theatrically, presenting it to the tracker like jewels to the pharaoh. The tracker raised up off my pack and limply waved it away with his gun, telling me that the man wanted us to sleep all day. I told him that it had made the night somewhat easier. Goliath, still seeking good grace, took the lid off the crock of banana beer and jabbered something that probably meant he would get more. The tracker seemed to think that was a good idea and Goliath showed hope of regaining favor.

I grabbed my pack while the tracker wasn't using it for a pillow and told the kid that we should get some air. I was feeling faint. It was time to eat the bread. We weren't prepared for what was outside the shack.

There they were, maybe forty of them, all between the ages of three and ten, all sitting quietly in the mud. When they saw us come out, they all got up at once without a word. They looked terrified. They were terrifying. A muddy graveyard of standing children with visible maladies of death. We all just stood there gaping at one another, until I said, *"Jambo!"* and then changed it to *"Bonjour!"* There was some tittering. I said it again, this time waving at them with my fingers, looking at their faces, trying not to see them. I had no idea if they spoke any French, but I guessed it didn't matter. One by one they began a timid wave.

Then, confirming his lack of predictability, the kid tried it. *"Bonjour!"* he said, waving back at the children. They mimicked him, followed by giggles. Just then the sun popped over the mountain. There was a murmur from everyone and a long sigh, nearly in unison. The kid pointed to the sun and said, *"Oui, oui!"* and then clapped his hands, applauding the sun's arrival. They all laughed and clapped their hands, crying out, *"Oui, oui!"*

I'd spotted the woman sitting near the middle of the bunch, a very small child on her lap. All those kids couldn't have been hers. Still, she seemed to have accepted responsibility for them—and the madness that went with it. She was undoubtedly Goliath's wife, or at least one of them, and he could very well have been the father of the entire bunch. I knew that Watusis, and other African tribes, fathered as many children as possible without regard for the women, particularly when the death rate was high: personal insurance for the strongest instinct of any man, continuation of his lineage. And there, standing in front of the group, was Johnny, an only child with total responsibility for his fallible father's lineage.

The woman was laughing, all her teeth shining in the sun. She now had hope, an aspirin for desperation, waiting for me to announce which lucky children would go with me. I was wondering what to do next, when the kid startled me, calling out, "Sunshine!" The children all called back something that sounded surprisingly like "sunshine!" Then the kid sang, "You are my sunshine!" The children coarsely mimicked, "You are my sunshine!" Line by line he went through the entire song, waiting for their timid voices to sing out the sound they'd heard. When he finished, I applauded them and the kid too. He bowed, and all the children bowed, giggling like real children do.

Johnny had been holding back a few things. An expensive smile, energy. He could sing, on key. But the kid wasn't through. He started another song with the same results, and when the clapping and tittering were over, he began another. The sun shining on all those kids' faces, their eyes gleaming, seemed to light up the side of the mountain. I couldn't see their sores anymore, so I went to the edge of the group and took a seat in the mud. I sang too, a kid on my lap and one sitting on my pack. When we clapped, they would squeeze each other with their sharp limbs, then me, rubbing their runny noses everywhere.

All at once the kid ran over to me and said, "Take your share of the bread! I'm giving mine to them!" He made a swirling motion with his fingers to indicate the children. I asked him how many he intended to feed with our little loaf, and he said, "All of them! Take yours!" He motioned toward the pack, indicating I should hurry. "Come on!" he barked. "I have to do this!"

I moved the child off my pack and got out the bread. There were some oohs and aahs around me. Handing the kid the whole loaf, I nodded when he said, "Are you sure?" He held the bread in his hands and closed his eyes. I guessed he was praying. Then he held the bread over his head for his cheering audience to see. When it was quiet, he walked around among them until he'd spotted the oldest and shyest two girls. He tore the loaf in two and handed them each a half. They looked at it for only a second or two, then, tearing off a small piece, they passed their half to another. The next two children did exactly what the first two had done. I watched the ones on my lap and those close at hand. Carefully, they tore off a piece of the bread and held it in their mouths, as though hypnotized. I supposed the piece was too small to chew.

As far as I know, the bread made it through the entire group. The kid was in an altered state. He came and kneeled by me just long enough to exclaim, "Can you believe it? They all ate! I fed the masses with a single loaf!" Then he skipped off, the born-again leader of a parade of sick children. They followed him up and down and around our muddy brown patch of quilt, clapping and singing, the sickest being pulled along by the others. Regardless of what was going on in the kid's head, those children were having a day they wouldn't forget in their brief lives.

Goliath returned, a shadow against the sun, stumbling along in his muddy shoes with a fresh crock of beer. He was obviously having a difficult time understanding what he was seeing, pausing a few moments before he went into the shack. I followed him. There was another surprise for both of us. The missing tracker! He and his wounded colleague were chatting, both of them all smiles when they saw the fresh crock of beer. They were into it with both mugs and had them swilled before they acknowledged the bearer. When they did, it was with a barrage of questions that backed Goliath right back out of the shack. I stood at the door watching him plod away, rejected, up the trail to wavering voices singing, "Old MacDonald had a farm, E-I-E-I-O."

Delighted, eager for the story, I sat down in the mud next to the wounded tracker, close enough to hear his tired, weak translation. His partner had reached the poachers just as they were positioning themselves to open fire on the mother gorilla and the silverback. Shooting quickly, he hit one of the poachers with a tranquilizer, dizzying him, causing him to stagger around and finally fall backward over a rock face. The tracker fired again at the second poacher but missed. By now, the mother gorilla was in a rage, and the baby was screaming at the top of its lungs. The poacher was again taking aim at the mother, when he was charged from the side by the silverback, who knocked him about twenty feet from his gun. The silverback didn't let the maimed poacher up. He jumped up and down on him, again and again, pounding his chest and roaring.

The tracker had kept his concealed position in the rocks until well after dark. He said that the silverback continued his tirade, stalking the area, bellowing warnings, sometimes pausing at the side of the mother to beat on himself and sometimes jumping up and down again on the poacher. After dark, the silverback led his family to a night nest in the trees. The tracker followed and took a position nearby, assuring himself that there were no more than two poachers. When it was nearly dawn, he went back to the cave and then came to the shack.

The trackers were obviously happy. They said the Watusis who lived above the shack wouldn't be, but the poachers wouldn't care; they were both dead.

I waited for the kid to wind up "Jesus Loves Me" before I told him the tracker's story. He jumped up and down and cried out, "Baby gorilla's alive!" The children mimicked him and began an echoing chant across the patches. I think I was glad that the kid and I were the only ones who understood.

I had hated every minute at the shack, but the last were the worst. The Hutu workers came. They hit the Watusi woman and children with cane sticks and threw dirt clods at them until they disappeared into the jungle. Johnny tried to protect his parish, pleading tolerance, peace, and love, but after a couple of well-placed clods in his face, he retreated to the shack.

We made a litter out of bamboo and the door blanket, loaded the wounded tracker, and were off. We had trekked only a short distance in the mud, when the Watusi woman came running down the hill. She tugged on my shirt and began her ragged sermon with renewed desperation. Her flock was lined up along the edge of the jungle, some of them waving. I gritted my teeth, took both her leathered hands in mine, and looked her square in the face. I could see the panic in her black eyes. I closed mine, cowardly, while I shook my head firmly. We stood there, holding our ground, both of us refusing our emotions, tears welling but not spilling.

The newly ordained Johnny interrupted. He had set down his side of the litter, slopped through the mud, and was giving the woman a hug. Puzzled, if not frightened, she backed away, but the kid's face glowed triumphant. The tracker, still holding on to the litter, barked a threat and pulled out his machete, causing the woman to run back up the hill to her charges.

That was the last, and the worst, of the Watusi woman. Small, empty, without answers, I stood a moment waving to her, as did the tracker with his menacing machete.

Johnny, pausing before he picked up the litter again, called out to her, "I'll be back!"

It seemed a long hike to the truck. No one said a word the entire trek. I was sure the trackers were thinking about losing the money in their pockets and being fired. Even though they had effectively caused the death of the poachers, they could surely be in trouble for taking us in without authorization. Concerned about our safety, I cussed myself for not being better prepared for the inevitable decision the trackers would have to make. The knife in my boot was insignificant considering their weapons. Killing us and dumping our bodies would be easy. The kid stumbled along, responsible for his side of the litter, oblivious to the danger.

At the truck, we loaded the wounded tracker without incident, and Johnny and I piled in with him. For the first half hour, the driver had his hands full keeping the truck front first, sliding along down the mountain. When the ride was somewhat smoother, the wounded tracker, his head in the kid's lap, asked if we would like some food. I nodded, knowing from his look that there was a price. He rapped on the glass to stop the truck. I inched the knife from my boot. In a moment the driver appeared at the rear. He was holding two white plastic boxes. I breathed a sigh of sheepish relief. We made the deal: two lunches via Brussels, albeit several days old, for our silence.

Rumbling along eating our peanut butter on croissant, I wondered how many mountain gorillas had to die in zoos before the message was clear. Dian Fossey with her passion had tried to save them. All those lonely years and then a brutal death, for the love of mountain gorillas. Fossey was a heroine, for sure, but from the back of the truck, looking at where we'd been, I felt most humbled by the Watusi woman. Only the flock of children she tended would ever know her name, but for them she gave her entire life. I wondered if they had ever met—the Watusi woman and Fossey. Most probably not, but I found it interesting to consider them sharing their passions. I had to risk the question, ask the wounded tracker if he had known Fossey. He nodded, so I asked him if he knew who killed her, and why. He said that she had many enemies, that she was considered a witch. I supposed that was how she survived as long as she did. I asked him if the Watusi woman was considered a witch. He said that she certainly was by him. I was glad.

The next day in Kigali, waiting with the kid for his plane to Brussels, I tried to think of something to say, a clever epilogue to the trip. Nothing came to me. Since our experience at the shack, he'd been more alert to his surroundings, but he still had little comment. We were both going to be happier when he was on his way home, although happiness wasn't something I thought the kid capable of. The only times I'd seen him smile were with the baby gorilla and with the children he had entertained so divinely. Sitting there on an airport bench waiting to say good-bye, the last time we would ever see each other, we were still pretty much strangers. I was wondering about his sanity, still, when the Belgian woman walked up to our bench. She was wearing her arm in a sling, a new hat of native origin, and a crooked smile.

The kid popped off the bench and extended his hand, his enthusiastic greeting startling me. "Hello! *Bonjour,* madam, are you all right?"

She began gabbing away about her bruises and about her arm, which she said was a mystery until she could see her own doctor. Punctuating her sentences with her horsey cough, apparently real, she made it clear that she was still mad as hell, and if she lived long enough, nothing would stop her from returning to see the gorillas. She would go home, rest, and do Egypt next while she waited on the goddamn Belgian government.

I indicated the bench and she sat down, tugging at the kid's sleeve to sit with her. She wanted to know about our trek. The kid sat between us and began, shyly, telling her about the antics of the baby gorilla. She was eager for details, and when he stopped talking, she questioned and prodded. At one point, I nudged him, reminding him of our confidentiality agreement with the trackers; he gave me a look that said "I'm not stupid!" then turned back to her as though their conversation were really none of my business.

The kid wasn't effervescent, but he was conversing and at times almost lucid, certainly a different Johnny than I'd experienced. He and I were probably incompatible under any circumstances, but watching him, I suspected that he was pushing up some new, or renewed, feelings and that the Belgian woman was a motherly foil. Leaving them to it, I wandered around, checking back from time to time.

Finally, the sound of the approaching plane caused everyone to queue up. I walked with them as far as the gate. They were exchanging addresses and checking the calendar. The kid wanted the woman to accompany his mother to Egypt; they had so much in common, and he was sure they would hit it off.

Before they disappeared, I managed to get the kid's attention and shake his hand. For lack of anything better to say, I asked, "So, Johnny, have you decided what you will do about college?"

"Yes, I'm going," he announced, showing me his expensive smile, "but not to Harvard. I'm going to be a missionary." The Belgian woman was nodding, as though he'd already told her.

Stammering out some sort of congratulatory remark, I imagined— a tad of retribution—Dad receiving the news that Johnny's African experience with Kelly had been a religious one. I asked, "Is this a decision you've made as a result of our trip?"

"Yes, yes it is," he said, tentatively. "I did promise the Watusi woman that I'd be back, and, well . . ." That seemed to be all he could say to me. I watched the two of them disappear through the gate.

Jonathan kept his promise and returned to Africa as a missionary. His father cussed about it until he died of a heart attack. Until I die, the Watusi woman will live in my head, an icon of passionate women with purpose.

Beira

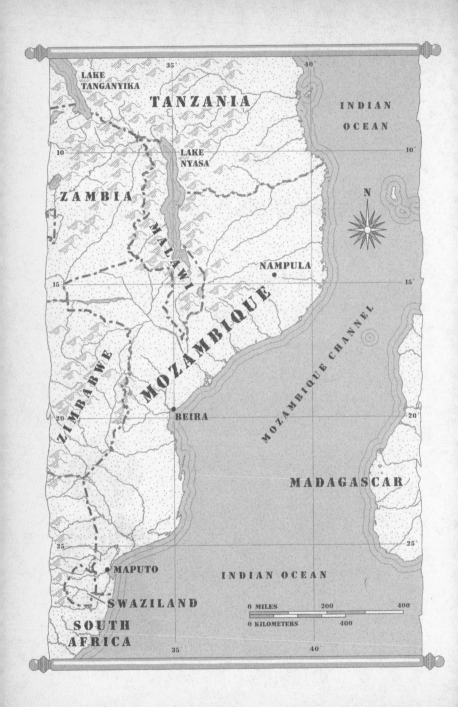

MOZAMBIQUE

The alarm on my cheap watch whined. I lay there listening to the engine, feeling the ship's motion. Captain Mac had said Beira by morning watch, but we weren't there yet. Perhaps the hurricane had cost us time. I wasn't ready for Beira again. I couldn't imagine ever being ready for Beira again. I'd regretted my inebriated promise to David all the way from Dar es Salaam.

David was surely awake too, lying in his bunk below in the crew's filthy quarters. This was his day. For ten years he'd grieved, hoped, and prayed about this day. For ten years he'd vowed to return to Beira. I had made it possible. I should never drink Tanzanian beer.

Still exhausted from our Tanzanian adventure, I was now beat up by the hurricane as well. David had to be in the same shape. Not that he could feel anything but the overwhelming emotion of returning home to find his mother and sister, as though they'd still be there, waiting, after ten years of bloody revolution. A hundred times I'd tried to talk him out of this audacious odyssey. I'd been to Beira the year before. I knew what to expect; I knew that today his heart would surely break. He'd been a kid, just fourteen, when he and Mrs. Braga had escaped, Beira in flames. The Bragas, prominent Portuguese colonialists, had owned his family as indentured slaves. Only he and Mrs. Braga got out, but not before they watched Mr. Braga and David's father being killed.

My watch whined again, 2:30 A.M., time to move. Reluctantly, I switched on the lamp, planted my feet on the floor, then examined my bruised body, procrastinating. Beira was once a Portuguese jewel on the Mozambique Channel, glittering in the tropical sun before the revolution, before the bombs. David had memories of a city made brilliant with expatriate opulence. Today, he would see shelled-out hotels, breadlines, and the rusted remains of war. The worst of the colonialists, the Portuguese raped Mozambique for years. Communism plunged it into hell. I headed for the shower, consoling myself by thinking that whatever happened, it would all be over in twenty-four hours.

The officers' mess was dark, everything confined safely to the cabinets. I'd put together tea and toast before Ensign Basso wandered in, blue eyes bleary. I handed him a cup of tea, admiring how he could look good even with a hurricane hangover. He gave me his best flirtatious smile, trifling with my hormones. Grateful, I mussed his blonde-streaked hair a bit, then left him, taking my tea and toast, balancing it up to the bridge. It, too, was mostly dark, only the lamp over the chart table subdued by the partially drawn curtain. The first mate had his face in the radarscope and, without looking up, grunted a response to the knock of my shoe. The window that had blown out was patched with plywood, the only visible remains of the hurricane. I sat down at the chart table to sip my tea and wake up.

My grandmother would have said that I was "pounded to fry." I'd hoped to get some rest on the trip from Dar es Salaam, but no one sleeps in a hurricane. My self-assigned duty, the three to eight morning watch, had stretched through the day and into the night while the ship tossed around like a toy in a tub. Green water crashed over the containers and through the blown-out window. Ensign Basso and I slipped and sloshed around in ankle-deep water catching birds—gulls, cormorants, frigates—and bats. One after another they floundered through the window seeking refuge. One by one we forced them back out into the storm.

The first mate stuck his head around the curtain and asked with a yawn, "Where's your buddy, Basso?"

My buddy Basso, the reason I did the three to eight. "It's five till three. I'm sure he's probably finishing his breakfast," I said, knowing he was. Sticking my finger on the chart table in the middle of the Mozambique Channel, I asked, "What's our position?"

"Here," he said, moving my finger to Beira, and then with his characteristic sinister smile repeated, "Here, 'port of hell.' I've called the captain."

Within a few minutes, Captain Mac, Ensign Basso, and Navigator Duncan were all on the bridge, starched and stressed. The captain demanded full dress for every port, his more snug by the year. His square frame and wide stance befitted a captain, and he was handsome enough, looking younger than his experience. Thick, brown, and wavy, his hair protruded from the sides of his hat. His jaw matched his frame, and he led with it. Navigator Duncan was thin-faced, red-headed, and red-mustached, the tilt of his mustache a barometer to his degree of drunkenness. Ensign Basso—young, tall, proud—always needed to be a hero. I did my best to oblige him.

At 4 A.M. the captain took me aside. "We've radioed the pilot at Beira. He's the Russian who usually comes, not a bad sort, and no worry to you, but as I've told you, the Russians have nearly all pulled out. One never knows in these bloody waters who might be with him or who's in command this week." He took my arm, pointing me to the door. "Off you go. You know the drill." As I started down, he called after me, "I've already sent for your charge! I'll send Basso for you when all is clear!"

The drill meant stowaways to the fo'c'sle, and on this ship it was a hatch at the bow—the safest way for Americans to enter and exit an African communist port. David, who was black and my "charge," as the captain disapprovingly referred to him, rode below with the Mauritian crew. He met me wide-eyed and full of hope. There was nothing to say. We hurried along, making our way through the rows of containers with a flashlight. Even at four in the morning, it was hot and humid, not a star in the sky. There were dead birds, dead bats, pieces of coconut, an oar—spoils of the hurricane. As we reached the bow, the ship slowed abruptly. David pointed at a dark horizon of land and then at the lights of the pilot boat.

We climbed in through the hatch. The fo'c'sle was dark, dank, and sweltering, just as it was when we'd left it exiting communist Dar es Salaam. We settled in on some piles of coiled line. David said, "I had a strange sensation looking at those birds, all dead, trying to get home, maybe an omen." I couldn't see him, but I knew this serious tone, the face. He didn't go on. We could hear the pilot boat.

For the next hour and a half we hunkered there, sweating quietly, plenty of time to ponder omens. I was regretting, still, my promise to get David back to Beira, a promise I'd made oiled on Tanzanian kerosene—rot-gut beer—and high with the celebration of an incredible victory. But what else could I have done? David had been a friend and comrade. His misadventures while on the road to Mozambique had led him unwittingly into a ransom situation that I was trying to solve in the Serengeti. He had helped me dupe the kidnappers and fight off lions, the Maasi, and huge spiders. His calm bravery had earned him the rank of hero, absolutely, which he hoped would convince me to take him to Beira. It was the least I could do for a hero: get his heart broken, maybe worse.

It would be a miracle if David's mother and sister were still alive, much less still in Beira. His sister would be twenty-six, his mother forty-one, about my age. And if they were alive, and if he found them, then what? David and I had discussed all the possibilities. I kept reminding him of his promise to leave with the ship, but I knew the fire in his belly cindered all reason. And there was reason. He'd had the finest education, including Juilliard in New York. He was a flautist, a tennis and chess player. Mrs. Braga had legally adopted him and doted on him, needed him. David had told me all of it. They had shared the same haunting nightmare, and there was comfort in their camaraderie. But his grief couldn't be satiated. He left her a note and asked her to forgive him.

It was getting light when Ensign Basso tapped on the hatch. The ship was tied off at its quay, and the Russian pilot had gone. As we walked back though the containers, David was trying for glimpses of Beira and asking questions concerning how long the captain would give him ashore. I told him all I knew. The ship's hold was full of beans, a gift from the French to Beira, and according to the captain, not to be received. He'd raged, cursing the futility of man, telling me that the Cubans, in exchange for liquor and cigarettes, would load it straightaway onto another ship bound for the docks of Djibouti. At best, David would have one day, this day. He wasn't pleased, but he wasn't surprised. I reminded him of his promise. He would leave with the ship and not look back. He nodded and went below.

The captain was waiting for me. He wanted to have a quiet breakfast, which meant he wanted to rant, rave, and lecture, that is, to impart his best advice. I looked forward to it. No one knew better the realities of East Africa, albeit spiked with personal politics. We'd been friends for years, Captain Daniel MacKinnon and I. I did him a favor once. He returned it several times and was doing so again now. Captain Mac's business was risk, silently servicing the harbors of East Africa in a politically forbidden South African cargo ship. He was always glad to see me, always eager to share his prized rum and swap stories.

"Here you go, woman, take your medicine." The captain passed me the bottle of malaria pills and then the coffee. Waddling his wavy head, a crooked smile, he said, "You're a crazy redhead, Kelly. I was daft to bring you in here last year, bloody hell! And just to look for some bloody bastard who did not want to be found!"

Laughing, I retorted, "I made money. You had the pleasure of my company."

"That I cannot dispute, but I tell you, Kelly, when I received the radio message from your man, Kumlesh, in Mombasa, that you wanted to be picked up in Dar es Salaam, I nearly didn't stop. You have no business being in these bloody waters, and . . . "

"And," I interrupted, "that's my job, contributing to your log of wild East African stories."

"That, too, I cannot dispute." He was nodding at me and at the same time making hand signals to the cook for scrambled eggs. "Nor can I deny liking the looks of you over the motley beasts who call this bucket home." The bucket, the *Osprey*, a small, antiquated cargo ship, about four hundred feet, housed seven officers of various ancestries, all Caucasians transplanted to South Africa. The seven crew members, including the cook, were Mauritian. The language on the lower decks was a mixture of Hindi, Urdu, and Bhojpuri; on the upper decks, it was English and sign language.

The cook came with scrambled eggs and scorched muffins. We loaded our plates before the captain began the lecture. "Beira is a graveyard; the situation has worsened. The Russians are pulling out. That drunken Rozdilsky, the Zar, as he likes to be called, he's still here, still flaunts his whore. The Russians will keep him here until someone kills him. Easier than exiling him somewhere else."

"We're opposed to whores now?" I teased.

"'Tis the flaunting I find distasteful," he quipped, jutting his jaw. He poured more coffee and ate his eggs. I asked him why the Russians were pulling out. He waved his fork in front of menacing eyes. "They are only here to keep FRELIMO alive, ride herd, as you Americans say, on these fifteen-year-old Cuban kids—all testosterone, no brains. However, as long as the Cubans are here, they have to be fed, and for that they're dependent on the harbor, on me and the other odd ship that may have food for the Mozambicans that they can steal." He was waving his fork again. "But they can't keep RENAMO out. RENAMO blew up the harbor again three months ago. Take a look when you can, all that work the Dutch did, for naught." He shook his head and made "tsk, tsk" noises to take his usual jab at the Dutch. "Bloody hell, the Dutch. They live in their bubble until it pops, then they blow another bubble. They have spent millions on this port. They repair it, RENAMO bombs it, they repair it." Pausing for another "tsk," he added, "and they bring their wives. Well, you know, you met them. Nurses to the wounded, saints to the dying."

Navigator Duncan, his red mustache drooping, half crocked already, came in with some papers for the captain to look over. I ate my breakfast and thought about what the captain had said, about the tragedy of Mozambique. FRELIMO, the abbreviated name of the Mozambique Liberation Front, funded by the Russians and Communist China, threw out the Portuguese in 1974 and turned the country into a Marxist-style black government fraught with dissension and general disregard for the people. RENAMO forces, funded by South Africa, white supremacists from Rhodesia (now Zimbabwe), and a number of other countries including the United States through the CIA kept up a military resistance that strangled the country's power, rail, and food supply. War, starvation, and disease were all the Mozambicans had known for ten years, with no relief in sight.

Duncan left, and the captain stood with his arms folded across his chest. "Now, concerning today!" he barked. "Duncan is loaning his passport again. Wear your uniform. Put your hair under your hat and put that mustache of yours on so you'll resemble Duncan, at least until we're through the gate, past those impetuous Cuban kids. The Russians don't care about you, a woman, especially in uniform, and you've met Rozdilsky, the bloody Zar. But you'll have to stick with me. Rebels from one bloody renegade faction or another could spot your white female face and find a way to use you. They're all animals now, hungry and mean." Eyes reduced to shiny slits, he rapped his knuckles on the table. "That Negro charge of yours cannot be paying you sufficiently."

"He's not paying me." I rapped my knuckles the way he had. "I'm returning a favor. You know how that works. He became involved in the situation in Tanzania, and . . ."

"I'll bet he put you in that bloody situation, didn't he?"

"Not true!" I snapped. "Listen, my dear captain, when this is over, and we're on our way safely out of here, and providing there's not another hurricane, I'll tell you all about Tanzania. It's going to take several hours and a bottle of your best brandy."

"You are on, my dear!" He shook a finger at me. "Hey, that was some bloody blow! I thought we were going to miss it, but these bloody hurricanes bounce around in the channel like Ping-Pong balls. You know, two years ago . . ." He looked up at the clock. "A story for later. We don't have much time here." Between the last gulps of his coffee, he said, "The beans will be unloaded today. The drought in the interior, the war, they continue. I'm certain there won't be cargo for us. We sail at sunrise tomorrow." Seeing the remaining questions on my face, he patted the top of my hand. "Providing the ship's jalopy is still here and running, we'll get your charge into town. If he dresses in rags and carries nothing on him, he'll blend. He can look through the breadlines and shelters." He paused for a grimace. "They're dead or gone, his family. Nobody lives in Beira for ten years." Grabbing his hat, talking over his shoulder, he said, "Now, you and I are going to see the Dutch, drink the beer I brought them. Of course, we'll probably have to share it with the Zar and his whore."

I followed him to the door asking, "Rozdilsky's whore, she was there last year. What's her name?"

"Labios Rubi! Portuguese for Ruby Lips! She's officially Rozdilsky's bodyguard. Ha! Wears a uniform and paints her face, ruby red lipstick. A real jewel." He turned around, a look of disgust dissolving. "The tenacity of the Dutch, here, against all odds. But then, bleeding hearts bleed till they're bloody dry, and their government continues to send them Heineken." He winked and plopped on his hat. "Now, you know the rules. Stay inside the ship, unless properly attired. Have your charge ready. We'll drop him"—he glanced at his watch—"say in about two hours; pick him up when the Heineken's gone."

I lucked upon Ensign Basso with his shirt off doing a check of the lifeboats. I asked him to get David from below. We met on the starboard deck out of view of the Cuban harbor guards who walked the shore. David was carrying his flute, not looking well. I asked him what they were feeding him. He insisted he was fine, just anxious. The crew had been giving him all kinds of advice. I gave his shoulder a pat and reminded him that none of the crew had ever been ashore in Beira. We chatted for a few minutes about absolutely nothing relevant, like a huddle on the pitcher's mound. It wouldn't do to hash things over now. The experience he was about to have was sure to rip him up, and there was not a damn thing I could do but trust his mettle. For all his sensitivity, a classical flautist, he was tough. I told him to find some rags, rest, and be ready.

The ship's bar, mostly empty during the day, was a good place to read and watch the shore. The Zan-Z-Bar connected to the poop deck, which overlooked a portion of the lower deck. We were tied on the port side, and through the curtains I could peer at the camouflaged uniforms on shore. The harbor was well guarded by Cuban soldiers. They were young, boys really, swaggering around with their Russian rifles, smoking, occasionally yelling at the few black, ragged, and barefoot workers who tended the port. The sounds of David's sweet classical flute wafting up from the lower deck gave the scene a sense of macabre.

Waiting, reading, and nodding off, I heard a commotion on the stern's lower deck. It was shouting and laughter—incongruous, delightful. I knew that Pepi had arrived. In uniform, I pulled on my hat, tucked up my hair, and stepped onto the poop deck. The first mate and navigator were already there. Looking down, we could see some of the crew, as well as David, gathered around the starboard side of the lower deck. Pepi was alongside in his small rowboat holding up one of his prize shells. His fourteen-year-old smile, sales chatter, and hearty laugh were as infectious as I remembered from my last trip. He traded shells for clothes, canned goods, whatever he could get for the shelter his mother ran for homeless kids. The crew loved Pepi. He knew a few words of several languages and used them all. One at a time, he would hold up his treasures, and the crew and officers held up their articles to bid. With an incredible amount of jesting and jiving, deals were made, after which Pepi would do a song, standing and waving his arms like a star on a stage. Officially not allowed by the port authority, this was done on the starboard side, out of their sight.

The shell bidding went on, getting noisier by the minute. David was mesmerized, no doubt seeing himself ten years earlier. The Cuban guard walking the shore looked over occasionally, but his view of the lower deck was mostly blocked by empty oil drums that the crew had stacked along the dock, probably just for privacy. However, the current in the harbor kept pushing Pepi's boat back toward the stern. Each time he finished a deal and the items exchanged were thrown and caught, he had to row back into position. Finally, when the activity was rushed, the current won and Pepi was in sight of the guard. The guard yelled out in Spanish for Pepi to get out of the harbor. Pepi's laughter ceased, his handsome young smile melting into old hate. He sat down and picked up his oars, but not before yelling a retaliatory remark at the guard in Portuguese. Before Pepi's oars hit the water, the guard had his gun to his shoulder. He fired two shots, two bullets into Pepi. Pepi slumped over his bag of shells. He was dead.

The first mate ordered the officers and crew inside. The captain came rushing into the Zan-Z-Bar with Ensign Basso. Basso pulled back the curtains of the stern window and pointed to Pepi's boat, which had floated off, coming to rest on the remains of a bombed mooring about fifty yards from the stern.

The captain stormed, "Which one of those bloody bastards was it?" Ensign Basso pulled up the portside curtain to reveal the guard still walking the shore as casually as he had before, smoking a cigarette. "Bloody, bloody hell!" The captain hit his fists together. "What's he going to do? Leave Pepi there to rot?" He walked in a circle with his hands on his hips and then asked, "How old was Pepi, fourteen, fifteen? I'm surprised he lived that long." He flipped up the curtain again, watching the guard and muttering, "That Cuban bastard is probably the same age. What a rotten bloody place! What a rotten goddamn bloody world! What a rotten goddamn bloody world for kids!" Everyone was quiet for a few minutes. The captain just stood there watching the shore.

The silence was interrupted by a call from the crew's quarters. Ensign Basso picked up the phone and relayed the message. "Captain, the crew wants to retrieve Pep . . . the body. They say, well . . ."

He didn't finish, and the captain asked, "What? They say what?"

Basso looked piqued. "They say he will be full of, of maggots, by the time the sun sets."

"And what in bloody hell will the crew do, embalm him?" He let out a long sigh and lowered his voice. "Tell the crew to retrieve the body."

Within an hour we were ready to leave. The port guards were paid in beer and candy for allowing us to return Pepi to his mother. His body was wrapped in canvas and stacked along with the goods for the Dutchmen. The crew pushed the ship's jalopy onto the dock, put in a can of petrol, and loaded our cargo.

Ensign Basso drove. The captain rode in the front seat, while I rode in the backseat among the boxes for the Dutch. At the main gate, Basso handed the gate guards the passports and a couple of cartons of cigarettes, the usual gate fee. They wanted more; the port guards had told them there was a body in the trunk. They didn't know that David was also there. The captain had a small bottle of whiskey in his pocket for the occasion. They waved us through.

Along the shoreline road, we passed the rusted piles of mechanical objects that had died without fuel, the Russian minute missiles that lined both sides of the harbor entrance, and the boarded-up, burned-out, and long-abandoned cafes and stores that lined the town's water-front. It was hot and humid. I could only imagine the horror of the trunk.

At what was once the Portuguese yacht club, now a shelter for children, we parked under a huge banyan tree, where an oil drum sat on bricks and smoldering dung, steaming, smelling of fish. Pepi's mother had taken over the responsibility of running the shelter when her husband was killed, leaving her alone with three children. Basso opened the trunk, and David crawled out, gasping. While we unloaded Pepi, dozens of people wandered around the jalopy and steaming drum, their faces blank, as though we were a mirage.

The captain, his stride wide and deliberate, went to find Pepi's mother. Basso waited at the car. David and I, and Pepi in his canvas shroud, waited at the pool under a moldy plastic shelter. The neglected pool was slimy green, floating garbage and reeking of a toi-let. The people coming and going were wearing rags, like David, but they were thin, some skeletal, all with the vacant look of depression and hunger, all waiting for the shark cooking in the drum. David, tall and muscular, sweat pouring from his well-chiseled ebony face, looked like an actor dressed for a play. I tried to talk to him, but he didn't seem to hear me. I'd seen him scared before.

The captain returned, sweating and pale. "What a rotten bloody place!" He looked about. "This was once a . . . oh 'tis long gone." He looked at me, a slow grin. "Your mustache is listing; you don't need it here."

David and the captain picked up Pepi and proceeded into the building. I followed. It reeked inside, too, maybe worse. There were children everywhere, the healthier ones playing, the sicker ones lying on blankets on the floor. In another room were the very ill on cots. The rooms had been stripped down to concrete and bare wood, and the acoustics were ghostly surreal: crying, coughing, moaning, and whimpering amplified through intense humidity. The heat was stifling, the faces of the children haunting.

Pepi's mother was where the captain had left her with the news, on the floor, weeping, rocking a baby. They laid Pepi next to her. I took the listless infant she was holding so that she could unwrap her son from the canvas. She saw Pepi's face, gasped, squeezed her eyes closed, and cried aloud. We left her to grieve.

The captain took a queasy-looking David back outside. I paced around with the child, talking to it as one does with a baby. The response—enormous black eyes in a skeletal head, wandering slowly over my face—felt like poison in my gut. I looked around for a more capable woman, but the few about were scurrying toward the loudest cries.

The child was sleeping in my arms when the captain returned and kneeled next to Pepi's mother. Through her sobs, she gave Pepi's epitaph, softly, in Portuguese. He was the lifeline of all the shelters in Beira, not just this one. The people of Beira loved him, counted on him. They would have to be told. She would have to tell them. The captain laid his hand on her shoulder and offered his assistance for whatever was necessary. Still sobbing, the woman thanked him but insisted she would manage. Now, she wanted to be with her son. The captain said he would send Ensign Basso back with all the canned goods the ship could spare. She smiled weakly, reaching for the child I was grateful to hand back. Holding it close to her face, she let her tears wash over the sharp edges of its head. Looking up at me, she told us that this child was also dead.

A crowd had gathered around the jalopy. They wanted something, anything I suppose. Ensign Basso, with the authoritative experience of a South African, yelled at them in English to back off, but they didn't understand. The captain, humbled by the stench of death, handled it in Portuguese, gently. We loaded into the car and drove toward town.

At the La Mar Hotel, laundry hung from windows and people queued around the block waiting to get into the bombed-out lobby in hopes of getting food or medical supplies. David remembered it, the most beautiful of the castles, forbidden to blacks. It was now a shelter for the sick, wounded, and starving, exclusively black. Those who lived long enough at the La Mar might be placed in one of the more permanent shelters. It was a place for David to begin his search. He got out of the car as though sleepwalking. I handed him a bottle of water and reminded him again not to use English. He reminded me again how to pronounce his family's names: Malawa. His father had been Paulo Malawa. His mother's name was Marie; his sister was Moana. He would meet us back at the La Mar at dusk. I hated sending him off alone, but I was anxious to talk with the Dutch people, particularly the wives. They had been in Beira three years and employed servants. David's family had been servants, albeit ten years ago, to the prominent Braga family. There were questions that begged asking.

The two Dutch couples lived together in a harbor view turn-of-the-century mansion in such bad repair that it resembled the proverbial haunted house: the mansard-style roof patched with rusted tin and bits of plastic, the carved wood extrados over the doors and windows chipped and cracked, and all traces of paint long gone. They had seen our ship in the harbor and were waiting at the front entrance. The men unloaded the jalopy. There was beer, cheese, candy, cigarettes, canned goods, and their mail. We couldn't have been more welcome.

When we were settled into the walled garden, Heinekens in hand, the captain told them about Pepi. Everyone knew Pepi, but still I was surprised the news had such an emotional impact on veterans of fourth-world horrors. The shorter of the two wives, Gilda, hurried back into the house to hide her tears. The taller one, Heather, sat clenching her fists and biting her lip. The men bombarded the captain with questions in Dutch and Portuguese. I went to the kitchen. The tall woman followed.

Gilda and Heather leaned against kitchen counters. I slumped in a chair. Finding a place to settle our gaze, we remembered Pepi. For me it was a memory of the morning, the sound of the gunshots, the speed of death. I swore out loud. The women wept. After a while we began to talk quietly. It was with difficulty for me; I understood Portuguese but spoke it poorly. The women gave Pepi's epitaph through their tears, the same as his mother had. He was a legend in his very short time, the lifeblood of all the shelters in Beira. He never failed to deliver a song, a poem, and an enormous amount of good cheer, every day, and he never went empty-handed. Some days it was canned food, some days packaged goods. Some days a little, some days a lot. The locals said he was a superboy with extraordinary diving skills and uncanny trading expertise. But the Dutch lived above the port and knew the few ships that did not frequent Beira. Pepi obviously had other traders, other connections. Why were the labels on the food always removed? The Dutch women, still drying their eyes, were angry. With whom had he been dealing? Why had he been killed? I offered my theory that he'd just been unlucky with the wrong guard, but the women shook their heads. They had always worried that Pepi was involved beyond his years and would meet with the statistics of war.

The women wanted to go to the children's shelter. They needed to comfort Pepi's mom—Velha, they called her. Their presence would be needed to maintain calm. The people of Beira would be angry. I wanted to go with them. I still had questions, and I could better help David by going with them than by swilling beer with the Zar and his whore, who were expected any minute. The captain gave me permission only if I remained with the women and Ensign Basso. Basso, he said, would be returning to the shelter with the goods promised and should be instructed to stay with me. As we left, the captain barked, "Don't take off your hat!" He was feeling the Heineken and looking forward to giving Rozdilsky grief over Pepi. The Zar wouldn't like unfavorable information, like the killing of children, to leave his port.

There was a large crowd of people around the yacht club now, mostly women, all ragged, all talking and making worried sounds. They hushed as the two Dutch women began touching and consoling their way through the group. I followed as far as the pool and decided its stench was slightly more bearable than what was inside. I pulled up a concrete block and sat down to wait. It was only a few minutes before the ship's jalopy arrived. Ensign Basso sprang from the driver's seat, opened the trunk, and motioned to me for direction.

We were about to unload the trunk, when Pepi's mother came out of the shelter followed by four women carrying Pepi on a litter. All of the women were wearing aprons, covering their shabby dresses. Their hair, short and tight against their heads, framed somber faces, masks focused on a somber task. Pepi's mother's apron was covered with the same blood that soaked the litter where Pepi lay, his arms folded and tied across his blanketed chest. The Dutch women followed behind the litter, the procession parting the crowd that began to wail out loud. As they passed by the jalopy, I caught the mother's attention, indicating the open trunk crammed with foodstuffs, wondering where she wanted them. She stopped, glanced back at Pepi, and then went straight to the trunk and, without hesitation, began unloading the cans and packages and placing them around Pepi on the litter. So deliberate was her action, so emphatic was her placement of the food around his arms and between his legs, that it did not seem appropriate to help her. Basso, confused, just stood holding the trunk open. The litter bearers braced themselves as the weight shifted and the load became increasingly heavy. Finally, Pepi was completely decorated and the procession began to move again, down the dusty street, the crowd of women following. Asking Basso to stay close by with the jalopy, I slipped in with the Dutch women, the street's dust wafting up to meet the white trousers of my uniform.

The procession grew, still mostly women. I managed to talk with Gilda and Heather about David's family of servants, the Malawas, and their employers, the Bragas. It was disappointing and difficult for me to believe that they hadn't heard of any of them. They told me that ten years was an eternity in Beira.

We were a block long before we reached the La Mar Hotel. When the people gathered there saw us coming, they began kneeling and crossing themselves. Word of Pepi had spread. A whispered chant of "Pepi" began somewhere, growing into a reverent, sad chorus. Pepi's mother led the litter straight into the hotel. The Dutch women followed, and I followed them, pausing at the door to see a jeep full of Cuban soldiers stalking the growing crowd that continued the mournful chant, "Pepi, Pepi, Pepi." Ensign Basso was parking the jalopy on a side street under a tree.

Inside the La Mar, in what remained of the main lobby, a table was quickly cleared and placed in the center for Pepi and his mobile pantry. Slowly, one by one, the sick, wounded, and starving, with the help of would-be nurses and each other, came by the table to view their slain boy-hero adorned with the foodstuffs for which he was famous. They crossed themselves and knelt and wept and whispered to each other and to Pepi's mother, Velha. When everyone who could had passed by the table, Velha took several of the cans of food from the litter and proudly, symbolically, gave them to a nurse in the group. The nurse clutched them to her breast. There were no dry eyes, certainly not mine. Then, nodding to the litter bearers, who promptly responded, the boy-hero's mother led us back out on the street where we marched on to the next shelter, preceding an enormous crowd with as many men now as women, two jeeps full of soldiers, and Basso in the ship's jalopy. I constantly scanned the crowd for David.

It was another bombed hotel, this one a men's shelter. There were men with wounds and missing limbs; some of the younger men wore remnants of shabby uniforms from one of the several warring factions that divided and confused Mozambique. As the men stumbled by the litter expressing grief, the chants outside were growing stronger, less mournful. By the time Pepi's mother had presented the tokens of food, the chants had taken on an angry echo. As our procession exited the hotel, the jeeps moved closer. The captain hadn't anticipated a mass demonstration when he said, "Don't take off your hat." The white hat, the uniform, dusty as it was, could have been a flag in the sea of rags. I reasoned that the white uniform meant ship, and ship meant food to the Cubans. Basso, still following well behind the jeeps, was probably reasoning too. I crowded between the Dutch women and took up the chant, "Pe-pi, Pe-pi," as we proceeded to the next shelter.

Velha was gaining momentum. We all were. Nothing like chanting masses to spur righteous indignation. A hero had been slain by the enemy, who were foreigners in camouflaged uniforms. Most of the chanters probably had an opinion of RENAMO, or FRELIMO, even if they couldn't spell them or write them, but today, now, they only knew that their local hero had been shot down in cold blood. A boy who had made them smile through their pain was now a corpse, just another corpse like all the others they had buried. "Pe-pi, Pe-pi." In time with the chant, we were moving deliberately now, in unison. We were all going somewhere, and so were the jeeps, moving inside the crowd, raising swells of dust onto the marchers. "Pe-pi, Pe-pi." The chant was now a threat to any opposition of our hero. In the gutted-out buildings and piles of trash, teenagers were dashing about gathering rocks and bricks, stuffing them in sacks. I couldn't see David anywhere. I assumed Basso was still out there, still the hero.

The next shelter was in a church. It was for girls—adolescents and young adults. Their parents had been killed or separated from them. The Dutch women said that the shelter was primarily to feed and educate girls sufficiently to prevent them from becoming prostitutes to the Cubans—and pregnant. There were a few books and old magazines about, tattered, but none I could see of any consequence to emaciated persons, male or female. The young teens, seeing Pepi, began screaming, holding on to each other, the sides of their faces pressed together in horror. The older girls didn't cry, but softly, deliberately, took up the chant from the streets. When a tall woman of about twenty-five came and kissed Velha's skirt, several more followed and knelt about her. I asked them about Moana, Moana Malawa. A young man had been there already, asking, they said. No one knew her.

Velha presented the tokens of food from the litter, and the young women followed us into the street, still chanting, just in time to see the first rocks hitting the jeeps and the Cuban soldiers taking their gun slings off their shoulders. One of the soldiers raised a megaphone and began shouting in Spanish, orders to clear the streets. Rocks hit the megaphone first, knocking it out of the soldier's hand. More rocks hit his face and chest. I yelled at the young women to get back into the church and shoved the Dutch women to the ground, landing on top of them. Suddenly, Basso was on top of me and, from nowhere, David was on us both. Pepi's mom and the litter bearers stopped, but stood tall. We heard the guns cocked in unison. There were whimpering sounds and flashes of people crossing themselves, and then, the terrible screaming of bad brakes followed by the crunching of metal. Basso, David, and I got to our knees to see a huge cloud of dust covering both jeeps. A third jeep had just smashed into them. Several soldiers had been knocked out onto the ground.

As the dust settled, the crowd stopped chanting and became quiet.

The driver in the third jeep stood up, adjusting his hat, brushing his pants and jacket. But it wasn't a *he*. It was Labios Rubi, the Zar's whore and bodyguard. She climbed up on the seat to stand as tall as possible, put her hand on the pistol handle hanging from her hip, and began to yell at the soldiers in Spanish, her painted lips aglow. We were thirty yards away and didn't get every word, but the gist of it was that all military personnel were to report back to headquarters, and no one would interfere with the funeral procession. Then, even louder and in both Spanish and Portuguese, she shouted that the soldier who killed the shell boy would be punished. The crowd immediately got to their feet and took up the chant again. The soldiers climbed back into their jeeps and in a minute were gone. Rubi, still standing on the seat of her jeep, looked over the crowd. Her Zar had apparently sent her, probably so that he could stay with the Heineken.

Jabbering to each other under the sound of the chant, the Dutch women were helping each other up, using their aprons to dab at the dirt on their faces. Feeling guilty, I tried to help, but Rubi was shouting again. She had spotted the Dutch women—or me—and was motioning us forward. Gilda told us emphatically to stay where we were; she alone would go. We waited nervously. She made her way through the chanting crowd. It seemed a long way. Basso and David whispered something about the identity of Labios Rubi. I whispered questions to David about his search. None of us took our eyes off Gilda.

Finally, Gilda was back and Rubi was gone. Gilda had satisfied her that Basso and I were with the ship in port and had brought canned goods for Velha. The Dutch women were thankful that Rozdilsky had sent Rubi in time and believed the captain was responsible. We marched on.

David and Basso walked with us for a while. David wanted to follow a lead that would take him to the outskirts of Beira and wondered if I could cover the remaining shelters. I assured him that I could. His water bottle was empty, his heart heavy. As he trotted off, I reminded him to be at the La Mar at dusk, as promised. Basso trotted off, too, back to the jalopy, hat cocked, still looking his part.

The afternoon steamed on. There were stray soldiers here and there, but apparently they had gotten the word. Nonetheless, I was trapped, a dirty, hungry, and tired captive. I looked at the dusty faces of the Dutch women and felt humbled. They were faces of hope to the women of Beira, hope that someone from outside their hell was offering a light, a voice for their pain. I wondered what these faces would be doing in Amsterdam or The Hague, or wherever they came from. Do-gooders, by the captain's words, bleeding hearts, marching from one shelter to the next in support of mothers, children, and decency.

By the time Pepi's body began to bloat, only women remained in the procession, with the exception of Basso trailing in the jalopy. Old women with fans walked alongside the litter shooing flies. The shelters we traipsed through now were in houses. No one had heard of David's family, the Malawas. We spared little time. A brief glimpse, a few cans of food, and we were gone. There were shrieks and sobs, but no surprises. By now, everyone knew Pepi's fate before we arrived.

The last shelter was on a hill, up a steep path and behind a thick, unruly hedge. We could smell the sea, just beyond. The house had recently been sloppily whitewashed. Inside, a few calendar pictures hung on walls that had been painted green or blue, much of it splattered on the bare wood floor. Stuffed chairs were scattered about between beds, and plants hung in the open windows. Although its structure looked friendlier, it reeked with the by now familiar smell of the half dead, and worse, it sheltered the insane of Beira. Women and men, mostly old and hideous, with hollowed-out faces of doom, tottered about, muttering and drooling. They all stared at Pepi; maybe they knew what was happening. I was trying to communicate with the attendant, asking her about David's mother, when a woman with incredible burn scars came and threw herself on Pepi, knocking the last of the canned goods onto the floor. As she was pulled off and placed in a bed, she screamed something over and over, a word that pierced the ears like a spear. The litter bearers quickly picked up Pepi, and we hurried out. The woman continued to scream her one word. We could still hear her as we tramped back down the hill and toward the cemetery.

It was finally over, finally dusk. Gilda, Heather, Basso, and I waited at the La Mar for David. Nothing had been said since putting Pepi in the ground. There was nothing to say over the despair that ached in us for the people of Beira. David came, finally, silent too, his face telling us of disappointment. We piled into the jalopy and went back to the Dutch mansion overlooking the port.

We found the captain and the husbands louder and happier than when we'd left, but our demeanor quickly quieted them. The women told them of the day, the confrontation with soldiers, the rescue just in time by Rozdilsky's bodyguard. Gilda was thanking the captain for his influence, until the captain shook his head and the men explained that they hadn't seen the Zar. He hadn't shown up. They quipped that he was drunk somewhere and probably didn't know the ship had arrived, much less about Pepi.

"Labios Rubi, bloody hell!" the captain exclaimed. "She has enough authority to stop soldiers when they're being pelted?" I reminded him that she had mowed them down with her jeep to get their attention. He bellowed like a bull and turned in a circle. "But she did say the Cuban was going to be punished for killing the kid?"

Confidently, Gilda said that the Cuban would be punished. Then she added something to the effect of "That woman feeds Beira. Pepi made the deliveries." Gilda's husband jumped in, making it clear that his wife was speculating, as she often did, but that if it was true, it was probably why Pepi was shot.

"I've had all the communist intrigue I can do this day," the captain replied, exasperated.

Gilda and Heather served up some kind of stew. I ate with David in the kitchen. Slumped over his bowl, listless, his heart was as broken as I'd dreaded. There wasn't a single clue that his mother and sister had ever lived in Beira. He could find no one who knew of the Braga family. Ten years ago they had been the most prominent family in an Indian Ocean seaport famous for its giant crayfish and posh hotels. But today, David could find only the pile of overgrown rubble where their home once stood. The Dutch women came in and sat with him awhile, talked to him in Portuguese, consoled him with hope, offering the possibility that his mother and sister were both still alive living in a village somewhere.

After good-nights and good-byes, we packed David in the trunk of the jalopy, and Ensign Basso drove us back to the ship. The captain didn't want a nightcap, but I did. He poured me a brandy, and I asked his permission to talk with David for a while on the poop deck outside the Zan-Z-Bar. He consented as long as David was below before change of midnight watch. He poured another brandy and said, "Give this to the kid, the poor, goddamn, bloody bastard. He should have stayed in New York and played his flute. Maybe now he'll appreciate the grace of God, or this woman, the rich Portuguese, Braga, who rescued him from hell." With that, he barked instructions to the officer on watch to have David brought to the poop deck, then tramped off to his quarters.

David stared at the brandy and gulped it down like medicine he loathed to take. He was quiet for a few minutes, cradling his head in his large hands. There was no sound but the groans of the ship, until he began to sob. I had seen David sob once before, without brandy. I hated it then and I hated it now, but I couldn't think of a thing to say either time. Finally, he was quiet, and I went back to the Zan-Z-Bar for another brandy. When I returned, he was at the rail. "How can I just sail away without them? I came for them!" He pounded the rail with his fist. "I came for them! They must be here somewhere! They couldn't be d . . ." Pounding on the railing again, he let his head drop, murmuring, "I can't just sail away."

I chugged my brandy, rubbed David on the back, and gently reminded him of his promise to me. Then, I pulled up a chair and asked him to share some memories. He had some good ones to keep. Why not share some with me, make him feel better? To my surprise, he did. He sat down and began telling stories. Some I'd heard before, about his sister, his mother and father, things they'd done together, sweet stories that his memory made maudlin. He used to dive for shells, like Pepi. Only then there were lots of shells and lots of ships to trade with. He had made a beautiful necklace for his sister to wear on her first date. He'd made another for his mother that she always wore on Sunday when she accompanied Mr. and Mrs. Braga to the big church, walking behind them, carrying their gloves or hats or their prayer books or fans. His mother loved to go to the big church. She had dreamed that Moana could someday be married there, even though she knew it would never be allowed. He rambled on with his reminiscing, feeling better, I hoped.

I was beginning to nod off when I heard him say, "I could almost hear her calling me. Dee Dee, Dee Dee. I must have been hallucinating. I was pretty hungry by then. Maybe I was hallucinating, but it sounded just like my mother."

"Where were you?" I asked, coming to.

"I was down in what's left of the basement of the Braga house. I used to play down there and get into the mister's fishing stuff. Mother would miss me and go to the top of the stairs and yell for me. She knew I'd be there."

"She called you Dee Dee?" A knot was forming in my stomach.

"Yeah, that was what she called me, and today I heard her—well almost." He leaned back, a tired sigh.

Clumsily, I got out of my chair. "David, where exactly is the Braga house, or what's left of it?"

"Up on the hill, on the far side of town. Not this hill by the port where the Dutch live, but on the far side of town. It overlooks that beautiful beach and the lighthouse."

"What time were you there?" I asked, hating to know.

"I went there last, a while before dark. Why?" He got to his feet, unsteadily. "Why, what are you thinking."

It was a long shot, but a shot. "David, it was the last shelter we went to. It was for, well for insane or senile people." I looked at him squarely. He appeared to be holding his breath. I took his arm and said, "David, this is just a wild shot, but there was a woman there . . . it was difficult to tell her age because she was very badly burned. When she saw Pepi, she threw herself on him and had to be restrained." I paused, remembering how terrible the scene was, how Pepi looked by then.

"Yes, so, this woman, what was her name?" He was frowning at me, impatient.

"I don't know her name. She had to be restrained, and we left in a hurry."

"Kelly!" David's voice cracked. "Please! What?"

I groaned, tired, wishing I didn't have to tell him. "It was before we went to the cemetery, about an hour before dusk when we were there, maybe the same time you were at the house. This woman screamed over and over, she was screaming 'Dee Dee' at the top of her lungs, at Pepi. We could still hear her screaming at the bottom of the hill. I wouldn't be surprised if that's what you heard today, not a hallucination but this woman screaming, 'Dee Dee.'" David was standing very close to me. Sweat slipped down his temples. I said, "Pepi is the same age you were when you escaped the bombing. Maybe she, I don't know, but . . ."

David fell into his chair, silent. I sat down too, reminding him again that it was a shot in the dark and that nothing could be solved now.

All of Beira was as black as the hour, even if the captain would sanction a midnight jaunt past the guards, and I knew he wouldn't. I was prepared to argue, but surprisingly David wasn't. For a long few minutes he sat seemingly complacent, quiet. Then he got up, sauntered around the deck, and sat back down again. I tried to imagine what he was thinking. I wished I hadn't been so descriptive of the woman's hideous scars. Then again, I wished I hadn't told him anything, even that I knew the way to Beira. Finally, I said, "David, I will do everything I can to talk the captain into taking us into town again in the morning before we sail. He'll be up early, planning to sail at dawn. That's the best I can do, and I'll do it, but only if you promise me you'll get some sleep until I send for you. He stood, nodded, and started off. I couldn't read him. He was sleepwalking in his own nightmare. "David." I caught hold of his arm. "Don't do anything that will jeopardize yourself." I was thinking about sharks and barbed wire and Cuban soldiers. I still didn't know what he was thinking.

At 3 A.M. I climbed up to the bridge. The first mate was snoozing, his head on the chart table; apparently it was an uneventful night in port. I wanted to send for David, to know for sure he was still on the ship, but I resisted in favor of waking up.

Ensign Basso was in the officers' mess. That helped. We made tea together, tossed a few smiles, said a few grim words about yesterday. On the way back to the bridge, he leaked some information to me. Apparently the captain was planning to see the Zar before leaving port. He wanted a promise that the Cuban who shot Pepi would be punished.

Sitting at the chart table, I told myself that the captain's plan was good news for getting David into Beira one more time, to identify what remained of a tormented woman who had a remote possibility of being his mother. And then what? Even if she was his mother, would she know what had happened to the sister, and if so, or if not, what would satisfy David enough to keep his word to me to leave with the ship and not look back? I went back to the mess for more coffee.

By four, I was tired of holding my breath and had Basso contact the crew's quarters. David was there. I breathed a sigh and sent word for him to hang tight until dawn.

By the time the captain was on the bridge, dawn was on its way. "You look fit for inspection," he snapped. "How did you get starched overnight? And why?" He looked at me with his head cocked suspiciously, then barked a few instructions to Basso before walking me by the coat sleeve off the bridge to breakfast.

"Take your malaria pill and listen to me!" he demanded. "Basso told you I'm going to see Rozdilsky, give him my thoughts on murdering kids. Apparently he didn't tell you I'm going alone." He shoveled the eggs on his plate and passed them on to me. "I gave your charge a day, as promised, that's it. No more! There's no way of knowing what kind of bloody hell is going on, what the fallout will be from yesterday. Maybe the drunken Zar isn't even in power anymore. He didn't show yesterday, had his whore doing his job. Maybe she's running things now!" He held up the coffeepot. I shook my head, but he poured anyway.

I talked fast and convincingly. David could ride in the trunk again, and if the guards were in trouble for Pepi's death, as Rubi had promised, they would be easy to deal with at the gate, and how long could it take to give the kid a peek at the woman?

The captain listened, all the time shaking his head. When I'd finished my spiel, he challenged me with "And if the Cubans have taken power?"

"If you believe that's a possibility, then I concede," I said, with a shudder of reality.

"In this part of the world, anything horrific is a possibility." He stood up and tossed his napkin on the unfinished plate of eggs. "Have your charge ready in ten minutes. If I'm going to make an impression on the Zar, it will have to happen before he starts drinking." He looked at his watch. "And the sun is on its way!" He slammed his hat on his head, started off, then turned around and said, "If he's discovered, your charge, he's a stowaway on his own!" Then he jabbed a finger at me. "And don't forget your mustache."

The captain drove. I was right about the guards at the gate. They saluted him and waved us through, Basso still holding the passports. The sun breaking through the craggy remains of Beira felt like a drumroll. I pointed the way through the empty streets. When we reached the path that led to the shelter on the hill, the captain stopped and we let David out of the trunk.

"Two hours!" the captain barked, slamming the trunk shut. "I don't care if you stay here, young man!" He was wagging a finger in David's blank face. "You would be the fool, but it's your decision. I'm only telling you that my ship sails in two hours, with you or without you!" He grabbed the jalopy door, flung it open, and then stopped to look at me. "You can take that mustache off until we go back through the gate, but keep your hair under that hat, and under no circumstances"—he motioned toward the hill—"do you leave this place." Slamming himself into the jalopy, he pushed the gear forward and pointed toward the shabby remains of a children's play area. "There! One hour and forty minutes!" A pop of the clutch and they were gone. David and I stood watching the dust settle before we started up the path.

The whitewashed house was quiet and dark in front of the rising sun. Heavy, tattered curtains covered the open windows, and the front door was shut. I needed to say something before we went in, anything. I asked David why he wore an orange shirt. I knew the answer. "Don't you recognize it?" he asked. He pulled the front out straight to display the faded picture of Jerry Garcia. "It's my good luck shirt. I wore it in Tanzania, for a week straight."

We smiled at our bond, and he walked up to the door, made a fist, and knocked loudly. Someone inside made indiscernible sounds, and David knocked again before partially opening the door and turning to look at me. His lips were pursed together tightly, eyebrows raised. He took a deep breath. The time was now.

The house was dark. Nothing moved except the stench, wafting to meet us. Remembering approximately where the woman's bed was, I shuffled carefully in that direction. When I thought I'd found the right bed, I fumbled with the drape on a window. Sunlight exploded through the room. Shrouded bodies moved and moaned simultaneously, stirring dust into diamonds. Bathed in this surreal light, David and I stared down into the woman's small bed. There she was, the scarred face. But someone else, too. There were two women in the bed. David whispered, "Mother, Moana." I looked at his face. Glistening tears welled and spilled. A young woman removed her arm from under the disfigured woman and sat up. In the sparkling light, her face was angelic, beautiful. She stared at David and said something about dreaming. David reached through the diamonds and took his sister by the waist, pulling her from the bed. Her thin dress draped her dangling legs as he held her to him, whispering "Moana," again and again. I went outside to weep and wait.

Within a few minutes, the woman was yelling "Dee Dee!" again at the top of her lungs. I stepped to the door in time to see her pushing David's face away. "*Nao, nao, quero Dee Dee!*" she screamed. One of the attendants who had been there the day before came staggering sleepily from another room. I walked back outside. In a short while, David came out holding on to his sister. She was wiping her eyes, her wide-set beautiful eyes, her brother's eyes. I took her hand. She held my hand firmly and put it to her lips. "Thank you," she whispered.

Moana led us to a bench beyond the thick hedge. She was tall and graceful, her head nearly bald. Her faded dress flitted at her slim ankles and bare feet. David had told me she wanted to be a dancer, like the dancers in Mrs. Braga's ballet magazines. She looked like a dancer. She took a place on the bench and pulled David beside her. I sat on a stump nearby. She spoke in a voice that was soft, like David's, stroking his arm or his face as though consoling him for what she had to say. At first I tried to hear what she said. She came to visit her mother at night, and on some nights, bad nights, she stayed. Yesterday, a boy had been killed. At this point she paused to weep again. I looked at my watch and decided to take a short walk, maybe find the remains of the Braga house.

I found the ruins of the house farther up the hill on the bluff of the sea. A pile of broken concrete and charred wood covered with vines, it had obviously been a mansion with a view. One could see for miles down the coast, including the lighthouse. What I saw was smoke. Several miles down the coastline and perhaps a mile inland was a huge amount of smoke billowing up from the green of the land. There was nothing else visible there, just black smoke. I looked at my watch. The captain had been gone forty minutes. I went back to the shelter. David and Moana were still on the bench talking. I felt an obligation to remind David of the time. He frowned when he heard but didn't look up.

I sat back down on the stump and tried not to look at my watch or to hear David. He was pleading with Moana to come with him, and she was pleading with him to go. She could never leave her mother and her mother would die if she were moved. It was her fate, but not his. He must return to Mrs. Braga. David had her by the shoulders. It was then that I heard my name being called out. Ensign Basso was running up the hill.

Basso, gasping, tried to tell us what was happening. RENAMO forces had taken the outpost, a bastion that guarded Beira from the south. The forces were now marching toward Beira. The captain had been with Rozdilsky when the news came. We were to return to the ship at once. We would sail immediately.

David looked horror-struck as he interpreted the news to Moana. She jumped to her feet and ran to the top of the hill, David following. I ran after them both, pleading, followed by Ensign Basso, also pleading. The smoke was as I'd seen it, black, made uglier by the news of its victims. Moana leaped at David, hugging his neck and telling him to go. Ensign Basso was nearly shouting. We should all go, and quickly. The captain had said he could not wait. I took Basso's arm and said, "Two minutes! Give them two minutes!" Then I told David, "She has a decision to make, and you have a promise to keep. We'll wait two minutes in front of the shelter. We can carry your mother to the jalopy."

It was five minutes when Moana marched back into the shelter, David calling after her. At the door, he turned and looked at me wildly. "I can't leave them! I can't! You've got to understand, Kelly! Please understand!" Then he went through the door, turned, and yelled, "Go!"

Basso grabbed my arm and we started down the steep path. My heart pounded with anger as noisy as my yelling and cussing. My worst fears! I should never have brought him. Basso shoved me into the jalopy he'd left running. I was screaming now, screaming at David as loud as his mother had screamed the day before. Basso was scattering people. News had spread, waking the town. At the port, one guard waved us through the gate; the other guards were assembling bunkers. Everything on and around the ship was in motion.

The captain greeted us with "The stupid, bloody bastard decided to stay! Get on the bridge, both of you! See if you can sober up our navigator. There won't be a pilot to get us out of here."

Thirty minutes later, we were still waiting for the Dutch women. The captain had offered to take them out, return them next trip to whatever was left. The men had accepted for their wives. We waited, listening to artillery in the distance. I talked to myself about why David had to stay, why his sister wouldn't leave, what their chances were for survival. Survival for what? Starvation, disease? If lucky, a hopeless way of life. I knew I couldn't come back. The captain had made it clear at the outset: This was my last trip to Beira. It might be the ship's last trip. There was little left of the port the way it was. I would leave the ship in Durban, South Africa, fly home, report the news to Mrs. Braga. I cursed war, communism, capitalism, racism, and goddamn Tanzanian communist kerosene.

Finally, the Dutch women arrived, arguing above the sounds of loading their belongings. They had been invaded before but had never been forced to leave their husbands. When their cases were on board, the captain marched up to the bridge and gave the order to release the lines.

The first mate called out the order, but it was not to be heard over the roaring of a truck headed down the hill, straight for the ship. "Bloody hell!" the captain shouted. "This is trouble! Kelly, get to your quarters!"

I started off but paused behind a lifeboat to watch as the truck came careening around a crane and slammed into the empty oil drums stacked along the dock. Some of the drums landed on the ship, one on the truck's canvas top. The door of the truck opened. It was Labios Rubi! She jumped down, adjusted her gun sling and her hat, and marched around to the rear of the truck shouting orders. Two Cuban soldiers popped out of the back and began unloading something, a large bag. They carried the bag around and placed it on the dock and then opened it from one end, pulling out the contents. A soldier! A dead soldier, soaked in blood! Rubi walked over to the corpse, stretched a leg, and straddled him, her gun held high, shouting through her luminous lips toward the bridge. The captain stepped out on the quarterdeck to listen. It was the soldier who killed Pepi. Rubi was proud of this revenge. The captain said nothing. The entire ship was quiet, and then Rubi was shouting orders again toward the back of the truck. Something else was unloaded. A large canvas-wrapped package. The Cubans carried it to where the gangplank had been and set it down. Rubi shouted up at the captain again. The package was a gift from Beira to the captain of the *Osprey*. She wanted permission to bring it aboard. The captain denied permission, thanked her suspiciously, and assured her that the crew would load it. With that, Rubi ordered her men back in the truck, climbed into the cab, and proceeded to back out of the oil drums. Once clear, she gunned the truck up the hill and was gone in a cloud of dust.

"See what it is, and be quick!" the captain shouted, and the first mate translated to the crew. "And mind it could be loaded with, God knows, anything!" Not taking time to replace the gangplank, two Mauritians leaped onto the dock and began prodding the bag, opening it gingerly. The artillery fire was close now and we could see smoke rising from behind the hill. I joined the captain on the quarterdeck. The Dutch women were chattering directly beneath us.

The two crewmen jabbered excitedly, one of them shouting out something. The captain muttered, "Dear God," then whispered, "Bloody hell, it's another body."

There was shouting now from the crew. Someone yelled, "David!" I was down off the quarterdeck, onto the deck. I tried to jump onto the dock but was restrained. I watched the two crewmen lifting David's limp body out of the canvas. The gangplank was hastily replaced, and I scurried across in time to follow them back onto the ship. David was laid in the shade of the poop deck. I kneeled beside him and took his hand. He was alive! He wasn't moving, but he was breathing! The captain was there, pulling back the orange shirt, looking over his head and neck. "He's been drugged," he muttered. "Someone wanted him spared."

Artillery fire thundered. The gangplank was removed. Lines were cast. We were under way. I sat there holding David's hand, waiting, wondering. We passed by the minuteman missiles lining the harbor. Several barefoot, ragged black men paced around the missiles, watching the smoke over Beira. The crew called out to them. They didn't respond.

Finally, the sea breeze was blowing across the deck. In a few more minutes the salt spray was glistening on David's face. I thought about how he looked a few hours ago through the dust diamonds in the morning sun, his tears, his joy, his terror—the culmination of a long ordeal of love and tenacity. "Goddamn you, David!" I tugged at Jerry Garcia, wiping my wet face on his. "Goddamn you, David, wake up! Tell me what happened!"

But David didn't wake up for hours. The crew hauled him off to their quarters, where I wasn't allowed to go. Basso brought reports on his condition: sleeping, groggy, quiet. The captain decided not to make any more ports of call in Mozambique and steamed straight through to Durban, South Africa. It wasn't until our last night on the ship together that I learned what had happened to David.

All the officers had gone, save Ensign Basso doing watch on the bridge, waiting for good-byes. David and I sat in the Zan-Z-Bar alone, sipping brandy.

"I may learn to like this stuff," he said, flashing me the first smile I'd seen since before Beira. "My mother, my stepmother, drinks this stuff before she goes to bed, says it makes her sleep. I'm still feeling half asleep, even after several days the effects of the drug are . . ." His smile and words had trailed off. In a coarse whisper he said, "I loved them such a long time, from such a long way!" I tried to say something reassuring, but he went on. "Mother was so . . . beautiful, an angel to me. My sister, too, beautiful, graceful, smart. They were my life; I was part of theirs. I loved them more than I'll ever love anyone, anything." He sat for another minute gazing off at a memory in his mind.

I sipped my brandy and tried to think of something comforting, for both of us. Finally, he went on. "Even if I were there, still with them, I would be loving them from a distance. I couldn't reach either of them. Maybe that's the way with women, women like my sister." He looked at me squarely. "You know what I mean?" I shook my head, which didn't seem to register with him. He slumped back in his chair, sipped at his brandy, and muttered, "Heroic women."

I thought about Velha, then the Dutch women, who were already on a ship going back to Mozambique. Maybe they could get into Beira, maybe not, but by God they were going to get back there one way or another and continue being saints. I poured us another brandy and said, "David, are you going to tell me what the hell happened to you?"

"Yes, of course." He sipped and asked, "Are you ready?"

"For several days!"

"When you and the officer ran down the hill, Moana and I ran down another trail to the beach, to the road that comes from the hotels. There was a jeep waiting there. Moana and I jumped in it, and she drove to a hotel, or what once was a hotel on the beach. We went in underneath, at the basement, to her office." He paused, a deep breath. "Within a few minutes, she was in a uniform, painting her face, and all the time telling me that Mother never knew I was gone.

The bombs that burned . . . burned my mother, well, it affected her mind. Very soon, Pepi became her son, Moana's brother."

"David!" I suppose I wasn't as surprised as I sounded. "Are you telling me that Rubi, the Zar's, well . . . is your sister?"

"Oh"—he rolled his eyes—"she's much more than those things. She runs an army, an entire underground army. She robs the other armies of food and medical supplies. She knows everything and controls everything through the Russian, Rozdilsky, the Zar."

"Jesus Christ!" I swore. "So Gilda was right about Pepi."

David gave a hopeless shrug. "Pepi was her partner, her best friend, her brother, like I used to be."

"So then what happened?" I asked. "Did she . . . drug you at the hotel?"

"No. We got into a truck . . . there were some soldiers she was ordering around who got in the back, and she drove, like a crazy woman. She drove to some barracks, soldiers' barracks." He stopped, sighed, and sipped his brandy. "She told the soldiers in the back to go and get someone, named, I don't remember, but it was the soldier who killed Pepi. Anyway, they went and got him and threw him in the back, and we drove to another place on the beach." David was looking at me now, intently, curiously, as though I might be telling the story. "She ordered everyone out of the truck, including me. She told the guy, the soldier who shot Pepi, to start running. He did. She shot him." He was still looking at me, waiting, I suppose, for my reaction.

I'm sure I looked shocked. "My God, David! You had to see that, your sister. Why didn't she . . ."

"Why didn't she drug me first?" he interrupted. "I think it was her way of settling the matter, of telling me I had no place there anymore, shocking me into never returning. I don't know. But she got back in the truck, opened a box that was under the seat, took out some tablets, and told me to take them."

"And you did?"

"No! I refused! I told her that I could replace Pepi, that . . . well, it didn't matter what I told her. She called her soldiers up; they held me down and gave me the pills." He let out a long breath, as though he'd been holding it. "Like you give pills to a dog. The last thing I remember was she was driving again, driving like a wild, mad woman." He shook his head. "Like Joan of Arc, I suppose . . . " His last words trailed off, an analogy I'm sure he wished he hadn't made. We sat for a while longer. The story just hung there, suspended in time, probably as it would for as long as David lived.

The last time I saw David, he said that if he were a writer instead of a flautist, he'd write about his sister. This one's for you, David.

Witchdoctor

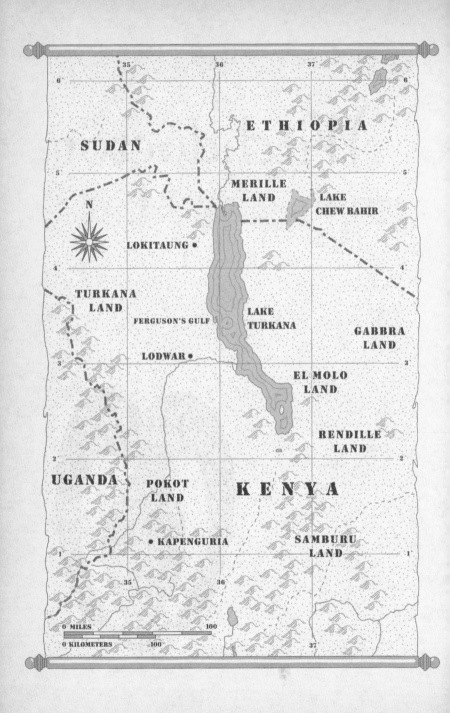

The Truck

TURKANALAND, NORTHERN KENYA

Kiuka was dead. From the back of the truck under a half-moon, just enough light to imagine anything, every shadow was suspect, even the rocks we'd piled on Kiuka's grave. Lua had done some magic before she left, something she said would keep away evil, but I couldn't give up the watch. They'd be back. They killed Kiuka easily, a spear through his gut. They took the can with the dregs of our muddy water, but the bastards could not take Kiuka's gonads for a neck ornament or whatever decoration they might want from Lorraine and me. They didn't get our clothes, our watches, our first-aid kit, our tents. I had interrupted them, scared them away with one shot from the tiny single-shot pistol, our one weapon, now with only two bullets left. Lua's magic or not, when the moon set, they'd be back.

Even before we buried Kiuka, I took all the tires off the truck, all six of them, an interminable job in the blistering heat. I made two stacks at the back of the truck bed, a barrier of sorts between the hostile environment and us. Over the tires my eyes filtered the night, midnight. I listened to Lorraine breathing heavily, sleeping, exhausted from retching up her guts all day. Her bedroll was just behind the cab, between the folded-up tents with all those medical supplies and the remaining cans of petrol for our broken, son-of-a-bitchin' truck. There wasn't much air, but it was the safest place for her to be. It was dead calm now, a haunting silence after the relentless roar of wind all day. I could almost hate Lorraine for sleeping while I watched, for keeping me here instead of with Lua, for our being here in the first place, insisting we take the truck off the track. English women, such royal pains in the ass, so determined. The day I met her and Roger on that dusty strip at Lodwar, determination was written on her like a ritual. The plane pelted dirt in our faces, stinging hot in our eyes and nose, and she just stuck out her hand and in perfect Queen's English said, "I'm Dr. Lorraine Covington, here to find Dr. Kali." As though Kiuka and I hadn't already sweated off a pound a day for ten days on those filthy camels in 120 degrees of hell looking for the good doctor.

I still didn't know the connection between Roger and Lorraine, only that Roger had some sort of responsibility for Kali, and Lorraine had been her guardian. Maybe. I wasn't sure. There had been little opportunity for details. Whatever their relationship, I knew that if we died there in that truck, if the Merille or Turkana or whichever renegades came back and put a spear through Lorraine and me, Roger wouldn't grieve. Whatever his liability was for Kali, he wanted it over, finished, a peremptory conclusion. Somewhere near forty, single, rich, Indian handsome, English-educated, he had been caustic with abandon about almost everything. In the Rover, trekking from the airstrip back to Kali's dirty little one-room cement clinic, Roger scoffed at Lorraine's determination. "No one, not even Kali, disappears in this bloody country for three weeks and is ever found, particularly in the middle of a bloody drought!" He hated being in Lodwar those two days. Lodwar had history for him; I guessed it was ugly history. He would spit words at Lorraine, then withdraw, hapless, stooped, his heavy brows a furrowed shelter over his anger, perhaps agony. The minute the keys to the worthless truck were in my hands, he bolted back to Nairobi. He had other "urgent business." He'd said to let him know when Lorraine exhausted her obsessive search for every trace of Kali's existence.

The stars in the Turkana sky went on forever into the past. Sitting there on that piece of Earth, where, according to the Leakeys, human evolution began, I was probably seeing the same sky, give or take a few explosions, gazed upon by the woman who began my gene pool. I wondered if she'd been terrified and thirsty, watching and waiting for an enemy. I loathed admitting that I was terrified, but I was sure as hell thirsty, sunburned, cloaked in a layer of dirt, lips blistered, eyes two flames, brain shrunken. We had invaded a place in time where we were not welcome. Humans may have begun here, but we did not evolve here, and neither did the land. It was difficult to imagine any tribes more primitive than the Turkana and Merille. And the land, if it could be called land, was black lava surrounding a huge saline lake filled with fish and crocodiles, predating humans by 120 million years. Day after day, year after year, the temperatures reached 120 degrees and the ferocious winds blistered everything between the lake and the horizon of ancient volcanoes. Periodic droughts, like this one, drained the tiny reservoirs of water, bringing widespread death to people and wildlife. Teleki, the first white explorer, an Austrian, lost hundreds of men in a failed attempt to circumvent the lake at the end of the nineteenth century. Nothing much had changed in a hundred years, or a thousand. I knew this hell could claim Lorraine and me as easily as it had claimed Teleki's troops, as swiftly as it claimed Kiuka. Jesus, yes, I was terrified.

Nothing moved but the moon. The potion or spell or whatever Lua had used to keep evil from the truck was Kali's magic, at least that's what I thought Lua said. She should have used it the night before. Instead, she had assured us we were safe because she and Kiuka were Turkana. But at four in the morning in total darkness, how could the attackers have known, or cared? After we buried Kiuka, Lua said it had been Ngorokos, tribal outlaws, who attacked. She knew from the spear in Kiuka's gut. We were lucky they only had spears. The Turkana and the Merille knew about guns, which they had been given on occasions when the whites were at war and needed expendable soldiers. They knew the gun I fired was small, too small to stop their lust for robbing and killing. They'd be back, maybe with guns of their own.

Roger could have seen to it that we were armed with more than a single-shot pistol and three bullets. Roger could have seen to it that we had a truck that didn't break down. Still, I knew a truck in Lodwar was a premium, that parts were impossible. He had supplied us with enough petrol to circumvent Turkanaland, and we had plenty of water and food, which unfortunately went mostly to people we encountered who were dying of the drought and hunger; the renegades took the rest. Maybe Roger did all he could, considering

Lorraine was determined to trace every track of Kali's to the ends, or beginnings, of the Earth.

Lorraine was waking up. I heard her groan and the truck shift. "Kelly? Kelly, is everything all right?" Her voice was weak and coarse. She needed water. We both did, but I hadn't been vomiting, and Lorraine was at least twenty years older, only once before out of England, she'd said. She was a doctor and frail, probably hadn't exercised a day in her life. I assured her we were still alive and encouraged her to sleep, but she came crawling to the back of the truck. "What is the time?" she asked.

I pushed the light on my watch. "Midnight, about. How do you feel?"

"Better, but what about you, Kelly? I should watch now while you sleep?" It was a timid question, politely asked. Lorraine didn't want to watch, and I didn't trust her to watch. I told her to get into the duffel and find a can of fruit. She said the fruit was gone, only two cans of chickpeas were left. Chickpeas would do; we needed the liquid.

We sat behind the tires on our camp stools. Every few minutes Lorraine would sigh, her perfectly round face and gray hair glowing, ghostlike. Her determination had left her with Kiuka's last breath. Guilt came with the burial, self-flagellation with puking and sobbing. For a doctor, she had little stomach for blood and death. I had threatened slapping her to shut her up, to get her to save her energy and body fluids. Now she just sighed.

The peas gone, the cans drained, she asked, "Has Lua had sufficient time to return to Lokitaung? She departed at sundown, six hours now."

"Maybe, depends." I didn't want to answer questions. I didn't want to talk.

"Depends?" She rubbed at her throat, voice cracking. "Depends on what?"

"On what she found on the way. She needed water, and she needed not to run into any more renegades, not to break a leg, the usual kind of luck needed traversing hell. And we don't know that she was going back to Lokitaung. She may have gone to the lake, to the encampment—the alleged encampment."

"But I distinctly heard the two of you talking about Lokitaung."

"Lorraine, as far as I know, understanding the Turkana language as little as I do, Lua was not going to decide until she began walking. Kali would send her magic, give her direction."

"Dear God!" Another long sigh before another damned question. "Which way do you think she went?"

"Don't know."

"You must have some idea. The two of you talked about it for hours."

"Hours is how long it takes for me to understand Lua, if I understand her, but I know she didn't like the people at the Lokitaung post. They were Kikuyu, spoke Swahili. Turkanas don't trust people who speak Swahili, believe they're an inferior race." I shot her an impatient look, a plea to shut up, then jumped down off the truck to check my fuses, my own magic. The tiny pistol in hand, keeping my back to the truck, I walked the length of the rope fuses, pouring more petrol from the coffee can into their troughs, a water hose I'd cut in half lengthways. The four separate fuses each connected to a five-gallon can of petrol. The four cans were in a semicircle fifty feet from the back of the truck. Timing would be the factor. To survive, though, it would take luck more than bombs. If Lua didn't bring back camels and water, Lorraine and I would die right there in that truck, more renegades or not. Lorraine wouldn't last another day without water in the scalding wind, and she sure as hell couldn't walk out. Lua had the best chance to make it, alone, at night, when the wind rested. She knew the country, she knew where to dig for water, and, for whatever it was worth, she was Turkana.

Lorraine was standing between the two stacks of tires in her white tunic shirt like a flag, a bull's-eye in the moonlight. I hopped back up onto the truck, barking at her. She began to sob, her thick hair falling around her face. "I should have been here weeks ago! Every day I was to leave, but my invalid sister, she was having terrible problems, she always has bloody problems when . . ." She sobbed on, her words muffled under hair. When she surfaced it was to wail, "Dear God! I failed Kali. I should have been here last month." I reminded her that if she'd been here sooner, she'd probably be lost with Kali. That really made her howl. Jesus, the woman demanded more energy than I had left. I liked her better when she was a drill sergeant. I told her that she had to go back to her hovel to sniffle. She did.

In a few minutes, she was back on her camp stool. She'd changed into a black shirt. Clearing her throat, she said, "Roger informed me that you agreed to do this only because it was a woman who was lost." I waited for her to go on, but she didn't for several minutes. Finally she asked, "Well, is that true?"

"Probably."

"But you do not seem to like women," she said in her haughty English. "Indeed, you do not seem to like me."

"Of course I like women; I am one," I retorted. "I just don't like you here in an environment inappropriate for your . . . experience." I was being kind. I wouldn't have liked Lorraine anywhere.

"But I had to come. Did you not see that? Roger would never have searched for Kali otherwise."

"Roger didn't search for her anyway."

"But because I came, he did organize it!" She was emphatic. "He hired you. He sent you here for the initial search, then came with me, bought this truck." She laughed suddenly, too loudly. "This bloody awful truck!" I indicated for her to keep it quiet, and she did for a few minutes, taking her comb and a can of lip balm out of one of the big pockets in her shorts. Using her finger, she smeared the greasy salve on her blistered lips, offering the can to me. I did likewise, wincing as she had. Then she began combing her shoulder-length hair with that god-damn red comb, as she had a hundred times a day, thoughtfully, as though it stimulated her brain. "Do you know, with the exception of myself, Roger is Kali's only family?" Pointing the comb at me, she went on, "Kiuka had explicit instructions—Kali assured me of that in her letters. If something, anything, were to happen to her while she was doing her research here, Kiuka was to immediately contact Roger and Roger was to contact me. But I was certain Roger would do nothing unless he knew I was coming, unless he knew I would be here, to be sure."

I was stumbling over the idea of Roger, an Indian, and Kali, a Turkana, as family, but I didn't ask. I didn't want to talk to this woman, and if we made it out of this predicament alive, I sure as hell wasn't going to talk to Roger again. I'd done a couple of small jobs for him before and never liked him. He was a Birla, a high-caste wealthy family of importers and exporters based in Bombay, and a friend of Kumlesh, the Indian in Mombasa who kept my Kenya business straight. Kumlesh had told me that Roger's family history, what-ever it was, had caused his general mordant disregard for everyone, particularly the blacks. Other people had theories about Roger, too, but I hadn't listened.

Lorraine was pointing her comb again. "Why would you not have hired on to do this if Kali were a man?"

"I don't like the working conditions in this part of Africa."

"Indeed." She was impatient and pushed her face close enough for me to see her sharp blue eyes. "Then why did you come?"

"A woman, a Turkana woman, made it out of the tribe to become a doctor and came back to the tribe to do research. She seems pretty important, someone worth saving in a country where women are fairly expendable."

"Good," she said resolutely, pausing to cough. "Kelly, listen, please. I feel certain that I understand the gravity of our situation, and further, I am quite certain there is a much better chance of you surviving than me." I began a protest, but she coughed again and went on, her tone hinting once more of determination. "It is important that some-one, someone who cares about the work of women, has an under-standing of what Kali was doing here. Her research records may yet be found, and Roger would do nothing with them, burn them per-haps." Aiming her comb again, she fired on. "I want you to know Kali's story, and if the records are found, I want you to take them to the institute. I have left the name of the person and the address of the institute with the hotel in Nairobi, where I was staying the night before we came to this godforsaken land." She shook herself. "Dear God, it is difficult to believe! You would think I would have been bet-ter prepared, hearing Kali's stories over the years, the descriptions of her people. Her stories, the books, the pictures, are all so colorful, so exotically beautiful. Nothing prepared me for the rawness of this land, the heat and wind, the smells, the flies, the savages. And now, after all I have been through with Kali, we will both . . ." She was coughing again, covering her mouth, wrapping her frail hand around her throat. I hoped she was done, wished she would go back to sleep, but she continued to drag her comb through her hair. She asked, "Do you understand that Kali was considered a witchdoctor by the Turkanas?"

I reminded her that I'd spent two weeks with Kiuka before she arrived. Even though I understood only every fifth word of Turkana and didn't speak it with the guttural sounds necessary to be readily understood, it had been easy communicating with Kiuka. He was all over every subject with gesticulation and mimicry, loving to talk, a Turkana trait, although when he didn't agree with me, he would withdraw and act as though I wasn't there, also a Turkana trait. Such expressive people, so all-or-nothing for the moment. When Kiuka talked about his beloved Kali, his long, chiseled, coal-black face glittered with excitement, and his rawboned body bobbed around as though he were dancing. He truly believed Kali was a witchdoctor, as did Lua. He'd demonstrated to me the way she did things with bones and sticks to forecast how to treat the sick. She read the signs and heard voices that told her to give an injection or tablets, or cast a spell. A pastoral tribe constantly on the move, the Turkana were mired in superstitions, curses, spells—magic. It was easy to understand why Doctor Kali could roam from encampment to encampment as a witchdoctor.

I heard something, a noise, a piece of brush cracking, a stirring. I smelled it, too, maybe the foul smell of Turkana. I put my hand on top of Lorraine's head, pushing her down behind the tires, hearing her whimper. Crouching low, I felt for the fuse ends and reached for the matches. Poised, ready to strike, eyes screaming, I saw it. A hyena! "Shit!" I exclaimed. "A hyena."

"Thank God!" Lorraine whispered, trembling. "I assume hyenas are not a threat."

I didn't tell her differently. Apparently the hyena, a striped one, was hunting alone. There wasn't much game in Turkanaland for hyenas and the drought had animals moving in all directions in search of food and water. We were close to the Ethiopian border and the boundary of the Merille tribe to the north, where game was somewhat more plentiful. Maybe the hyena was attracted by Kiuka. God, I hoped that wasn't true. Kiuka was in a canvas duffel, buried with all the dirt we could find, covered with a layer of rocks, plus the rocks marking his grave. But there was dried blood everywhere, from Kiuka and possibly from one of the renegades I may have hit. The hyena slinked around, sniffing, seemingly ignoring the grave, glancing up at us a few times. Then it was gone. I hoped.

It was a good time to tell Lorraine that she couldn't talk unless she spoke in a low voice or whispered. I also told her that if she was going to sit there, she could help me watch. My magic was in limited supply, and we couldn't waste it on hyenas. With my fingers crossed, I told her that we would make it out of here together and she could take care of Kali's records, if they were ever found. She was contrite and perhaps scared enough to keep quiet. I needed quiet. I needed to conserve my energy. Kiuka was killed at two in the morning, when there was no moon. It was nearly midnight and the moon would be gone in less than three hours. That's when they'd be back. I had to count on it. I had to be ready.

I had hated burying Kiuka there in the middle of a lava field, with only a few black, jagged rocks, like all the other rocks, to mark his grave. But he had to be buried. We couldn't just let him lie in the heat rotting. I considered burning him, in order not to attract hyenas and vultures, but Lua said it was bad magic, and Lorraine, the doctor, couldn't stomach it. I wasn't sure I could, either. Lua had searched for a crevice of dirt big enough to dig in, but we shoveled only three feet and hit more lava. It was a shallow grave, maybe too shallow in this harsh land, but it was Kiuka's land. He had known no other. He'd been an assistant to Kali for nearly a year, when the drought had driven him starving and near dead to Lodwar. Kali had given him magic, and he survived, vowing his life to her. Lua had been with Kali for six months. She'd had a disease caused by sharp granules of lava dust entering her lymph glands—not uncommon in women who walk barefoot over lava. Kali gave her leather boots. Lua left her life and family to follow the witchdoctor to Lodwar. Both Lua and Kiuka were grateful to the witchdoctor to whom they had pledged their lives.

Roger had been brutal to Kiuka and Lua. The first hour he and Lorraine were in Lodwar, we all sat around the flat rock that served as a table in Kali's one-room cement clinic, drinking black tea and fanning ourselves, while Roger insulted, prodded, and badgered Lua and Kiuka. They were Kali's assistants, why were they not with her? They were incompetent, mindless savages put in a position of importance bigger than their tribal brains. He was completely ruthless, and surprisingly, he was fluent in Turkana. He raged on until he collapsed in a chair, dropping his head in a handkerchief to soak up the sweat. Lua and Kiuka had long turned their backs on him, the Turkana way of saying, "Piss off!"

I knew that Kali made them stay in Lodwar. Kiuka had told me. They were expecting Lorraine at any time. She was bringing more magic supplies that needed to be put in Kali's safe place, because the safe place was empty. Kali had taken the last of the magic supplies to tend those dying in the drought. She'd said that she might be gone longer than usual. She had gone alone before, before she had Lua and Kiuka as assistants.

When Roger rose again, his anger renewed, I told him I'd had enough of his bullshit. I reminded him of the facts: Kiuka had done exactly what he was supposed to do. When Kali hadn't returned in two weeks, Kiuka hitched a ride to Ferguson's Gulf on Lake Turkana. Kali's Rover was there; she had gone on by camel with Goa, the camel tender, as usual. Several people saw them ride off to the north, the camels loaded with water buckets, baskets, gourds, and supplies. Kiuka took Kali's Rover north on the track from Ferguson's Gulf and encountered a caravan with one of Kali's medical bags strapped to a donkey. The leader of the caravan told him that they'd found it lying south of Lokitaung, the contents scattered about. Kiuka came back to Lodwar as quickly as possible and wired Roger. Roger contacted Kumlesh. Kumlesh ran me down, and I called Uli, my pilot. Uli and I searched every mile we could from the air before Kiuka and I set out on camels. Ten days we sat on those beasts, going from encampment to encampment, searching in vain for the witchdoctor. We had returned only several hours before, parched, blistered, exhausted, and clueless. We hadn't found a trace of Kali, Goa, the camels, or any of their gear. There was nothing further we could do. I looked at Roger and Lorraine squarely and told them just that.

Roger, mollified finally, agreed. He was certain that Kali had met with renegades. He was ready to return to Nairobi. Lorraine was not. She stood up, stuck out her determination, and ranted. The medical bag may have simply fallen off the camel. The research records had to be found at all costs. It was unbelievable that none of Kali's records were in her clinic and a mystery as to why she would take them all with her. On and on she ranted, bickering with Roger, until finally they haggled off into the blistering wind leaving Kiuka, Lua, and me melting around the rock table.

We were asleep on the dusty concrete floor when Lorraine returned and announced that Roger had gone to get us a truck. We were going to Lokitaung. She was ready for me with her arguments. Lokitaung was where Kali was from, her home, and in her letters she told Lorraine that she had considered returning there, moving her research base closer to the more remote clans. I told her that Turkana people were from no particular place, they were pastoral nomads, and Lokitaung was nothing more than a remote government outpost near the Ethiopian border, much farther away than Kali's regular course. Besides, Uli and I had landed there and searched the post. The few people there knew nothing about a Dr. Kali, or a witchdoctor. Lorraine was rigid, insisting that Kali may have been in route when we were there. Because of the drought, she may have gone much farther north than usual. Once more, she pointed out that the medical bag was found near Lokitaung. Once more, we listened to the importance of finding the research records.

"What is that?" Lorraine whispered frantically, grabbing my arm. "Do you hear it?"

"No. Be still so I can." We listened, our eyes tracing shadows. I didn't see or hear a thing. Lorraine squeezed her grip again. She was hearing something, maybe in her head. I leaned toward her, cocking an ear into her space. In a moment, I heard it. A dung beetle—I recognized its scratching sound. It was next to her in the sack of dried dung we'd collected for boiling water. I told her what it was, and she pushed the sack off onto the ground. "Good listening," I whispered. "Keep it up." She put her head in her hands and began to sob, again. "Lorraine, Jesus, I know you're scared. So am I. But you've got to get a grip, woman. You're a doctor, don't you have any pills you can take? There must be something back there in all those supplies you brought for Kali."

"I am scared," she whimpered, "because I am quite certain that I shall die, just as that poor man, Kiuka, died. I know some things about the Turkanas. I have studied them, as much as possible, through Kali, and what little is written about them. They are a bloodthirsty people who love to kill, in fact they take pride in killing. They will kill us, I know." She kept whimpering. "I have been praying and praying, but . . ." She looked over at me, her tears glistening. "Roger told me that you practiced the Hindu religion."

"Not true," I said.

"But how did I misunderstand?" She was dabbing at her eyes. "He told me that he knew you through his Indian friend, who . . ."

"No. Kumlesh, a friend of Roger's in Mombasa, is my Kenya office. His brother, Hitesh, is a Hindu guru, a good friend of mine."

"You are a friend of a guru, but not a devotee?"

"Yeah, I suppose that's how it is."

"A strange friendship," she accused sharply.

"Not at all," I said, resenting the conversation but wanting her to stay calm. "He has a wisdom I appreciate. We enjoy each other's company. The temple is beautiful, has air conditioning, and I really like the big white plastic cow. My grandmother had one just like it—well, *it* was real. How about you? Church of England, no doubt."

"No doubt," she confirmed. "A proper compress for the soul, nothing to offend, sugarcoated, easy to swallow, indeed nothing to prepare one for . . . this!" She threw up both arms. "And it is not only my . . . impending death. I am so very broken-hearted. Kali has been so much of my life, my work."

"Okay then," I said, reluctantly acquiescing. "Maybe you should tell me about her." I reached over to pat her on the shoulder. "But do it quietly, and no crying. As a doctor you know that every drop of body fluid is critical right now."

She dried her eyes on her shirt and began in a shaky whisper. "Roger told me that your expertise is, among other things, the cultures, the geography, and history of Africa, so I am assuming that you know the historical significance of Lokitaung?"

"Do you mean the Lokitaung Gorge, the petrified riverbed that once joined Lake Turkana to the Nile River, or do you mean Lokitaung outpost, where we were, where Jomo Kenyatta was imprisoned?"

"The latter," she said, satisfied.

"And now that you've seen it, you can understand why the Brits put him there. They thought 'out of sight out of mind.' In the most remote, desolate place in Kenya, Kenyatta would be forgotten, and without him the revolution would be squelched."

"Yes, yes," she whispered, "and it is also the place where a missionary took Kali, when he found her wandering alone at the age of three. Her family, her entire village, had apparently been killed in a raid by the Merille tribe." She looked at me, a pinched face needing response. I nodded and she went on, her hoarse whisper beginning to crack. "The missionary, whom Kali remembered as Ben, must have taken a liking to her. He kept her there at Lokitaung, taught her English, taught her to read and write, and nourished her with proper food and water, to which Kali attributed her ability to learn. But Ben became ill and died, leaving her to fend for herself. She was only six." Pausing to cough, Lorraine swallowed hard, then added, "The time of Ben's death coincided with the time that Kenyatta was imprisoned at Lokitaung."

She was still trying to stifle her dry cough, perpetually rubbing at her throat. I was thinking about the dates aloud. "It was 1952, I think, yes 1952, when they held that mock trial to condemn Kenyatta, in the schoolhouse in Kapenguria in the Cherangani Hills, another place where the English were sure there would be no spectators. Then they locked him up at Lokitaung for seven years, I believe it was. Then they took him to Lodwar, kept him there another two years."

Lorraine was still hacking, her throat obviously raw. The scorching wind and lava dust had taken its toll on our eyes and throats, and without water it was becoming difficult to swallow. Her speech was faulty, but once again she was cloaked in determination, this time to tell me Kali's story. She went on. "You see, when Kenyatta was locked up in Lokitaung, Kali was made his servant, his errand girl. She could speak English, so she could communicate with him. She slept on the floor outside his door. She took him his food and water, and then began bringing him news, spying for him, running errands, giving secret messages to people still working to free him. He, in turn, was teaching her English, history, geography. He was a very educated man, you understand?"

"Yes, I've read his books. He was not only the first president of Kenya, but certainly the only good one."

"I agree," she said, a bit melancholy as she added, "Kali became very fond of him, called him Papa, perhaps a name he gave himself."

The story was becoming interesting, but my priority was watching and listening beyond the truck. I kept hearing the dung beetle in the sack on the ground beneath us. He'd probably been joined by some of his friends. They would soon be a choir. I hopped down and slung the sack off to the side, careful not to hit my fuses in their troughs of petrol, checking each one again, satisfying myself that all was as well as it could be.

Lorraine had moved from her stool to the edge of the truck. She looked pathetic slumped there, her skinny legs dangling into her boots. I told her to get back on her stool. She couldn't sit exposed like that, particularly with her legs hanging; all the fluid would be in her feet, where she needed it least. Reminding the good doctor to take care of herself seemed to hit a nerve.

"I do nothing sufficient to please you, do I, Kelly?" she growled. "I have been a thorn for you from the beginning." I got back on the truck and told her I was sorry she felt so bad, but as a doctor she should know the importance of conserving energy and body fluids. That wasn't what she wanted to hear. "Are you quite certain you are a woman, Kelly?"

"Yeah, Lorraine, I am. Sometimes it surprises the hell out of me, but I am a genuine, cardcarrying female."

A long sigh. "You look female, but you don't have the compassion or gentleness of a woman. In some ways you remind me of Kali, and maybe that's why you irritate me!" She clenched her fists and pounded her knees.

"Jesus, Lorraine!" I whispered loudly. "Calm down!" It looked as though she was going to lose it again, start vomiting again, dry heaving. I needed to lighten things. Difficult as it was to chuckle, I did and said quietly, "Lorraine, I'm being paid to do this; you're my responsibility. If you dehydrate and die here, it's not going to look good for my . . . expertise, plus I'll have to dig another hole." I did the chuckle again and gave her crossed legs a pat.

She let out a groan, shook herself, and ranted, "Why would you, a woman, be working anyplace in Africa?" An angry question followed by "The entire continent is extremely inhospitable, especially to women! What made you want to come here and do . . . these kinds of things?"

This woman made me grind my teeth. "I never wanted to do *this kind of thing,* any more than you did. But Africa, well, I seem to have a an affinity for the continent."

"But how, why?" she demanded, staring at me. "The reason Kali was here is obvious, at least to me, but you?"

Still placating, I said, "When I was a kid, I read about Sir Richard Burton in *Search for the Source of the Nile.* Everything and everywhere I wanted to be was in that book."

"Sir Richard Burton was a nineteenth-century African explorer, a man," she said incredulously. "You are a card-carrying female, so you have stated!"

I was barely containing my irritation. "Burton's wife said that if she had been a man, she would be just what her husband was, an explorer. Well, I want to be Burton, and I don't know what the hell sex has to do with it."

"Well! It looks as though I have hit a sore spot," she huffed. I thought we had settled things, but in a minute she asked, "Do you feel your profession to be a noble one, over here helping the unfortunate . . ."

"No. I accept Africa on Africa's terms, or did so before this trip." I couldn't talk to this woman another second. "Lorraine, look, why don't you finish telling me about Kali, another woman who obviously wanted to be in Africa."

She clutched her throat, swallowed hard, and raised a stern finger. "All right, but please listen. It is indeed an important story." She began, finally releasing her finger. "So, for seven years Kali was a confidante and spy for Jomo Kenyatta, and when he was moved to Lodwar, she went with him. She was thirteen by then. That is when she met Gil Birla, Roger's father. Perhaps you know of his involvement in freeing Kenyatta." I didn't and shook my head. "Yes, he worked very long and hard for Kenyan independence. Kali became Gil's right-hand . . . girl. She was a native, a tribal girl, could move around without notice, and she spoke Turkana and English, and by then she had learned Swahili."

I heard something. I put my hand over Lorraine's mouth and then grabbed the matches. Listening hard, I heard it again—snarling, the snarling of hyenas—and there they were, slinking into view, a pack of them. Now I was hoping it was Kiuka they'd smelled. Food was scarce in Turkanaland, the drought taking its toll. A pack of hyenas would attack anything if hungry enough. Lorraine had ducked behind the tires making squeaking sounds and ordering me to do something. I told her to get off her ass and hand me things to throw at them. I began with Kiuka's spear, taking careful aim and missing entirely. With the same results, I flung the Ngoroko's spear, the one we'd taken from Kiuka's gut.

"Well, there went our weapons!" Lorraine barked. "I hope you will be more successful with these tent pegs!"

"You see if you can hit them, Doc. They're your hyenas, too!" She tossed a peg, hitting a hyena hard enough to make him yelp. I threw the shovel, missing again, difficult to do considering there were four, five, maybe six of them, none of them particularly interested in the piled rocks over Kiuka. We threw the folded tents, the duffel bags, even the first-aid kit, but the hyenas kept moving closer, close enough now to see bared teeth. The air was foul and hot with their stench. Their chorus of snarling chilled my bones.

Lorraine was dancing around behind the tires, asking questions in a panic. "Do they want to eat us? Do you have experience with these creatures? Will they come up here on the truck?"

"That's their next move!"

"Dear God, Kelly, do something!"

I sure as hell had to do something. There were only two bullets left for the pistol. If I were able to stop two hyenas, there would still be enough to take us. I couldn't afford to fire my bombs, but maybe I couldn't afford not to.

I took the pistol from my belt, took aim at the closest hyena, and fired. It went down. Grabbing the coffee can of petrol, I flung it on the writhing hyena and then lit a match and threw it. It went out. The scattered monsters moved back around, drooling, their snarling crescendoed. Lorraine yelled at me, "What in God's name are you doing?"

"Nothing in God's name! Here!" I handed her another can I'd just filled. "When I say go, throw it, can and all, on the hyena!"

"This one?" she shrieked. "The one that is wounded?"

"Yes, of course that one!" They were all right there, ready to jump. "Go!" I yelled, leaning out over them. She tossed the can and I dropped a lit match, jumping back. There was a flare of fur in all directions and a terrible stench. The wounded hyena was on fire, burning and writhing, the others scorched and gone.

"My God, that poor animal! Kelly, you have burned him alive!"

"You're goddamn difficult to please! Maybe they'll come back, and you can give them what they really wanted. Here!" I threw a couple of cans at her. "Fill them up!"

Three, four, five times I climbed on and off the truck, pouring petrol on the tents, the bedrolls, and duffels, soaking them, my hands shaking with adrenaline. Then I moved the soaked gear in a close semicircle around the back of the truck. There was no sign of hyenas yet, except the one still smoldering. I grabbed him by his hind legs and dragged him as far from the truck as I dared, lifting him over my fuse lines. Several times I dashed to his carcass, dousing him with petrol, setting him ablaze again. I doused the dung sack, too, taking it in the opposite direction and lighting it. Next I checked my artillery. The hyenas had damaged two of the troughs, the petrol spilled and the fuses left to dry. Exhausted, trembling, I repaired them, listening to Lorraine sniveling at the edge of the truck. Finally, with her help, I crawled back on. Panting like a lion, I said, "Let's hope like hell we've seen the last of the hyenas." She concurred with a whispered "Amen."

In silence, the stench too vile for us to open our mouths, Lorraine and I watched the dung sack and hyena smoldering. I knew we were not watching alone. They were out there, probably not far, waiting for the moon to set. Most likely they were renegades, men banished from their clans and living entirely without rules. The Turkana called them Ngorokos. Even if they were from a clan and not Ngorokos, robbing and killing across boundaries was rewarded with songs and special decoration. The Turkana men earned an ostrich feather for killing a human and the right to scarify their bodies, cutting cicatrices on the upper right arm and chest for male victims and on the left for females. The Merille castrated their victims and wore the genitals around their necks as proof of bravery, and until they did this, they were not allowed to take their first wife. These heathens were out there waiting for their moment.

The incident, the stench—the dreaded inevitable—had left me light-headed. Despite the difficulty concentrating, I needed to assess our arsenal and have a firm plan of defense. We needed a long torch to reach the semicircle of petrol-soaked camp gear. The hyenas could come back, and I sure as hell didn't want to get in the middle of them. We had three barriers now, if I counted Lua's magic. But we only had one bullet left. Only one bullet meant that if the renegades made it through, or the hyenas, Lorraine would get the bullet. I was being paid; she was my responsibility—I would have to shoot her. I looked at her slouched on her stool, her teeth chattering in the extreme heat, a doctor from England waiting to die in remotest Africa for a woman whose life and story were paramount.

I got out my knife and whittled on Kiuka's walking stick, notching the end where I would tie a petrol-soaked rag. It wasn't quite long enough, so I climbed off the truck and moved the gear closer. I also gathered up the tent pegs we'd thrown and the spears and shovel.

They might make decent last-effort weapons. I could feel the dehydration in my knees, the stiffness in my joints, the weakness exacerbated by terror. The last water we'd drunk, and only a swallow, was at midnight the night before, just before we'd bedded down in our pup tents, leaving Kiuka on watch. We'd begun rationing water twelve hours before, at noon, when the truck broke down, or rather blew up, which is how it seemed. It had made several loud noises that sounded like explosions, then belched black smoke from under the hood, spewed steam from the radiator, and quit. Even with my limited knowledge of mechanics it was easy to see the truck wasn't going anywhere, probably ever.

A tent peg in one hand, the pistol in the other, I walked around the goddamn squat, tireless, defunct truck, sizing up the rotten situation. One of my reasons for removing the tires was to put the truck on the ground and eliminate the possibility of renegades sneaking underneath from the front for a surprise attack. The cab of the truck was locked, the key zipped up in my pocket, but there was no windshield. Windshields didn't last long in Turkanaland, this one gone many years. But there was a solid partition at the back of the cab and no rear window, no entrance to the rear of the truck except over the tires and Lorraine and me. If the renegades knew we were just two women, they probably would attack head-on without hesitation, no sneaking around waiting for the moment. If I could see them coming in time, a gang assault could work in our favor. If my timing was perfect and the bombs went off at the moment the renegades all charged, it could do some serious damage to their assault. I'd tested a fuse and a plastic jug of petrol during the day. Lua thought it incredible magic. With the wind crosswise, it had taken twelve seconds. Without the wind it would take less, but even eight or ten seconds was a lot of time considering the distance I would be able to see them coming in the dark. Jesus, I needed more luck at once than I'd ever had. If they snipered us one spear at a time, my bombs could be worthless. There were four bombs, all with separate fuses. I could light them almost at the same time or individually. But without adequate warning, I could have a spear through me before I knew what to do.

I checked the heavy canvas that covered the rear of the truck. It was still mostly intact, but the metal frame over which it was stretched had been weakened by the wind and wobbled loosely. The renegades could set fire to the canvas, but they wouldn't want to burn the booty. All things considered, the situation was grim. Although I'd been in grim situations before, this one seemed worse. It threatened barbaric pain. I needed a dose of courage, my grandmother's courage. She would be howling. I thought about the time that she was attacked by four government agents. They had come to take her children away because she was living with them on an Indian reservation. The only weapon she had was a fire poker, but she chased them a mile back to their roadster, howling the whole way. The last she ever saw of them was their dust. But then, my grandmother was fearless. Hope was all I had.

Lorraine had moved to the side of the truck and was slumped against the canvas. She appeared comatose, depleted, I supposed, by the hyenas. I moved one of the two stacks of tires over in front of her. She raised a limp hand but didn't say anything. I sat back on my stool, pulling it closer to the fuse ends. The box of matches was in front of me on the tires, open. Kiuka's walking stick was at my right side, the rag end soaking in a can of petrol. Both spears were on my left. The pistol was stuck in my belt. The moon would set in less than an hour. I was as ready as I was going to be.

Waiting, I was angry, seething, at the vile renegades waiting to kill us, at Roger for abandoning us, at Lorraine for her determination now turned to worthless weakness, at Dr. Kali, at the entire human race. But I was to blame. I should never have allowed Lorraine's determination to bully me. I was insane to have taken the truck off the track, particularly on a barely discernible trail over a terrain of nothing but black lava that quickly became impassable. The truck may have broken down anyway, but not where there was little chance of a nomadic caravan for weeks, months maybe. Lorraine had bought a story given to us by a small caravan of Turkanas, just after we'd left Lokitaung. They told us that they had seen two people on camels, a man and a woman, near a lake encampment north of the track, very near the Merille boundary. They drew us a map. Lorraine grabbed the story and the map, saying, "Kali would do that, take off on an unscheduled trek! She never lived by any sort of rules, always unpredictable, always pushing toward the edge of things!" I argued like hell. Lorraine persevered. Lorraine had decided. Her determination propelled us to this death trap. I should have stopped her.

The moon hovered, taking its time, the same half moon I slept under the night before, snug in my pup tent, until Kiuka screamed, a spear through my dreams. On my knees at the tent flap, I could see dark figures dashing about. I got to my bare feet and out of the tent, tripping over the spear that was in Kiuka. I found his hand and the pistol. Then Lua was beside me. She yelled something as a figure lunged toward us, a spear flashing. I raised the gun and fired. The figures disappeared, and it was quiet, deadly, until Kiuka began to moan. He lived until dawn, bleeding, suffering as one could only imagine. Lua did Turkana magic with stones. Lorraine prayed out loud to her WASP God. I cursed at all of them. We wept. Kiuka died.

"This goddamn country!" I swore aloud. Lorraine didn't move. I stood up and hit my fist on the tires. It was then I heard them. It was faint, but I heard them, talking, Turkana, I was sure of it. I couldn't see them, not yet. It was Turkana, I knew from the "he he" guttural sound they made as though they'd had the wind knocked out of them. Listening hard, swallowing hard in order not to be sick, I grabbed the matches. They were still talking, making their "he he" noise, but I couldn't see them. The Turkana couldn't talk without their bodies in motion. Where were they? Just beyond my limited vision? Just beyond the hyena, the dung? Maybe just beyond Lua's magic? Why were they there before the moon set, discussing things? I was crouched, ready to strike, ready for the bastards. What the hell were they waiting on?

Several minutes passed. They continued to jabber. My legs cramped from crouching. I decided they were waiting just out of pistol sight, letting us know, as practiced in their culture, that we were of no threat to them, that they could stand there and chat, relaxed, before they killed us. It was tactically wise. I sweated the little liquid I had left. Worse, listening to them, my anger was dissipating into useless terror. I knew a few things about defending myself. I had to be angry enough to be violent. I had to work myself up again. I thought about the way they looked out there, visualized them: spears and knives in their hands, ivory plates in their lips, hair lacquered in a knot with dung, naked, their enormous penises hanging down like horses'. They were doing what they'd always done, what they would be rewarded for, notch their bodies for, strut about in feathers for. They were about to take their spears and knives and carve us up like my grandmother butchered pigs.

Like hell they were! I stood up, threw my head back and howled, a long low howl ending in a shriek so sharp that it cut into my throat.

"Come on, you bastards!" I screamed, "I want to see your eyes in the moon when I blow you to bits!" Then I yelled something in Turkana, and in Swahili. Plopping onto the stool, I was out of breath, out of mind. My hands were trembling, but I managed to hang on to a match long enough to light it. I found the fuse to the bomb I wanted, put a match to it, and counted to ten. The bomb exploded with a deafening blast and an enormous, fiery plume that sent out a scorching wave across my face.

Silence followed. Not a stir. I couldn't afford a glance at Lorraine, but she was silent, comatose still, I guessed. I waited. The moon was touching the horizon. I saw Kiuka, saw the spear in his gut, heard his cry. I stood up and let out another howl, wringing my lungs. Cursing in every language I knew, I plopped down again and reached for another match. There was not a sound except for my own gasping. Should I? Could I afford to set off another bomb, just as a challenge, if that's what I was doing? What was I doing? Defending myself, goddamn it, from a hideous, son-of-a-bitchin' death. I struck the match and stuck it to a fuse. I counted to nine. The bomb exploded with another deafening blast and fiery plume, the heat wave flaring my hair.

It was suddenly black as Turkana skin. The moon was gone. My heart was all I heard. I had a match in my right hand, Kiuka's stick resting on my knee. Eyestrain made me dizzy. Where were those bastards? What were they doing? Surely a couple of bombs hadn't turned the mighty Turkana warriors. I had time to think about it. The silence went on like a clock. I ran all the Turkana warrior stories I knew through my brain. The indomitable Turkana, renowned as the most formidable warriors of East Africa, including the British, the Ethiopians, the Merille. The bombs should have been a challenge. They lived to fight. They were absolutely fearless, except, yes, except . . . they were incredibly superstitious. Whatever they can't explain becomes supernatural, an omen, a demon. The Turkana witchdoctors are renowned by other tribes. Maybe the bombs, my howling, maybe the hyena burning, hell, maybe Lua's magic; maybe something they considered magic spooked them. I waited, hope beginning a trickle.

Then, suddenly, they were there again, talking! Their voices slashed at my gut! The "he he" sound they made for every exclamation was louder than before. They were closer! I stood up to howl, my knees giving way, my howl a pathetic wail that tapered to a whine. I fell to the truck bed gasping, groping for the third fuse. The match head broke. I reached for another, lit it, shaking, sticking it to the fuse, both fuses, the last of my bombs, then to the soaking rag on Kiuka's stick, spilling the can, flinging the fire. I didn't count. The explosions stabbed at my ears, jarred the truck and lit up hell! Everything was burning! And there they were, ghostly black figures swarming the fire, chaos—donkeys braying, hooves clattering, the yells of men in a bloody charge. I struggled to my feet and grabbed for a tent peg, my arm limp. Flames encircled me. Lorraine. Jesus, there was Lorraine, fire lapping around her. "Lorraine!" I yelled, only a whisper escaping, answered by the flash of a spear, a black face at the truck edge, guttural sounds. I swung with the tent peg, tripping, falling, Lorraine underneath me, the gun digging into my belly. A hand grabbed at my arm, another my leg, lifting me. I found the gun handle, then the trigger. I was being thrown over a shoulder, my head swirling, arms flinging, my hand clutching the gun, trying to focus, find Lorraine. There she was, being dragged through the flames by a naked body. I brought the gun up, bouncing, pointing it at Lorraine's head, squeezing the trigger. The gun blasted. I was hurled into the air. Fire swirled, hot, red-hot circles, faster, faster, faster, faster . . .

The Hut

Someone was saying my name, a woman. She said it again. I opened my eyes. Someone was hovering over me, someone red. "Kelly, Kelly, can you hear me? Kelly, open your mouth!" She was angry. "You must drink! Kelly, open your mouth!" I hated this red woman. She floated away. Now a black figure hovered, prying at my mouth. Water trickled down my throat, foul water.

"Kelly! Kelly, wake up! You have to wake up!" The angry voice was back. I opened my eyes. She was there, red. "Kelly, can you see me?" I tried to nod. "Good! You can see me! Who am I?" I didn't know this woman. I wanted her to go away. "Kelly, look at me! Can you see my eyes?" I tried to nod again. "Good! Then what is my name?" I tried to speak. A sound hurt into my throat. "Good, Kelly! Talk to me! Tell me my name!" I tried, but the noise coming from my throat didn't sound like "I don't know your goddamn name!"

The fire was roaring again, deafening, but there was yellow straw all around. I was in my grandmother's barn. Yes, my grandmother's barn, hiding. I should have been collecting eggs, but I was hiding. It wasn't a fire I heard, it was the threshing machine in the field. I looked around. No eggs, just yellow straw.

The woman was back barking at me. "Kelly, you must wake up! Open your eyes and talk to me!" I opened my eyes. There she was, the red woman, her eyes bright, sitting in the barn with me, straw all around. Was this my grandmother? She didn't sound like my grand-mother. My grandmother wasn't English. "Kelly, how do you feel? Can you move? Move your hand, move a finger!"

My grandmother wouldn't bark at me like this, and my grand-mother wasn't red. I looked around the barn. It was small, very small, not my grandmother's barn. I tried to say, "You are not my grand-mother." It was almost discernible, so I also tried "Get the hell out of here!"

"Kelly, good! What did you say? I am not your grandmother and what?" The red woman sounded so happy, I tried saying it again with better results. "Indeed, Kelly, I am going. You are better. I am certain that you are better."

The threshing machine was roaring again. My scream came in a coarse whisper. "Tell that son of a bitch to turn off that machine!"

"What machine, Kelly? There is no machine." The red Englishwoman floated into view. Her eyes were bright, her teeth large. She was definitely not my grandmother.

Raspy words came slowly from my throat. "Who the hell are you?"

"Kelly, it is I, Lorraine. Kelly, think! I am Dr. Covington, Lorraine Covington."

"No! I killed Lorraine." The words choked me and I tried to sit up, but the straw began to spin.

"No, Kelly, we both survived." She had her hand on me, both hands. I wanted her to take her hands off me and leave, whoever she was. I opened my eyes as wide as possible to see her. "I am Lorraine," she insisted. "You are Kelly. We are safe, I think, but I do wish you would wake up and clarify that for me."

"I shot Lorraine in the head." My voice was better. "You are not Lorraine. You don't look like Lorraine."

"It is I, Kelly. I am bald, my head is burned. My hair, my eyebrows, it was all burned off in the fire. I am certain I look quite different."

"Turn off that goddamn machine!" My voice was better still. I tried to sit up again, but she pushed me down, sending pain everywhere. I tried to smack her.

"Kelly, listen to me!" She was hovering, a red ghoul, barking. "Kelly, I am certain it is the wind you hear, not a machine! The wind, remember the wind? We are in Turkanaland. We are on Lake Turkana. The wind is howling. The wind is perpetually howling!" Then a donkey brayed and she yelled, "That dreadful donkey! Why does he continue to come in here?"

Howling. Long low howls on the hill. It's the hill with the big oaks behind our house—Indian Hill. First, I listen to the coyote, understanding how he feels. Then I howl. My grandmother howls beautifully, the best. She howled when Uncle Jess died. She howls on New Year's. She always howls on her birthday. She howled when Aunt Lou died, for three days. That was the loudest and longest. I howled a long, low howl, a good one. I kept howling, but those bastards won. I did all I could, but it's their country. I lost. But why am I here on Lake Turkana? Did they leave me for dead? They must have left me for dead. Who is this who found me? Too many questions! Too tired for questions when the wind howls so angrily. Blow me out of here, wind, to my grandmother. She understands everything.

Jesus, there she was, Lorraine! It was Lorraine without hair, her round head like a tomato, red and slick, protruding from the scorched and frayed neck of a long-sleeved black T-shirt. She was sitting beside me on the straw, her skinny legs pulled to the side, her feet bare. I tried sitting up, but pain burst through my head. "Lorraine, Jesus, you're alive, I think. You are alive, aren't you?" She nodded with her eyes closed, wobbling her bald, red head as if to say that she might be. "Lorraine, I can't believe it! I shot you. In the head! My God, what did I do to you? You look terrible!"

"You did not shoot me in the head, Kelly."

"Where did I shoot you? Did I shoot you?"

"No, apparently you missed. Were you aiming at me?"

"Of course I was aiming at you, at your head!"

The tomato crinkled. "Bloody hell, Kelly! Are you still out of your mind?"

"Probably."

"You must eat, Kelly. Here, try to swallow some food." She stuck a gourd in my face and yanked my head up.

"Jesus, Lorraine, take it easy. My head, my side, hurts like a son of a bitch."

"I am certain, Kelly, but you must eat. If you do not eat, you will lie here and hurt until you die." She put her fingers in the gourd, holding something to my mouth. "This is very soft. You don't have to chew it, just swallow." It smelled like fish. I did what she said. "Good, Kelly! Now another bite."

"Let's wait and see what happens to that one," I said, still swallowing. "And if you stay in my face, I'm going to need sunglasses. Does it hurt a lot? You really do look like a tomato."

"Kelly, you are even more insolent in a compromising position." Dropping my head, she was gone in a swirl of red.

I lay there, dozing in and out of flaming dreams, trying to sort out images, the pain in my head keeping time with my heart. Several times I gave thought to getting up, seeing where I was, but a stabbing in my ribs kept me down. Above and all around was straw, reeds maybe. A wind shelter, no doubt, the kind built like a shell, a tunnel circling to the center. Subdued light filtered through the reeds, sufficient to see clearly. My boots, socks, and belt were piled at my feet, and I was still wearing khakis and a long-sleeved green T-shirt, both filthy. The howling continued, rising and falling, the demonic Turkana wind taking on form when I drifted into memory.

She was back, the tomato, barking, sticking the gourd in my face again. "Kelly, you must eat, I insist! Here, open your mouth." She yanked my head up again, sending pain to my toes. She was holding the fishy-smelling stuff to my lips. "Take it, Kelly! You will die right here in this godforsaken hell if you do not eat."

If I could have taken a swing at her threats, I would have, but I opened my mouth obediently and swallowed, exclaiming, "Are you sure you're not poisoning me? What is that shit?"

"Food, protein! I am the doctor. Do what I say or you will die right there. Do you understand? Now, water. Open again!" After I drank the water, she was gone.

The silence woke me. The howling had ceased, and it was black as midnight. Hunger rumbled in my stomach, and I needed to pee. I managed to get on my elbows, but the pain, the dark, forced me to abandon my notions. I lay there wondering what day it was in the rest of the world. A globe was spinning, the cities of the world lighting up as it went around. New York, Hong Kong, Istanbul, Paris, London, Cairo, San Francisco—home. The globe stopped spinning at the continent of Africa. I stuck my finger in the middle, the deepest part of Africa, Lake Turkana.

It was howling again, light again, hot again, and the beast was back, the same threat, eat or die. I told her I had to pee. She was ecstatic. I was getting better. "Can you lift your bum? I'll bring the chamber pot."

My dignity retorted, "I'll go to the pot, thank you!"

"You will do no such thing, Kelly! You are too weak to stand and much too weak to squat. I'll get the pot." Challenged, I tried projecting myself vertically, but in a flash she was back and I was only to my elbows.

The humiliation over, she sat down beside me and began a quiz. "Do you know where you are, Kelly? Do you remember how we got here?" She didn't give me time to guess. "We are on Lake Turkana, a fishing camp, I suppose you would call it. Do you remember the fire?"

In pain, I pulled up my disgusting green shirt in order to see my side. It was wrapped in black cloth, the cloth missing from the bottom of Lorraine's ragged shirt. Carefully, I felt my ribs, wincing. "I remember a spear in my ribs. What's it look like, Doc?"

"It looks like broken ribs, no doubt from riding like a sack of potatoes on your belly, tied in front of me on a donkey for three hours. You most certainly have not been speared."

"Are you sure?" It was unfathomable. "I remember the spear, and this pain in my side."

"I am the doctor. There was not a spear in your ribs." She raised the slick skin above her eyes where her brows used to be. "Are you disappointed?"

"Not really, I suppose, but I was getting used to the fact that I'd survived a spear, which would have been something. Everybody recovers from broken ribs."

"If it will make you feel better, you may also have a fractured skull, possibly two fractures, but most certainly a severe concussion."

"Are you sure, Doc? How do you know without an X ray?"

"I do not know. However, based on the information I have . . ." She put up a finger. "The fact that you rode three hours on your belly without protesting, the two very swollen areas on your skull, your state of drifting in and out of consciousness for several days, your two very black eyes, all substantiate my diagnosis." She waved four fingers at me while I felt my face. "Now then, Kelly, you need to know what is just outside . . ."

"I have black eyes? How black? What do they look like?"

"A full black mask, with lighter discoloration in the remainder of your face."

"Seriously?" My eyes were definitely swollen and hurt like hell, but she could have been putting me on.

"You hit your head hard enough to cause internal bleeding, which settled around your eyes. Indeed, I am satisfied that you will live, that is, of course, if you have a plan for removing us from this camp of savages."

"Jesus, Lorraine, do you remember how determined you were to get here?"

"I would remind you, Kelly, that you blew up everything we had, simply everything! We are at the mercy of these people! The sum total of your valuables is a watch on your arm that does not work and a knife in your pocket, and, oh yes, the key to that truck. The truck that was!"

"I blew up everything because we were under attack! I don't know quite yet what followed, but I do know that we were under attack by the same bastards that killed Kiuka!"

It was impossible to read her tomato face, but her eyes looked skeptical, and she did a bored sigh before she said, "I have memories of these people rescuing us from the fire you set."

"Memories! You were comatose! If up to you we'd have been digested by hyenas, or our dried pussies would be swinging from a neck! If you have memories, remember why you weren't giving a hand, or . . . a howl!" My head was screaming as loud as my indignation.

Someone had entered, a black woman wearing only a leather skirt. A couple of pouches and a knife hung from her waist, a few simple beads adorned her neck, and she wore boots! "Lua, Jesus, it's Lua!" I exclaimed, sending a jolt through my head. "You used to wear more clothes."

"It is vogue here to be naked," Lorraine said with disgust, moving her frail body to make room for Lua.

Lua sat down, her full breasts jiggling. She was all smiles, glad to see me awake. The high bones of her face glowed as she gestured and jabbered, her body keeping time. Before I could think of the Turkana words to ask a question, she was well into a conversation. We got through the part that she was okay and I was going to live. I asked her if my eyes were black. She confirmed that they were, giggling, exposing the yellow stains on her teeth caused from drinking foul water her entire life. She liked our new looks, my mask and Lorraine's color, and she thought Lorraine looked better bald. She pointed to her own head, shaved except for a tuft of plaited hair on the top, indicating that Lorraine could soon look as good as she did. Then we slowed down to my speed for communicating in Turkana. I spoke loudly and listened hard over the thumping of my head and the howling wind. It took a while.

We were in a Turkana fish encampment on the lake, the camp where Lua had gone for help, apparently where she felt Kali had sent her. She found the encampment just as it was indicated on the map that had been drawn for us by the people we had encountered in the caravan south of Lokitaung. And with exclamation in both her body and her language, her eyes wide, she told me that Kali had been here.

Lorraine was fidgeting, wanting to know what Lua was saying. She'd heard Kali's name and was impatient. "What about Kali? I have been here three days, and no one so much as looks at me. These people treat me as you do, Kelly!" I told her what I'd understood from Lua. "I knew it!" She exclaimed. "I knew Kali was here! Where is she now?" I told her we hadn't gotten that far.

Ignoring Lorraine, Lua continued talking as though she were conducting a symphony, her bare breasts swaying. She was conveying to me that she had awakened the entire encampment when she arrived, telling them that she was looking for a witchdoctor named Kali with three camels and a camel tender named Goa. They told her that the witchdoctor had been here and made a spell on two children that were going to die. Now they lived. But in two days, Kali was gone. She left her camel tender Goa and two of the camels. She just disappeared. It was part of her magic, they said, and Lua agreed.

I took Lorraine that far. She listened, standing in the very center of the hut where it was high enough for her to stand up completely. Turning around in circles, thinking about what I said, she resembled a red lollipop on a stick. "This must surely mean that one of her bags did indeed simply fall off the camel!" She stopped to wave her arms. "They were not robbed or molested at all! But what does it mean . . . she simply disappeared? She certainly would not load all of her things on a camel and leave without Goa?"

Lua went on with her guttural jabbering, "he he" sounds, and gesticulations, doing her best to help me understand the rest of the story, which seemed to take forever, the drumming in my head ceaseless. She had told the men of the encampment that she was an assistant to the witchdoctor Kali who had saved the two children. She showed them the sticks and stones in her blue bag of magic so that they would believe her. She told them that there was a battle with Ngorokos, enemies of the witchdoctor's magic. They had already killed another assistant and were preparing to kill two more witchdoctors. At this point Lua made it clear that she really only considered me a witchdoctor, not Lorraine, probably because she'd been impressed by my bomb test with the plastic jug. Then she went on to tell how the men of the camp, six or eight of them, she thought, rounded up spears, shields, knives, and clubs, and two camels and a donkey, and set out with her to battle the Ngorokos.

I told Lorraine what Lua had said, more or less, and filled in the blanks with probable explanations. No Turkana could resist a battle. They lived to fight. The Turkana who fished did so under threat of starvation. They gave away their pride; eating fish was considered lowly by the brave pastoral warriors. Lua had presented a situation that gave the fishermen an opportunity to redeem themselves.

I was more than anxious to redeem myself, as well, with the rest of the story, despite the pounding in my head and the spear that I still imagined in my side. I urged Lua on. When she and the men were nearing the truck, they saw a fire burst into the sky, and then another. Lua told them it was witchdoctor magic, she had seen it. She paused for confirmation from me. The warriors hurried on to the truck. The Ngorokos were waiting, watching the fire bursts.

I stopped her long enough to ask Lorraine, who was still twirling in the center of the hut, "Did you hear? Ngorokos! When they came to rescue us, the Ngorokos were waiting!" I hated her skeptical eyes.

Lua, her face lit up with excitement, her body bouncing on her knees, was anxious to tell the ending to her story. Suddenly, there was a huge fire burst, bigger than the two before. The Ngorokos were on foot and ran. The men on camels charged after them, but Lua convinced the two men on the donkey that they had to save the witchdoctors from the fire. She told them that Kali's magic was there, that she had encircled the truck with it before she left, and that it would protect them against the fire and they would be rewarded greatly. Fire was everywhere; even the truck was burning. The men were very brave. They pulled the witchdoctors out of the truck and loaded them on the donkey. Then, there was another huge fire burst, the biggest of all, and many things fell out of the sky. The men on camels returned from the battle. They had killed the Ngorokos. Now, the men, the entire encampment, and especially Lua were waiting for the reward, the reward of magic for saving the witchdoctors.

I told Lorraine the story with satisfaction, despite my exhaustion. She stopped turning in circles and said she remembered being dragged from the truck and loaded on a donkey. She said the donkey was dancing around, and then the truck blew to bits, scattering debris everywhere. Lamenting the scene, she said, "All of that medicine, all of Kali's supplies, up in smoke." She went on, "That dreadful donkey ran in circles and I continued to fall off." She raised her shorts to show me the bruises on her thighs. "They finally tied me in a sitting position, leaving my body and head to flop around. They tied you in front of me like a sack of potatoes. When the sun came up, I took off my shirt and put it around my head, but it was this black shirt that absorbs the heat—that I changed into for you, remember?" I remembered, sheepishly glancing at the part of it tied around my ribs. She lifted her short, ragged shirt to show me her sunburned chest accented by her dirty white bra. She said that she would trade the consciousness of the ride for broken ribs. Looking at her head, I was sure she meant it.

The part about the men waiting to be rewarded, the entire encampment waiting for more magic, troubled me. I asked Lua about the big new pouch that hung from her waist. She'd had the small blue cloth bag before; now she had an enormous leather one as well. She said it was Kali's magic bag. Kali had taken all of her things except her magic bag; that's how she knew Kali would be back. She opened it, placing the contents on her leather skirt. There were more of the bones, sticks, and colored rocks like the ones I'd seen in Lua's blue bag. And there were small containers—medicine, some magic, I hoped. I was anxious and began sorting through the stuff, but Lua took my hand away. This was Kali's magic, not mine. She was Kali's assistant. She would keep Kali's magic safe until Kali returned. I convinced her to show me the containers, let me read the labels. One was penicillin tablets, a cup-sized clear bottle, half full. Another was labeled morphine; the container was white plastic and apparently stuffed with cotton, so there was no way to tell how much, but it felt light. There were two larger bottles marked glucose, one full, one empty, and a large tin of aspirin that rattled half empty. There was also a small, clear plastic box containing a syringe, a rubber strap, suturing materials, a couple of tubes of ointments, and a half-empty box of gauze bandaging. Nothing much to make magic with, certainly not to equal giant bursts of fire in the sky. I asked her if I could have some of the aspirin tablets in the tin. She told me again that they were Kali's magic. She could only give them to people when Kali's magic told her so. I asked her again if Kali had left anything else. She was sure there was only the magic bag.

Lorraine, still standing, not much interested in Lua's pouch, demanded, "Where is Goa? Has he remained here?" I put it to Lua. She said that several days after Kali disappeared, Goa decided to go look for her. No one had seen either of them since. "That makes no sense entirely," Lorraine said with disdain. "Did Goa know where Kali had gone? Who saw her leave?"

Lua and I talked about it for a while, but I was out of bullets, exhausted from the charades involved in Turkana translations. As best I could interpret, Kali had simply disappeared. No one saw her leave. She had worked her magic into the night with the two children, and two mornings later she was gone with everything except her magic pouch. Goa had no idea where she went. He waited around a few days, then took the two camels and went off looking for her. When I asked whether Goa could have taken all of Kali's things when he left, she said that many people saw Goa leave. He was alone on two empty camels. She giggled about the camels, something they wore, something particular about the camels that had amused the Turkanas. When I asked her if she knew how much stuff Kali had with her, she made motions with her arms that indicated a great many things: more magic, like the magic in her pouch, and gourds, water jugs, a tent.

Lorraine grumbled when I told her. "How could she have possibly put all those things on her camel? And then she simply rode away with not a single soul to testify to her doing so?" She began turning in circles again, a red lollipop voicing discontent that anything Lua said could be laced with superstitions.

"She saved our lives!" I reminded her. "Jesus, Lorraine, she saved our goddamn lives by a hair on a frog's butt! Perhaps you could thank her and be grateful!"

"I have thanked her, but she has no idea what I say, and quite frankly, I am certain that she does not care. Kali treated people she disliked in exactly the same manner."

With the last of my energy, I spent a few minutes searching for words to tell Lua how grateful we were to her. She had saved our lives, and we would find some way to reward her. She said that seeing my magic again, rewarding the brave men, would be enough. That wasn't what I wanted to hear.

There was one more question I had to ask, and it was about the magic that Lua had used to encircle the truck. I seemed to remember that she had put it a long way from the truck. What was it? I had to know what had stopped those guys. They were about to cut us up. Why had they stood there discussing it rather than attacking? I put the question to her, poorly. I'm not sure she understood, because she gathered up her magic, stuffed it back in the leather pouch, tied it on her waist belt, and left.

Before collapsing, I managed to feed myself the fish and water Lua had left. Lorraine ate too, silently. She was thinking hard about something, probably Kali. Just as I was dozing off, the donkey brayed, and Lorraine scrambled to her feet, yelling, "Stay out of here, you beast! Go away!"

I woke to my pounding head. It was dark. I could hear Turkanas talking and laughing, lots of laughing, which they are known for—difficult to figure considering their lives. Considering mine at that moment, laughter sounded inviting. I felt the need to get up and go out to join them. I began the process slowly, carefully, painfully, wishing Lua had been generous with the aspirin. On my feet I was wobbly, the dark exacerbating my poor equilibrium. One step, carefully, then the next, and then I was back on my knees. Lorraine squeaked. I had tripped over her. "What are you doing here?" I muttered through gritted teeth.

"What do you mean, what am I doing here?" Her voice cut through the dark. "This is where I am, where we all have been since we arrived here at the Ritz."

"You've been sleeping here, beside me, the entire time?"

"Where else would we be? Lua as well." Lorraine wasn't happy that I had awakened her, and rudely.

"So we're all here, in this one hut?"

"This is the hut they gave us," she snapped in the dark. "And although it is far superior to any of the others, it is a small space for three people." She let out one of her long sighs and added, "I had to be here anyway, to watch after you, give you water, make you eat. Lua is not often here during the day, and she remains out late with the others. They sit around at night and talk." She paused, waiting for another round of Turkana laughter, and added, "as they are doing now."

I managed to sit down. "I guess I've been out of it, Lorraine. I didn't know you were here at night. Thanks for all your care. I'm appreciative."

"Sufficiently appreciative to make yourself well and find out where Kali has gone, I hope!"

She shouldn't have said that, not then—not yet. "Goddamn it, Lorraine, if you so much as mention Kali's name again, I'm going to break your tomato! If I live to be old, and at this rate it's not likely, it will be too soon to hear her name again! We have just escaped being sliced up, and the devil knows what else, and we still need every bit of luck we can conjure up! Believe it when I tell you, I don't give a hairy rat's ass about Kali!"

Silence followed, except for the hammering in my head. The Turkana voices stopped. They had probably heard my tirade. More than ever I wanted out of that hut. I made another painful stab at getting to my feet, but by then I had no idea which way was out. With a modicum of humility, I asked Lorraine to show me the way. She insisted that we must first put on our boots. She helped me with mine, then laced up her own, groping in the dark. Then she found my arm, pushed my aching head down, and led me slowly out through the tunnel. Everything was bright. The moon, somewhere near full, reflected onto the vast lake. The Turkana were talking again. We could see them sitting in a circle not far down the shore and tottered off to join them, Lorraine supporting me.

The Turkana watched us coming, falling silent. Choosing a place in the loose circle next to three women, we sat down carefully. The women, stacks of seeds around their necks jingling, got up and walked away, their tits and leather skirts flopping. Then, one by one, the several men got to their feet, picked up the stubby stools they were sitting on, and walked away, penises swaying. Only Lua remained. The three of us sat there in the dirt watching them disappear.

"This is what I mean," Lorraine whispered. "These people will not even look at me, and they have never come close enough to speak . . . if I could speak to them."

"I'm guessing it has to do with the magic they believe we're capable of."

"Frankly, I am most happy not to have to look at them or smell them any closer. It is almost impossible to believe that Kali came . . ." She covered her whispering lips with two fingers.

"Maybe they're afraid of you, Doc." I began laughing. "They've never seen a tomato." Laughing would have felt good except for the pain.

"Wait until they see you, my dear! You look like a redheaded Zorro!"

"Jesus, that's great! I love Zorro!" God, it hurt to laugh. "Too bad we don't have a camera for posterity. We're unidentifiable, hopefully, although we do seem to be cleaner, some of the dirt wearing off."

"That is because I have washed us in the water from that foul lake, both of us."

I was a bit humbled. "No fooling, you washed me, as in gave me a bath?"

"As best I could. I needed to see your face, how bad it was, and your ribs. I could do nothing with your hair. My comb simply would not go through it."

"Your comb? You still have your red comb?"

"Yes, my pockets are deep and they were buttoned. The lip balm melted away."

"But now you don't need a comb," I giggled, unable to control an obvious need to turn reality into absurdity. "Seriously," I said, "I really don't like pain. How are you dealing with it? It must be terrible."

"No, not anymore, unless I have to go outside during the day, in the sun and wind, which I do not do, except to empty the chamber pot . . . gourd."

"Well then, that could explain why these people don't like you. The only time they see you is when you're carrying a pot of piss." I laughed again, wishing I hadn't. I turned to Lua for an opinion on the subject. She was gone.

"Even Lua is evasive," Lorraine whined. "You see, she has gone to bed. I sit by the entrance to the hut all day, just out of the wind. No one, not even Lua, so much as acknowledges me. At dusk, when the wind stops, I have tried walking around the encampment. They separate in front of me and vanish. The only thing not evasive here is that bloody donkey! See, here he comes to torment me." The donkey ambled near us and brayed once or twice, probably hungry.

"Lorraine, you told me on the truck that you knew something of the Turkana. Do you know their history with the English?"

She shrugged. "I know that the English have never been able to bring them under control."

"Did you know the English have slaughtered them at times, women and children too?"

"Kali has told me that is true."

"Well, you're English, Doc. You're a white woman and you speak . . . very English. Granted, most or maybe all of these people have never heard or seen an Englishman, but they know about them, and Lua has seen them. She's been around Lodwar for a while, she knows you're English. I'm sure you're suspect, plus she may be jealous of you because you're a friend or colleague of Kali's. Exactly what are you anyway, friend or colleague?"

She gave me a wary look. "You have requested in no uncertain terms that I not speak of her."

"That's good, Doc, the request stands."

"Right!" she said with a lilt, then, "Why does Lua like you? You are as white as I am."

"I'm not at all certain she likes me, but she probably trusts me somewhat. I don't speak like you, and I know a little Turkana. I went with Kiuka to search for Kali. Plus, I know how to do magic."

"Absolutely! You know how to blow us all to bits!"

"You still won't give me credit for saving our scalps. Well, most of them."

"How do you know that it was not Lua's magic that stopped the Ngorokos, Kelly?"

"You are an obstinate bitch, Lorraine! When we find out what her magic was, you're going to eat crow."

She gave me a ho-hum sigh and then said, "Perhaps you could tell Lua that I am the person who purchased her boots. Perhaps that will impress her enough to like me. Kali asked me to get them, a very specific kind. I finally had to order them from Italy."

"Jesus, I was sure that on the truck you told me you knew something of these people! Lua doesn't have a clue what, much less where, Italy is. With my very limited ability to communicate, you want me to first convince her that the world isn't flat and then give her a geography lesson? They do believe the world is flat, you know."

"You could simply tell her that I am responsible for them."

"Yeah, okay, maybe," I grumbled, then asked, "Who brings our fish and water, the foul stuff we're consuming?"

"Lua brings it three times a day, in two gourds, as though we are prisoners. The water is soda—salty, alkaline, hideous, but Lua drinks it. I feel slightly sick all the time, but I daresay it won't kill us, certainly any faster than other things. The food is fish, enormous fish; I have seen them. They dry them in the sun. I have been pounding the fish with a stone, so that you might swallow it without chewing." Again humbled, I started to thank her, but she blurted out, "Kelly, I have truly been terrified that you might die, leaving me here with these savages!"

"Lorraine, it was savages that killed Kiuka, and were about to kill us. Those were the savages we had to worry about. These people saved us from a death far more horrific than spending the rest of our lives here drinking foul water and eating huge fish."

We moved back in front of our shell, taking a seat in the dirt near the entrance. The donkey followed. Watching the moon and the lake, we sat in silence. I did reruns of the night at the truck. Like it or not, I supposed I always would. We could hear Turkana voices, some laughter still. They had moved their circle somewhere else.

The sun and wind came simultaneously; the shell became a furnace. I sat cross-legged on the filthy reeds, shoulders back, trying to keep weight off my ribs. I had a need to be upright. I was remembering and choosing Turkana words, practicing for a talk with Lua. I couldn't see Lorraine, but occasionally the wind pushed one of her long sighs past me. She was near the shell entrance, watching, as I supposed she'd been doing most of the last three or four days. She was just out of the sun, but it was windy there, too windy I thought, considering her condition. She insisted that her outer skin was dead, without feeling, and served as armor for her new skin. She was the doctor. She was beginning to change colors, looking more like a kiwi now than a tomato. I'd asked her to send Lua in when she came with the fish and water.

Lua came and I was rehearsed, dreading the necessary use of my hands and arms. The first subject on my agenda was why the locals were keeping their distance. She understood quickly and said it was because we were witchdoctors, interjecting, again, that she wasn't convinced about Lorraine. But she waved her arms to make the point that the entire encampment knew of our power. The witchdoctor Kali had done good things with her power—she had saved two children—but she was Turkana. We were very different, not Turkana. They were suspicious that we might use our power against them. My red hair meant witch. Lorraine's red face meant demon, or something similar. They were waiting to see some good magic, to be rewarded with magic that would prove we were good witchdoctors. They were less aloof with Lua, keeping about arm's length was my understanding of what she was saying. She was able to interface because she was Kali's assistant, she was Turkana, and she didn't have a red face or red hair.

Lua's information was about what I figured, but beyond that there were questions. What kind of magic would appease them, and if we didn't come up with any magic, what would they do? Lua didn't know. She hadn't considered that. As a good witchdoctor, why wouldn't I do good magic for them? She had me. Groping as long as possible, I told her we were recovering. We were wounded witchdoctors. We had fought a bloody battle against the enemy in order to get here to bring Kali more magic. We needed to rest, to heal ourselves before we could do magic, and before we continued our journey to find Kali. My painful gestures more effective than my poor Turkana, Lua watched intently. She was giving me her "he he" exclamation, doing the exaggerated nod. It was apparently what she wanted to hear.

I asked her then why we got the best hut. That was simple. They had built it for Kali. When she made the children better, Kali asked them to build her a good shell hut. They did, immediately, exactly where she wanted it, near a reed clearing on the lakeshore where she could bathe privately. They had thought she was going to stay a while. Lua became very serious while telling me that Kali always asked that a hut be built for her separate from the others. She was the witchdoctor; she needed a special place, which made sense to me. Dr. Kali had been Europeanized. She didn't like the smell of these people much more than we did. What didn't make sense was that if she had a new hut and two critical children, why did she leave, and without Goa? I asked Lua what was wrong with the children and how they were doing now. She said they'd had an accident; she didn't know how. They were bleeding badly and nearly dead when Kali arrived to cure them. They were doing fine now.

Next, I asked her about the encampment; how big and how much livestock? The Turkana who fished did so to keep from starving and were short on possessions, particularly livestock, the measure of Turkana wealth. We would need camels to transport us out of here. Lua confirmed that these Turkana were very poor, a few families with only two camels, one donkey, and several cows between them.

The next subject concerned the missing witchdoctor. Why did she think Kali disappeared, leaving only her magic bag, and how did she physically do it? The second part of the question was difficult to gesture sufficiently and took time, causing my ribs to feel as though they'd come apart. Lua's explanations, if I had them right, were that she didn't have a clue. She wasn't a witchdoctor, only an assistant. She had hopes to become a witchdoctor, and when Kali returned, she would go on with her training.

I sat picturing the dilemma, scouring it for something positive, something we could use. Lua started to leave, but I caught the tail of her leather skirt and groped for words to ask again about the magic she'd used around the truck. I needed to know what had stopped those Ngorokos. Had it been my bombs, the burning hyena, Lua's magic, or all of the above? She turned her head away. I let go of her skirt and tried asking why she wouldn't tell me, but it either took too long or she wasn't interested in answering. She was gone.

Lorraine, listening just out of sight, heard Kali's name, apparently enough times to put her in a stew. She came in, face crinkled with questions that I'd buffaloed her into not asking. Without conversation, we ate the few bites of foul fish from the gourd Lua had left. I thought of us as wounded prisoners of war in a concentration camp, the image dark and disturbing. The need to think of something else spurred me into conversation from the top of my head.

"Lorraine, tell me the truth. How have you been able to deal with the pain so well? You've suffered a terrible burn. Maybe you had something in your pockets, those big pockets of yours, besides your red comb? You're a doctor, maybe some codeine or morphine, just in case?" She looked sheepish. I was excited. "Morphine, you have morphine? Lua has morphine! We can drug a few people, make a miracle, hell, drug the entire encampment and take their camels! Well, we could do a drop shipment later, pay them in, what? How about tartar sauce?" I laughed, amusing myself. "How much morphine do you have?"

"I did have morphine," Lorraine said shyly, "sufficient to do myself in, just in case, as you say." I used some of it the night . . . at the truck, after it became apparent that something, the hyenas or worse, was going to kill us."

"So that's why you were comatose!" I gave her my most disgusted look. "You took morphine, left me sitting there to defend us alone, and then you criticize how I did it."

"It was you who said that I was your responsibility. After all, you are being handsomely paid."

"Yeah, if I live to spend it! Jesus, Lorraine, if I'd known you had morphine, I could have used the last bullet on myself, instead of wasting it on you."

"Did you actually try to kill me, Kelly?"

"Of course! And if I'd known you had morphine, I'd have killed myself. Well, maybe . . . yeah, I guess I would have." I was believing it, surprisingly. Yes, I would have, rather than die by the hands of the Ngorokos. Lorraine was looking at me, considering what I'd said. We sat for a minute or so staring at each other as though we were each watching the same movie. I don't know what prompted it, but suddenly I began to snicker, then really laugh, then hoot. My ribs screamed, but hysterics rendered me helpless. Maybe it was euphoria because we had lived through the nightmare at the truck, or fear of what was ahead. Maybe it was looking at Lorraine. She stared at me in disbelief, and then her face began to crinkle, and then she burst out with a cackle she had seemed incapable of. We rolled around in the dirty reeds as though we'd been given laughing gas, tears streaming, partially from pain. When the hysterics began to taper, we giggled, first one, then the other, until I asked, "Okay, so do you still have some morphine?"

"Yes," she wailed, trying to compose herself. "But only a little. I took quite a lot of it on the donkey."

"So you were anesthetized on the donkey, too!"

"Not sufficiently," she snapped, then giggled. "And I used more the first day and night we were here. But after I had a good look at this place, the people, and . . ." She had another short giggle. "I thought it best to save the rest. Indeed, I may still need it."

"Indeed you may, but show me what you have!" While she dug around in her big pockets, I tried to get in a position that didn't hurt. She pulled out her comb and several small prescription bottles. "Jesus, Doc, how much have you been holding out on me?"

"Well, these two are thyroid and estrogen. This one is for diarrhea, thankfully, which I need! This is the morphine here, the red label." She opened it and poured the tablets into her palm, four of them. "This is just enough to put me to sleep for about twelve hours."

"And to get rid of this pain in my head and ribs!"

"Kelly, one cannot be administered morphine with head injuries."

"And why not, Doc?"

"Because it is better that you hurt and be alert than be comfortable and unconscious."

"Better for who?"

"For me." She let another small giggle escape.

I was sorely disappointed. Only four tablets, probably enough to put two or three people to sleep for a short time. Not hardly a miracle or sufficient to let us get away with camels. "Okay, Doc, how much morphine do you think Lua has in her pouch?"

"I would not have the slightest . . . except that the bottle is not very big. If it were full of tablets, not cotton, there would only be sufficient morphine for ten, perhaps . . . twenty people to sleep several hours."

"That's more or less, of course?" I said, mocking her vagueness.

"More or less, of course," she defended coolly.

The day blew on, hotter and hotter, too hot to talk even if we'd had something to say, such as a new thought about our predicament, an idea, a plan. But nothing came to mind, other than the idea of drugging enough people to steal the camels. Lua sat with us, primping, shaving her head with a sharp piece of metal she kept in her blue bag, redoing her tassel of plaited hair. Lorraine was having intestinal problems and was continually on the gourd in the tunnel. I encouraged her to drink more water, but she was sure that was the source of her problem. My head pounded and my side ached, nonstop. Sometime in the middle of the day, Lua brought more fish and water. Even ravenously hungry, the few bites were difficult to choke down. Lua ate with us, quietly. She said she was thinking of Kiuka. I was thinking of a persuasion sufficient to entice her to give me some of the aspirin, when suddenly the donkey brayed, startling us all. He had come into the tunnel, his long head poking around the corner at us.

Lorraine snapped, "Please ask Lua why that bloody beast continues to come inside!"

I did, and took glee in translating Lua's explanation. "The beast, this donkey, the one who carried us to safety . . ." I indicated his dejected face hanging there. "He cannot go with the other animals to graze because he was hurt carrying too big a load, and burned as well. He only wants to come in out of the wind." Lorraine groaned and buried her bald head between her knees.

Later in the afternoon, Lorraine's diarrhea pills seemed to kick in and she was somewhat better. I asked her if she wanted to accompany me to the lake. I knew I wasn't going to like it out there in the middle of the day, but I had a need to wash up. She agreed, telling me there was a good place in front of the hut where she had been able to immerse herself. It was secluded on both sides by reeds, and not so windy. The place Kali had selected for her baths, no doubt.

We hobbled out barefoot, pushing our way against the wind toward the lake. Green and vast, it looked inviting. Wading into the sheltered water, she in shorts, I in khaki pants rolled to the knees, felt almost like fun. We splashed water up into our faces and over our arms, and then at each other. Very soon we were both soaking wet, laughing and shedding our shirts, tossing them toward the bank. A few more splashes and everything came off. Lorraine was a portrait painted by Salvador Dalí: a reddish brown, perfectly round head set on top of a bright pink torso surrounding English-white breasts. She thought that my mask and nudity looked sadomasochistic, suiting me well.

We went in to our waists and Lorraine doused her head, telling me that she'd been doing it several times a day, thinking the soda water was helping her heal. She was convinced that the layer of dirt she'd had on her face kept her from being burned more seriously. I told her that if she hadn't combed her hair so much, maybe the dirt would have saved it as well. Over the screams of my protesting head, she rinsed my hair. When the water turned from rust to clear, she shrieked something about how much redder my hair was and how much more I resembled a witch. Beginning to scorch, we reluctantly collected our clothes and started back. In the short distance from the lake to the hut, everything on us dried.

When the sun was low, Lorraine stayed inside and I went out. Dusk is short at the equator, and I wanted to look around the encampment before dark. The wind was doing its last gusts for the day, rattling the reeds at the edge of the lake and forcing a list to my already faulty walk. The other huts, five that I could see, were seventy-five yards down the lake's shore and off the bank about a hundred feet. This side of the huts, there was a dugout fishing canoe on the bank, and four men gathered around it putting a spear through the gills of two large Nile perch. All the men were naked, save for the knives tied at their waists. They wore earrings or ivory spools and ornaments of this and that in their dung-slicked hair. Their bodies were scarified. They could have been the men who saved our lives and killed the Ngorokos, but they weren't wearing ostrich feathers. Perhaps they wore feathers only for ceremonies or special occasions, I couldn't remember, or perhaps they didn't have access to ostrich—probably not, being too poor to do any trading. Two of the men had large ivory plates in their lower lips, a sign that at some time they'd had wealth enough to trade. They stared at me, not moving from the canoe. I gave them a wide berth.

I could see one or two women sitting in the shade of each hut watching their children play with the donkey on the muddy, reedless part of the beach. Two of the children were wearing filthy, ragged bandages on their legs, surely the kids Kali had fixed up. As I approached, the mothers called to their tots, and everyone disappeared inside, except the donkey. He sauntered my way with a slight limp. Most of the hair on his right side was missing. I reminded him we'd attended the same party.

The five huts were smaller, squatter, and more poorly constructed than ours, some so flimsy that I could see children moving about inside. Alongside were forked stakes supporting drying fish. When I reached these huts, I looked back toward ours. It was clearly visible, as was the land and lake around it, with only our secluded bath area blocked from view. I couldn't imagine everyone in the encampment looking the other way long enough for Kali to disappear. If she walked or rode out of there, at least during the day, someone had to have seen her.

We continued gimping along, the donkey and I, past the encampment and down the lake's shore where the reeds grew thick on the bank. Flamingos, on their last pass before nesting on the soda bars, made a pink haze across the water and disappeared to the north. Looking east, the lake and rising moon were all there was, the green waters becoming murky as the sun approached the volcanic horizon to the west. There, I could see a couple of cows and the two camels coming across the lava, herded by a naked boy with a long stick. No doubt he had been with the animals all day, maybe several days, in the blistering wind, searching for the small clumps of grass here and there in the crevices of lava. He may even have risked everything to graze across the border into Ethiopia, Merille territory.

The rank smell of huge Nile perch skeletons heaped at the edge of the reeds halted me. These enormous fish swam up the Nile River when Lake Turkana was part of the Nile system millions of years ago, but only recently had the Turkana been forced to fish for them. Judging from the size of the pile, either the fishing camp hadn't been there long or the fishing was poor.

The sun melted into the horizon, and I turned back. The donkey had disappeared. The moon was already bright, and I stumbled along making my way to the dark form of the dugout where the men had been earlier. Placing my hand on the bow, feeling the crude wood, I peered inside. Except for long poles used to navigate in the shallow water, it was empty.

My walk was reality smacking me on an already lumpy, throbbing head. The stark emptiness and hostility of the land—the wind, the heat, the razor-sharp edge of human existence—flooded doom over me. Groping my way back into the dark hovel, taking my place on the dirty reeds, it was as though I'd been sucked into a black hole. Lorraine asked, "Well?" I said, "Hell!" There wasn't anything else to say.

When the moon was high and we heard voices laughing, we ventured out. We couldn't see anyone; they were keeping their distance. We sat down at the entrance of our hut in the dirt, trapped in gloom. In a few minutes, Lorraine was sobbing. "Jesus, Lorraine, I hate it when you do this. Is it really necessary? Does it help you somehow?" She paused in her sobbing to look at me and then began again. "Knock it off, Lorraine! They'll think we're performing witchcraft. They'll be up here waiting for rockets!"

Fortunately, she quieted down; no hysterics. My head, amid perpetual pounding, worked hard looking for a solution to our situation—an idea, even a lame one. Nothing came to me but dizziness, maybe from my wounds, maybe from hunger. I needed to stop thinking about it, let it rest. Tomorrow there would be something, a little thing maybe, but something to give us hope. I pushed my thoughts to pleasure—food, music, sex—but was unable to taste a thing. Lorraine's sighs were the cello of our depression.

"Okay, Lorraine," I said as a last resort. "Talk to me about Kali, but only if you can tell me something good; something funny would be nice. What happened to her when Kenyatta was freed? That's where you left me at the truck, wasn't it? She went with Kenyatta when the English took him to Lodwar for two years. She was the right hand of Gil Birla, Roger's father, right? Then Kenyatta was freed. What happened next?"

She stared at me and then at the moon for a few minutes, muttering something about my good memory considering my head injury. I waited. Finally, she said, "She came to London to live with me. She and Roger both."

"Roger, why Roger?"

"I suppose it will be necessary for me to back up and tell you something about Roger's father." She dipped her head at me, a sarcastic expression. "Would that be allowed?" Not waiting for my response, of course, she launched right into it. "Roger's father, Gil Birla—certainly you know of his family in India." It wasn't a question; she didn't pause. "Gil made his home in Kenya, near Nairobi. He had fallen in love with an Englishwoman—she had been living there—and he occupied nearly all of his time romancing her. She was very beautiful." Lorraine drifted off, the moon in her eyes. I wondered then if she might be the beautiful woman Gil Birla was in love with. I asked her. "Oh no, it wasn't me," she said, coming around. "This woman was an incredible prize! She gave Gil an awful time. She was wild and promiscuous, as I have been told the Nairobi social life encourages. Gil, of course, had all the money necessary to play with her, and he did so with wild abandonment, until she finally married him." She paused to smile at me, as if to say, now isn't this a nice story? But I'd seen enough movies to know it wasn't going to be a nice story. The Turkanas were laughing loudly—Turkanas, who have the worst life on the planet.

"Their plantation was beautiful!" She gave a sarcastic "Humph! He built it for her exactly as she dictated. I was there once, the only time I ever ventured out of England, until now. It was a palace beyond an Englishman's imagination, England being what it is, since the war." She paused a few moments, I supposed to lament the war, and then continued. "There is no question that they were beautiful together, she so fair, Gil so dark, so very, very handsome."

Surprised at Lorraine's esteem for beautiful people, I interjected, "This sounds like a Lana Turner, Tyrone Power movie."

"Perhaps it is," she retorted dramatically.

"Of course, Tyrone Power wasn't Indian, but Hollywood would have made him so." A Turkana was talking, a speech of some kind. I picked up a couple of words that sounded like the words for fire and witchcraft.

Lorraine turned to me, the moonlight sad in her eyes. "After Roger was born, Lana Turner left husband, child, and Africa for an English barrister." There was a long pause while she continued looking at me, then the moon, then me, the moon. This story had been big in her life. I kept nodding, and finally she went on. "It was indeed a scandal for the Birla family. Gil, of course, was devastated, that was apparent. He went into seclusion, he and his baby son, Roger. No one knew where they were for several years."

"What about Jezebel, Lana, back in England? Wasn't she concerned about her baby?"

"Of course not! She was never concerned with anyone but herself! She was vain and ruthless, with everyone. Frankly, one can quite easily see her reflection in her son."

"Sweet Roger? Damn, Lorraine, are you as mad at him as I am?"

"I am always mad at Roger, but you must remember the blood, Kelly. So much of what we are is in our blood. Life mostly only happens to us." The Turkanas were jabbering away, seemingly all at once.

"With that, we are in agreement, Doc. Okay, so little Roger with

Jezebel's blood is off with Daddy somewhere, but no one knows where."

"That is correct. What he was doing, I was not apprised of until several years later. He and Roger appeared at my door; Roger was seven by then. Gil said that the long rains had begun in Kenya, and he needed a rest. Indeed, that was all he said. They were there nearly two weeks before he said anything else, really. One night he had drunk brandies, I have no idea how many, but sufficient to talk to me at last. In fact, he . . ." She might have been choking up. She turned her head away. In a moment she cleared her throat and went on. "He poured his heart out to me, so broken he was, so completely devastated, still, after those many years."

"Okay, it's time you tell me your connection with Gil Birla. Why did he show up on your doorstep?" She didn't answer, just sat there holding her head in her hands.

The Turkanas had grown very noisy, chanting and singing in their guttural sounds. They could have been doing a ritual of some kind. I got up, trying to see them. There was some movement down the beach near where the canoe was, but I couldn't tell what was going on. I was about to sit down for more of the story, when I saw someone coming. It was Lua. Walking toward us, her straight, proud Turkana gait was slow and contemplative.

She sat down in front of us. She had news. The Turkanas were sending a message. They wanted to meet with us tomorrow. They wanted us to reward the brave warriors. By the time I'd translated that much of Lua's message, Lorraine was on her feet. As she ducked into the hut, I could see tears in her eyes.

Lua went on, body and word. There was more. A mother with a new baby was very sick and needed magic. I asked about the mother's sickness, how long she'd had it, if the baby had it too, did she need attention immediately—everything I thought Lorraine, a doctor, would ask. Lua didn't have the answers, only that we were to meet the elders tomorrow. I asked if she'd told them we were wounded, recuperating, unable to do magic until we'd recovered. She had, but we were witchdoctors. We had use of our own magic. Surely we had recovered by now. I could see that Lua was in agreement. She got up and tromped back to her people, Kali's large leather pouch bouncing off her leg.

"Lorraine, are you all right?" I asked, feeling my way into the gloomy, dark hole. She murmured something I didn't understand, so I asked her again.

"No," she said clearly. "I am not all right, and neither are you. Look at us!"

"Would that I could," I said, trying to laugh. "Tell me why you're crying."

"It would be much simpler to tell you why I do not cry, when I do not cry," she blubbered.

"Okay, just tell me this. Are you crying about the story you were telling me, or are you feeling bad physically?"

"Both!"

"Okay, then let me give you something else to think about." I gave her Lua's message. She didn't respond, not even a question. "Lorraine, do you think we should try to do something about the mother tonight?"

"What? Do what? Give her the last of my morphine, perhaps one of my thyroid pills?"

"You're the doctor. Maybe if you just take a look at her . . ."

"Maybe if I just take a look at her, I could contract whatever it is that she has. We could spend the last few days of our lives with typhoid or something worse!" She was approaching hysterics and climbing. "This is one of the women who has refused to look at me for four days? Do you honestly think that she will allow me to see her? It seems these, these savages, have . . ."

"Knock it off, Lorraine! You might try to remember for more than five minutes in a row that these savages saved our asses. And you might also try to remember that you're a doctor. You seemed to believe your dear friend Kali's work was so important that we had to risk our necks to find her records, but you can't lift a finger to help the same people she was helping, the same people that saved your hide, well most of it anyway."

A long silence followed, broken only by the pounding of my head, the donkey braying, and the occasional sounds of the Turkana talking, quietly now, their voices barely reaching us. Finally, I couldn't stand the indecision and groped my way out of the hut. The donkey greeted me. The moon was brilliant. We walked down to the shore, which was painful for both of us, nearly to the dugout before I saw them. They were in a circle about twenty yards away from the bank. There was a hush as I approached. I couldn't see which was Lua, but luckily she got up and said my name. She was surprised and uneasy. As best I could, I told her that I was concerned about the mother and wanted to see her. While Lua translated, I questioned my actions, watching the Turkana fidget. If I did nothing, showed no concern, and the mother died, they might hold us responsible. Of course, if I looked at the mother and she died anyway, it would be my fault as well, and what the hell did I know about making her better? I was probably doing the wrong thing, but suddenly I was committed. Three of the women got up. Lua told me to follow them.

We walked to one of the huts and got on our knees to crawl inside. There were holes in the reed and stick structure, but it was too dark to see anything. Lua came in behind me and indicated where the mother was, but I was lost. I asked if she could be moved into the moonlight. There was some talking between them, and then Lua and I moved outside, followed by the mother helped along by the women. They laid her on a cow skin, and I knelt down beside her, barely able to make out her features beyond her decorated head and the pile of wired seeds around her neck. Her breasts were large, full of milk I supposed. She was staring at me, terrified. I put my hand on her face and she winced. The women gasped—the witch at work. The mother was hot, very hot, a fever, obviously. I asked how old the baby was. There was some discussion before one of the women went inside and brought the baby out, probably believing that was what I wanted. She held it close, below all of her neck ornaments, her eyes flashing terror at me. The baby was sleeping. I felt its head and belly, to the sound of more gasps. It wasn't feverish. Unable to think of anything else, I told Lua that they should take water from the lake and put it on the mother, that she needed to be made cooler. The women understood as quickly as Lua and obediently gathered up a couple of gourds and started off to the lake. I told them I would be back shortly and hurried off, tripping over one of the stakes holding the dried fish.

"Lorraine! Doc, wake up!" I felt my way to her shoulder and shook it. "Wake up and give me your morphine!"

"Stop yelling!" she yelled. "I am not sleeping! What do you want with my morphine? Are they going to kill us now?"

"I'm not sure, but I have a half-assed plan. Come on, give it to me."

She began digging the bottles out of her big pocket. "Here, this is it, the one with morphine. What are you going to do with it?"

"The mother has a fever," I said, feeling the bottle in my hand. "A high fever. Fever means infection, right?" I waited for the good doctor's response, which was a grunt. "Lorraine, fever means infection, am I right?"

"Probably, but morphine will do nothing for an infection."

"The morphine isn't for the mother. It's for Lua, so we can steal her penicillin. Come on, you've got to help me! How many of these pills mixed with water will put Lua out for the night?"

"Bloody hell, Kelly! How do you anticipate pulling this off? And how can you be certain the penicillin will do the woman any good? God knows what she has!"

"What I know is that the woman has a high fever." I was out of patience. "If she dies, it's going to be our fault. As far as I know, the only chance we have to come out of this with any points at all is the penicillin in Lua's bag. Now help me, damn it! How many pills for Lua?"

"Two, I suppose," she said tentatively. "Yes, two. She should sleep all night soundly with two pills."

"Okay, dump the other two in with your thyroid, mush the two for Lua into powder and put them back in the bottle."

"I cannot do that in here. I cannot see a thing!"

"Then get outside in the moonlight!" She grumbled something as we made our way out of the hut. Nervous or sick, Lorraine's hands shook as she sorted out the pills. I asked her if she was all right, but she just shrugged. Finally, with the small bottle of powdered morphine in my hand, we walked hurriedly down the shore. I told her the general plan. She didn't have time to protest.

The mother was still lying outside the hut. One of the three women with Lua was holding the baby, another was dipping her hand in a gourd of water and splashing it on the sick mother's breasts and arms. I announced that Lorraine had come with me because we were going to do a magic ceremony. It would take two witchdoctors and an assistant. By the time they understood, they looked horrified, including Lua, who wanted assurance that Lorraine was a real witchdoctor. I convinced her that the ceremony would make her a believer and sent one of the women for a gourd of fresh water. She was back quickly and stood with the others in trepidation, their piled jewelry glistening in the moonlight. I told Lorraine to sing something, something sad. She wasn't happy about the part, but surprisingly she did so almost without hesitation. I'd never heard the song, which sounded like a lullaby, as best one could tell with a voice like Lorraine's. While she was wailing, I took one of the empty gourds, poured some of the fresh water into it, and swirled it around while I turned in circles. Then I ceremonially had the mother drink it, all of it. Filling the gourd again, swirling it again, turning in circles again, I gave it to Lorraine. She stopped wailing long enough to tip the gourd high and drink to the last drop, as instructed. She resumed her wailing. I did the hocus-pocus again, this time drinking myself, dramatically draining the gourd. Then I filled, swirled, turned, dumped in the powdered morphine, and handed the gourd to Lua. She drank it as dramatically as Lorraine and I had, draining the gourd. I did the hocus-pocus one last time, giving the gourd again to the mother, putting my hand on her head while Lorraine finished her song.

The ceremony over, I told Lua that the baby should be placed in the mother's arms and they both should remain outside the hut until morning. I would stay with them and continue the magic, but everyone else should go to bed and rest for their duties tomorrow, when the witchdoctors would again need them. I thought I saw Lorraine try to smile at Lua, probably for the first time, and they walked off together.

In less than an hour, Lorraine came stumbling back clutching the leather pouch. The mother and child were sleeping, but I wasn't sure the women inside the hut were. There were sufficient gaps in the reeds and hides of their hut to see out, if they had a mind to, and I didn't want them to see us with Lua's pouch. With one of the gourds, we crept off farther down the shore. Lorraine was nervous and muttering her concerns, which went right by me. I was trying to remember which container had the penicillin. We sat down near the reeds and began taking things out of the pouch, holding them up in the moonlight, trying to remember which was which.

"This one is the penicillin," I said happily, unable to read the label but remembering the size and shape of the container.

"Are you certain?" Lorraine asked, putting the other things back in the pouch.

"No. Yes, I'm certain, but no, don't put this stuff back. I want some aspirin for myself, and we'll give Mom some as well, and let's see how much morphine there is." I took out a dozen or so aspirin tablets, popped two in my mouth, and put the rest in a pocket. Then we decided which was the morphine and emptied it into Lorraine's hand. There were ten tablets; they were bigger than Lorraine's tablets, more milligrams we assumed. "Do we keep them?" I asked. "Do you think Lua has ever looked in these bottles, even shook them, not being a real witchdoctor?"

"No!" Lorraine said, emphatically. "Put them back! We cannot risk Lua's support, if indeed we have it now."

I agreed, but took the bandaging and the ointments out of the box. Those kids Kali fixed up looked like they needed new bandages. There were probably seventy-five penicillin tablets in the bottle, and it seem to take Lorraine forever to decide that we needed thirty-two of them. "Four a day for eight days," she finally said, tentatively, followed by a terrible groan.

"What is it, Lorraine?" I asked, alarmed.

"Eight days! Will we be here eight more days? Can we live here another week?"

"Jesus, Lorraine, I thought you were already dying. Let's take thirty-three, give her two to start, get her going. What do you think?" She grunted.

We finally had it sorted out. I had the gauze and ointments in one of my pockets, the penicillin in another, except for two in the separate bottle along with two aspirin. Standing at the water's edge, I was shaking the bottle vigorously, breaking up the tablets, preparing to pour them into the gourd and add water. Suddenly, there was a crashing noise in the reeds! It seemed nearly on top of us, and we could see the reeds ripple in the moonlight. The donkey, very close, brayed once and then it was quiet.

Lorraine squealed and ran a few feet up the bank. "That bloody donkey is going to be the death of me!" she ranted, loud enough to wake the entire encampment. I told her to be quiet, and she whispered, "I hate that beast."

"You've made your ingratitude clear, several times," I snapped, peering toward the reeds, trying to make out the beast. I couldn't see him and decided he was probably feeding on the wet grass that grew there. "Let's go, Lorraine, before everyone is awake, if they're not already."

The mother and baby were awake, the baby suckling. I swirled the water around in the gourd and put it to the mother's lips. She drank all of it, seemingly thirsty. I hurried back for a refill, tripping over the fish stake again. After three gourds of water, mother and child drifted off to sleep.

Lorraine left, and I felt around for a part of the hut substantial enough to sit against. Propped there, I searched for thoughts of something other than gloom. Lorraine's story of Roger's father and his broken heart over a Jezebel wife floated around in my throbbing head for a while, along with a lot of questions, but soon I was worrying about the next day. The Turkana wanted to meet. They wanted to be rewarded. If the mother showed progress, maybe they would give us a reprieve. We could argue that it took a lot of energy to perform magic—of that I was sure—and we needed to rest between acts, an intermission of several days to conjure up something for the brave warriors. Jesus God, we needed more than magic; we needed a miracle. Maybe we could pull off some kind of mass ceremony and drug the entire encampment with the ten or so pills of morphine in Lua's bag, coordinating it with a time when the camels were not off grazing in Ethiopia or wherever, but then what? If we traveled south, we'd sooner or later run into the track. We could steal dried fish, and I'd seen a couple of gourds around with lids for water, but we were not in good shape physically, either of us, without consideration of injuries. Lorraine had diarrhea. I would be next. We were both so dehydrated we looked like shedding snakes, our pants bagging over bony hips. One day on a camel in the sun and wind would probably finish us both. We'd have to travel at night, and we could get lost or attacked. I didn't want to think about Lorraine and myself on camels in the dark being attacked again, but I did.

The baby cried, and I woke with a start. The baby was suckling and quiet before I could make out the mother. I think she smiled, but I wasn't sure. I grabbed a gourd and went to the lake for water. Just beyond the muddy part of the beach, there was movement and the sound of reeds crashing. I guessed the donkey was probably still feeding. Suddenly, my gut grumbled and diarrhea overcame me. I squatted there, sick and empathetic for Lorraine.

I drank, downed more aspirin, refilled the gourd, crumbled in a penicillin tablet, and marched back to the mother. She drank down the magic, and as far as I could tell, she didn't want any more water. Resuming my place in the dark against the hut, I spent the remainder of the night listening to my cramping intestines and trekking to the reeds, weakness consuming me.

The sun and wind came out of hell, whistling over mother and child and through the hut, stirring everyone inside. The mother, whom I could see clearly now, was only a child, maybe fourteen. She seemed improved, or at least not as hot. I prepared another dose of magic and gave it to her. Lua came, yawning and rubbing at her eyes, the large leather pouch swinging from her waist. She talked to the mother and confirmed there was improvement but still much pain. I asked about the pain, where it was and for how long. Lua pointed to the woman's pelvis and indicated that there had been a problem there since the baby came. This was obviously Lorraine's department. I told Lua to get the mother in out of the wind; I would be back with the other witchdoctor.

The wind blew my beating head and screaming ribs into the hut, where Lorraine lay curled with her knees to her chin. She was awake but didn't move. "Lorraine, how are you feeling?" She murmured something I didn't understand, and I knelt down beside her. "What's happening with the diarrhea?" I asked, not liking the looks of her.

"I believe it to be a standoff," she answered. "The more water I drink, the more diarrhea I have."

"So then, are you better or worse?"

"I am worse. I was unable to sleep in your absence, of course." She looked up at me as if to say, "I told you so." I rolled my eyes at her, and she said, "No, it was a good thing. I lay here alone long enough to come to terms with my life, which I suppose is what people do, wait until the end to deal with realities."

I sat back and crossed my legs, spying her diarrhea pills next to the water gourd. The bottle was still half full. I popped a couple along with two more aspirin, wincing at the taste. "Okay, I'm ready. What are the realities you face now that you're at the end of your life?"

Still curled on her side, she hadn't moved. "Firstly," she said, with her signature sigh, "that I and I alone have caused not only the premature end to my life, but of yours and Kali's as well." She was not only sick, she was pathetic. "Secondly," she said, in a coarse whisper, "my entire life's work has been a dismal failure."

"Okay, Lorraine," I said, getting to my feet. "That may all be true, but right now, here at the end, you have work to do. Who knows, maybe it will redeem you somehow. Now get up and come with me."

"I am going nowhere," she stated flatly. "I have decided that this is the place I shall die. I have the right to . . ."

"No, you don't!" I exclaimed over the goddamn gusting wind. "You don't have one single, bloody right! You're at the mercy of the people who saved you. Now get your butt up, and let's go have a look at that girl. She says she's in pain, her pelvis. That's your department."

She sat up, alarmed. "What do you mean, my department?"

"Just that. You're the doctor. Now let's go!" She didn't say anything and she didn't move. "Lorraine, I'm warning you. If you're not out of this hut in one minute, I will drag you all the way over there, which I'm sure will amuse the Turkana!" She got up slowly, watching me as if I might jump her, and I might have. Out into the blast of heat we stumbled, pulling the necks of our shirts up over our faces, the wounded to the rescue of the wounded.

On our knees, we crawled inside the squat hut, the stench watering our raw eyes. Lua was speaking with authority to the three young women—girls somewhere between thirteen and eighteen—who were feeding the mother bites of dried fish. It was the first time I'd really looked at these girls in the light of day. Their colorful ornamentation was typically Turkana, rows of stacked beads made from seeds, as many as fifty, from the top of their breasts to the bottom of their chin. Their heads were shaved up to a plot of plaited hair, just like Lua's. The area between their breasts and navels was scarified. Several children, hunkered on the reeds, were decorated in the same manner, less a few beads and the scars. The girls sat in a squat, knees to shoulders, their long legs separated by their arms, bare breasts, and leather skirts. Lua's modest fashion, by comparison—just a row of simple beads, her pouches, and boots—appointed her as someone special, an assistant witchdoctor with obvious influence. She made a motion with her fingers and barked instructions. Everyone left except the mother, Lua, Lorraine, and me.

"Okay, Doc," I said. "See what's causing this girl's pelvic pain. It must be the source of her fever, don't you think?"

Lorraine was still on her hands and knees. Her eyes, red and watering, protruded from her round, scaly brown head. In a grating voice, she said, "These women are terrifying."

"Next to us, Doc, they're beautiful. Now get to work."

She didn't move; only her bulging eyes traced the anxious mother and suckling baby. "Please, Kelly," she whined. "I cannot do anything for her."

"Goddamn you, Lorraine! Examine this girl or I'll stick my boot up your ass!" Lua and the mother, alarmed at my tone, lowered their heads and stared up at me like scolded children. "Lorraine, I'm dead serious. Perhaps you don't understand our predicament; it's more than our tits in the ringer here."

"Kelly, I have been here the entire time and know precisely our predicament." She sat back on her butt, frail hands on her skinny legs, palms up, her wet eyes on me. "It is my cross, our being here, one that I will carry through the fires of hell. Please forgive me."

"You are pathetic. As a doctor, as a woman, you . . ."

"Kelly, I am not a medical doctor."

"Excuse me! You're not . . ."

"I have a doctorate in human behavioral research." Her round head fell between her shoulders.

"You're a shrink!"

"In a manner of speaking. I was certain that you would call me that."

Confused and furious, acutely aware of the alarm on the faces of Lua and the mother, I asked as calmly as possible, "And why did you lead me to believe otherwise?"

Her longest goddamn sigh. "My expertise being human behavior, I knew the moment I met you that you would never respect a . . . shrink." She closed her eyes. "I needed your respect in order to find Kali, and therefore I allowed you to believe that I was a medical doctor. If you had not believed me, you might not have eaten or drunk the foul . . . shit to survive."

"Jesus, you are a trip!" I wasn't finished with her, a dozen questions coming to mind, but the mother and Lua were growing conspicuously anxious. "Okay, Doc." I mustered my most sinister smile. "You and I are going to lift this girl's skirt and see if we can tell what the hell is going on."

"Dear God," she whispered.

Lua removed the goat hide from the poor girl, then pulled up her skirt, spread her legs, and propped up her knees. Trying to suppress anger, trying to ignore the stabbing pain in my ribs, I got on my belly between her legs, motioning for Lorraine to get down there too. She leaned over the girl's leg and peered squeamishly at her private parts, or what could be made of them. They were swollen beyond belief, fiery red, and reeked with the smell of infection. "Jesus," I said. "Dear God," Lorraine whispered again. Some of the area was yellow and looked like pus. I put my fingers to it, confirming that it was. The girl flinched. I told her I was sorry and sat up to face Lua.

When I was through questioning Lua, my suspicions were more or less confirmed. The girl had been circumcised—her clitoris removed—and then immediately was married and became pregnant; my guess was not necessarily in that order. The circumcision hadn't healed properly, and she'd had a premature birth; the birth tore open the wound and it became infected. I told Lorraine. Surprisingly, she was matter-of-fact. Kali had told her of the horrors resulting from the African tribal tradition of circumcising girls. I asked Lua about the husband. She said that he was presently with another wife in an encampment to the south. I crawled out of the hut and went to the reeds trembling, nausea and diarrhea overcoming me.

At the lake, I prepared more penicillin and aspirin in a gourd. When the magic was administered, I gave instructions to Lua and the girls that the mother would have to be washed in lake water three times a day. My spirit felt spent, but I had one more thing to do. I asked Lua to take us to the children Kali had saved. She didn't think it was a good idea, but I convinced her that Kali would want us to follow up, make sure that her magic was continuing.

The two naked boys, about six and eight years old, were playing by the lake with sticks, their bandages nearly unrecognizable as such. Lua, shouting over the wind, told them what we wanted, and they ran like hell back to their hut, round butts bouncing. We followed, and somehow Lua talked their reluctant mother into letting us remove the bandages and see the wounds. Both boys had jagged deep cuts on their left legs. Kali had sewn them up, and aside from the dirt, they looked okay, I guessed. I slathered the ointments on the stitches, not knowing what else to do, and wrapped their legs back up in clean bandages. I asked how they'd been cut so badly and watched the nervous mother tell about the boys' bad luck falling on sharp lava rocks.

Playing doctor had sickened me in body and spirit. Diarrhea sapped me. I felt finished. Back in our hut, just before I crashed, I told Lorraine that she was responsible for the next batch of penicillin to the mother. I put myself to sleep, exhausted and depressed beyond the limits of my experience. Occasionally, I would wake, flooded with thoughts I couldn't handle, then retreat back into my subconscious. I was done. The dull thud in my head was in sync with my pulse, and that's as far as my consciousness could go. Whatever was, was. The girl with a pussy of pus who'd had her last good time months ago was not my problem. Whatever happened to those little boys was their fate. Whether Lorraine was a doctor or a whore was of no consequence. Kali was dead somewhere, and I wasn't responsible. Lua came and went, and I didn't give a shit. Lorraine sobbed. Good. I was done.

Lorraine was shaking me. "Kelly, they are everywhere! Kelly, wake up! Something horrid is happening! There are people here, a great number of savage people!" I sat straight up, my first impulse to punch her. She had her scaly, bald round head in my face, her bright blue eyes bulging. "Kelly, something very important is going on! There are men with feathers and capes and big ivory plates in their noses and lips! Bloody hell, Kelly, what does it mean?"

I was shaking myself, trying to focus, when Lua came in jabbering. The Turkanas had sent for other members of their clan, their extended family. Apparently they had done so the first day we were there. Today, they arrived. They brought two witchdoctors. There was to be a big ceremony of witchdoctors, including us. It would begin immediately. The dancers were doing the last-minute things to their hair. We should come and take our place.

I couldn't see how any of this concerned me. I wasn't up for a ceremony, and I was fresh out of magic. The wind, howling sweet as my grandmother, beckoned me back into sleep. I returned to my position, and over the sounds of Lorraine futilely barking instructions at Lua, I drifted off.

And there she was again, Lua, with fish and water, Lorraine still barking. "Kelly, you haven't eaten today! You must eat and drink! Here, sit up and eat!"

"Or what, Doc?"

"Or you will be sick, more sick! You need strength!"

"For what, Doc?"

"For them!" She was jabbing a thumb over her shoulder.

I thought about it. I sat up. I ate. I drank. Lorraine gave me diarrhea pills. There was no way out. This was going to be another really bad time. I got up and walked out of the hut, blasted sideways by the wind, Lorraine and Lua on either side.

There they were, a large semicircle of Turkana in all their finery. A structure of skins, sticks, and straw had been constructed as a wind-break behind them. If my white feather count was right, there were fifteen warriors with plaited leather armbands and cicatrized bodies, most with ivory implanted in their face somewhere. They all sat on their squat little stools wearing dark capes of cloth tied around their necks. Their hair was slicked back in dung caps, and cloth headbands held the ostrich feathers in place. Spears and shields rested by their sides, knives hung from their waists. There were a few women at one end of the semicircle, probably favorite wives. They, too, were decked to the hilt. At the other end there were two men with lots of ivory around their necks and animal skins on their shoulders—our colleagues, no doubt.

The three of us approached the circle, Lua instructing us to sit next to the well-adorned witchdoctors. We did as we were told, planting ourselves right there in the wind-slicked dirt and scalding sun, Lorraine in filthy khaki shorts and what was left of a black T-shirt, I in filthy khaki long pants and what was once a green T-shirt.

"What do you think we look like to them?" Lorraine whispered. She answered herself. "Considering your black mask and my head, probably aliens."

I said, "They don't know about aliens yet, and in fact, neither do we."

"Then why is not one person making eye contact with us, not even these voodoo gentlemen next to us?"

"That's the Turkana way. They want us to know they're superior, that they don't need us."

"Then why do they want us to do magic?"

"They won't want it. They will demand it!"

A line of nubile girls had formed—the dancers, all smiles and giggles. They walked out in front of us straight and proud, and with no downbeat or cue, began jumping up and down, their breasts rising and falling like jellyfish. There was no music, no drums, no rhythm, just jumping. A short stack of dried fish carried by a small, naked boy was presented to one of the warriors; probably some trading was going on. Several women sat off to the side behind dozens of small pots filled with seeds. Alongside them, cowhides and decorated gourds were stacked in piles. The warriors conversed, told stories using all their "he he" sounds and all their body parts, laughing a great deal and occasionally looking at the dancers.

Beyond the festivities, there were children playing on the beach, their mothers watching from the huts. The sick mother's hut looked abandoned, but I knew she and her baby were there, probably wondering if the witchdoctors' magic would save her from death, probably wishing she were one of the dancers and mourning her lost youth. Past the huts there were a number of camels and donkeys, all lying down out of the wind. If I could have made it to the camels, I would have. I would have stood up, climbed on one of those camels, and rode away, damn the consequences. But I didn't have the energy to get to a camel, much less get on one, and with every minute that passed, the sun melted me further into the dirt. I was considering going back to the hut; it didn't look so far away, and anything would be better than watching the girls jump and jump and jump.

The girls finally stopped and wandered off, their part finished. The warriors began jabbering in earnest, about important business, clan business. I heard the word *Ngorokos* many times, spoken in conjunction with camels and cows, which probably translated to rustling. They devoted a great deal of time talking about a donkey. I didn't care. The sun swirled my vision and distorted my brain. One of the dancers, a girl of about thirteen, was brought out by an old woman with stringy tits and presented to a young warrior. He had bloody cicatrices on his chest and wore a white ostrich feather. Lua was jabbering. He had killed Ngorokos, the ones that attacked us. He had earned the right to take his first wife, this shy girl, no doubt recently circumcised.

It was time for the witchdoctors. The one next to me stood up, dramatically threw off the skin that was over his shoulder, and presented himself in front of the warriors. Taking a pouch from his waist belt, he pulled out some sticks and stones and then knelt down and carved a circle in the dirt with his knife. Over and over he tossed the stones into the circle, each time moaning and murmuring, the audience hanging on his every sound. I watched the stones, falling, bouncing, falling, bouncing. Dizzy, melting, I closed my eyes, but when I opened them, the swirling was still out of control. I changed my focus. I looked at Lorraine, studied the long crinkles of brown skin circling her bright blue eyes. In a moment, she turned her face toward me, and without changing a crinkle asked, "What does it mean?"

I had missed something. The witchdoctor was poised in front of Lorraine and me, a shadow against the sun. As clearly as I could tell, his legs were spread, his arms extended and his hands bent back. I asked Lorraine, "So, what'd he do?"

Barely audible, she said, "He spat at us."

Tired of his pose, or maybe aware that I'd missed his statement, he spat again, the potent-smelling brown spittle landing at my boots. He resumed his pose. I turned my head from him and the smell, nodding for Lorraine to do likewise. The three of us remained in our contrary positions until the whispers from the audience turned to jabbering, and the witchdoctor resumed his seat next to me.

"What does it mean?" Lorraine whispered again.

"He spat ekeriau, a smelly root to keep away danger and enemies."

"Does that mean we are enemies?"

"Probably."

"They seem to be anticipating something from us, Kelly. It must be our turn. We have nothing to throw in the circle he made, not a stone, even a stick. I think we should have come better prepared." Lorraine's whisper had a tremble.

I got to my feet, the motion in my head moving faster than my body, strength coming in short waves timed with the banging in my head. Focusing on the feather nearest me, I began addressing the warriors in English. I told them how grateful we were, how we appreciated the fish, how much we loved the dancing, and that now we were ready to go home and we needed a couple of camels, for which they would be paid. It was not until I took a break to widen my stance, steadying myself, that I comprehended their blank faces.

"Jesus," I said, "I forgot, we need Lua to translate. Lua, get up here and help me out." Motioning for her, I nearly toppled myself, again looking longingly toward the hut. Lua stood up tentatively, and I began arduously trying to make her understand what I wanted to say. She was not a willing participant, or maybe she didn't approve of my choice of words, or perhaps my speech was as blurred as my vision. It was becoming difficult for me to remain vertical. At some point in the translation, about the time I was telling them that we needed two camels, I felt a hand on my leg. It was Lorraine's. She had reached up under my pant leg and was trying to steady me.

Finally, I finished. I couldn't think of anything else that I wanted to say badly enough to stand there another second. I motioned for Lorraine to get up. She did. Hanging on to me nervously, she reached into her pocket and pulled out her red comb. Flamboyantly, she tossed the comb into the witchdoctors' circle. There was some gasping. We plodded off, hanging on to each other, listing into the wind.

I suppose that I was asleep even before I was horizontal, but I do remember Lorraine stuffing more diarrhea pills in my mouth. Images of white feathers and nubile girls dancing with their infected pussies hideously exposed and witchdoctors spitting in my face were probably just dreams. I remember Lorraine barking, many times it seemed. I remember swallowing fish, much more than I wanted. I remember the dark, the Turkana voices jabbering and laughing. But that's about all, until morning.

"Kelly! Kelly, please, please wake up! Dear God, please, Kelly! What does it mean? Bloody hell, what will become of us now?" I could feel Lorraine lying next to me. She put an arm over me and snuggled close. She was sobbing.

"What?" I asked, surprised to hear my own voice.

"Kelly!" she said, sitting up. "Oh thank God! Can you hear me?"

"I haven't heard anything else in years."

"They have gone! They have simply disappeared! Lua too! You must look. Can you get up?"

"Of course I can get up." It wasn't that easy. I crawled to the entrance. Blinking against the morning sun and wind, I looked where Lorraine was pointing, at nothing. There was nothing there, not a single hut, person, child, drying fish, donkey, or camel—nothing. The entire encampment had moved. "They do this sort of thing," I said, crawling back inside. Lorraine lay down beside me, her arm over me again, whimpering. I went back to sleep.

Someone was jabbering, a woman. Lua. I rolled over and opened my eyes as Lorraine was sitting up. "Lua!" she exclaimed. "Lua, you did not abandon us."

Lua sat down and began talking to me, something about food. She took off the leather pouch and pulled out a chunk of dried fish. She wanted me to understand that it was the only food she'd been able to steal. They'd left nothing, not even a gourd. Then she dug into the pouch again and excitedly, bit by bit, pulled out a long piece of string. The string was attached to a crude fishing hook. That's where she'd been, combing the shoreline for just that, some way to feed us.

I patted her on the shoulder and told her that we should eat the fish now, celebrate the fact that we were still above ground, even this ground. The goddamn Turkana had gone without killing us, which seemed to me a reason for a memorial breakfast, or perhaps a last supper. Either way, it didn't seem important, nothing did. Lorraine divided the fish, giving me the biggest piece, justified, she said, because I was the weakest and the tallest. We ate in silence, until Lorraine asked a whining question. "Why did they leave, Kelly? Do you think it could have possibly been because I threw my comb in the circle? Does Lua know?"

I chewed weakly on a bite of fish and then answered. "It was their way of saying they didn't trust us. They did this to Teleki. They've done it to missionaries, to government people. They just leave in the night, the ultimate snub."

"The way Kali did?" she asked, timidly.

"Maybe," I said.

She scowled, saying that it didn't sound logical. When I reminded her that logic was not logical here, she said, "Kelly, you are very sunburned, from yesterday, and your voice is faint, weak. Perhaps you should refrain from talk until you have had food and have rested."

"I believe I've been resting," I scoffed. "Maybe this is as good as I'm going to be."

She was still scowling at me. "Okay then. Who is Teleki?"

"Teleki, an Austrian explorer, the first white here. He named the lake, Rudolf, after Austria's Prince Rudolf."

"Yes, Lake Rudolf. That is the name the English still use."

"Rudolf wasn't pleased. The lake was described to him as a hell never before imagined on the planet. He killed himself a year later." Lorraine rolled her eyes, disbelieving. I did a steadfast nod. "It's true.

However, he may have had more insults than this lake. He also shot his girlfriend in the head."

"Ask Lua," she said.

"About Rudolf?"

"No," she said, impatient. "About why the Turkana left without a word."

It took a while, probably because I had difficulty sustaining interest. Lua's response was stern, a bit reprimanding. The Turkana weren't convinced that we were good witchdoctors, even though she herself was still a believer. They didn't trust us. We may have been from the government, English, although she was sure they'd never seen the English before. Also, there were too many crocodiles here now. They had lost a cow last week and yesterday the donkey disappeared.

"So that's what happened to the donkey." I lay back, too weak to sit. "Jesus, that was close!"

"What about the donkey?" Lorraine demanded.

I told her and she shrieked, "Crocodiles! There are crocodiles here?" Reminding her that Lake Turkana had the largest concentration of Nile crocodiles in the world, I had to admit that I hadn't given them any thought until now, but I should have. Lorraine wailed, "My God, that poor donkey!"

"The beast you hated?"

"Even a beast should not have to die by a crocodile," she said sadly. Then she remembered our bath in the lake. "We could have been eaten!" she exclaimed. I waited, knowing what was coming next. Her face seemingly cracked into a million pieces, her eyes flooded. She whispered, "My God, Kelly. Is that what happened to Kali?"

"Not unless she took all her things and a camel into the lake with her," I said, with all the assurance I could muster. "Lua said that the only thing she left was her magic pouch. Remember, that's how Lua knows she's coming back, probably the reason Lua stayed with us."

She swallowed hard. "That is true. Kali certainly would not have taken her baskets and gourds, her clothes, everything she owned into the lake for a bath, certainly not a camel."

"Surely not," I agreed, wondering if it was worse to be torn to bits and eaten by a huge Nile crocodile, or be cut up by Ngorokos.

Lua was telling me something else, which took me a while to comprehend. Although it wasn't a surprise, I loathed to hear it. The mother of the boys had lied to us. The boys had actually been with their father when he was killing a crocodile. It didn't go well, and the crocodile had struck at the children, gashing them. I knew the Turkana attached shame to eating crocs, but they did it because it beat starving. I'd heard it said there were places on Lake Turkana where the principal diet of man was crocs, and the principal diet of crocs was man. I didn't like to believe it, but starvation as it was happening at that moment, as it had happened many times through the centuries, made strange dinnermates for all the animals of Turkanaland.

Lorraine had been caught up in her own thoughts while Lua told me about the boys. I decided that she really didn't want or need to hear it. She was doing some of her short, quiet sighs before she asked, "Kelly, what about that poor girl, the mother? What do you think will happen to her?"

"I don't know, Doc. What do you think?"

Her eyes filled again, and she bit her lip. "I think she will die, as many girls do, according to Kali."

Lua wanted to go fishing. She told me sternly that if we didn't catch a fish, we wouldn't eat. She stuck out her well-defined chin and made it clear that because we didn't have a boat, and because of the crocodiles, it would take two of us, one to watch and one to fish. Lorraine, pretending to be a real doctor again, said that she would watch, because I had to stay in and rest. She also insisted, "Before we go, we must drink. We have had no water today, and there are no gourds, except the chamber pot." Shuddering, she cocked her head at me. "You will have to make it to the lake."

I did, but it wasn't easy. Maybe it was true that this was as good as it was going to be. The three of us lay sucking the soda water into our mouths, probably thinking the same thoughts. If we didn't catch a fish on the string and crude hook, we would die of starvation, just as hundreds of Turkanas were dying right then somewhere in Turkanaland. For whatever reason, physical or mental, surviving wasn't as important to me as it should have been.

I agreed to stay in only if we could make Lorraine a hat. Lua took her knife from her belt and was off to cut reeds. It didn't take long, or didn't seem to. Lorraine and I were tying the truck key on the fishing line as a lure, when Lua came in piling the reeds around us. Lorraine and I wanted to help, but Lua's fingers were a blur, weaving the reeds into a cone, occasionally fitting it to Lorraine's head. We braided two straps to hold it on in the wind, one from the front and one from the back. Lorraine agreed to cover the exposed parts of her legs with mud. Like a den mother, I lectured them about crocodiles, as though I knew something, and they were off.

Surrounded by reeds and no place to go, I decided to make a fish trap. I was less motivated than I cared admitting to myself and completely without experience. Fighting dizziness, struggling with the weaving, trying to remember Lua's flying fingers, and matching the notes of the wind to songs of my own, I felt like a retard in a cell. Finally, I figured out how to do it, crudely, but it was a while before I had what looked like a long, loosely woven basket. Somewhere, I'd seen traps that fish swam into and couldn't turn around and get out of, but there had probably been bait involved. The best I could hope for was a careless fish.

The trap was nearly finished when the women returned. They hadn't caught or even seen a fish. With her legs covered in dried mud and crowned with her reed hat, Lorraine resembled an Asian refugee. She held up her red comb. They had found it exactly where she'd tossed it into the circle. Lua was dejected, a mood I'd not seen her wear before. Hungry and exhausted, they were asleep within minutes. I slept, too, the wind a satanic lullaby.

When I woke, the sun was low. Lorraine was still conked out, and Lua was examining the fish trap. She knew exactly what it was and how to finish it, and she did so within minutes. Lorraine woke while we were in the middle of discussing how far out in the lake the trap needed to be and, the most difficult part, how the hell we were going to get it there. The lake was probably shallow enough to walk as far as we needed to go, but the big concern, of course, was the crocs. We agreed to set the trap immediately and that it would take all three of us. As fast as our fingers would work, we braided a long line from which to secure the trap to shore.

Lorraine daubed more mud on her legs and a bit on my sunburned face, Lua laughing. I walked between them, both of them holding on to me, bracing against the wind gusts. Lua pointed north. She had seen big fish taken close to the shore, beyond where the huts had been. We plodded on. Reaching the pile of reeking fish skeletons, Lorraine was encouraged. "One of these enormous fish would feed us for a week," she said. Then she peered at me from under her hat and said, "A week! Can we live another week in this bloody hell?" I reminded her that she'd asked that question before.

We continued on and not far before encountering another vile smell. At first we didn't see anything, and then Lua pointed into the reeds. Approaching cautiously, she parted the reeds enough for us to see the carcasses of several large crocodiles, hidden there in shame. We didn't talk about it. The stench was too strong for us to linger, and crocs or not, we had to set our trap.

The sun was near the horizon, and at last we reached a clearing in the reeds where Lua was sure there would be fish offshore. We approached the shoreline with trepidation and stood there scouring the water for demonic eyes. The clearing looked safe, but it was difficult to know with the last of the day's wind rippling the surface. It was time to decide who would walk the trap out. Lua wanted to do it. The best I could understand was that she thought Lorraine was too old and I was too weak. If we were going to eat, she had to be the one to set the trap. She took off her precious boots. I told her she was brave like a warrior. She liked that, and I sure as hell meant it.

The sun was touching the horizon, and the wind was dying. Lorraine and I hung on to the end of the braided line. If we saw eyes coming, or a smooth streak, we would yell at Lua. I tried to communicate that to her, but she was on her way. She was quick! Running in the water, she was to her thighs before she slowed. She held the trap over her head and kept going. Lorraine and I, our eyes racing over the water back and forth and beyond, held our breath. My heart and head pounded. Lorraine squeaked. Lua was to her neck, and we were nearly out of line. I yelled at her, and she pushed the trap underwater, holding it, letting the reeds soak and sink. It seemed to take forever. Finally, she was on her way back, holding on to the line. Faster and faster she came toward us, her knees rising above the water, then her feet kicking water behind her. Then she was in our arms. We flung ourselves at the shore and fell into a heap, gasping, laughing. In a moment, Lorraine was sobbing.

We walked back in the dark, far from the shore, silent. It was deadly quiet after the wind. We hung on to each other, exhausted, heads dizzy with hunger, three women sucked into a black hole together.

Sometime in the night, Lorraine came crawling out of the hut to join me. Yawning, she said, "I cannot sleep no matter how many sheep I count."

"Yes," I agreed, "I'm having the same problem. We need food. I'm sure there's a fish in the trap, just waiting for us. Tomorrow will be better."

She struggled into a sitting position beside me. "Kelly, if we do get out of this, will you ever forgive me?"

"Probably not, not either of us." I tried a smile and patted her knee. "At least I'm being paid. You're just here out of . . ."

"Love, love of my dear . . ." She stopped, her voice a tremor. I gave her another pat. She cleared her throat and said, "Roger said that you are well paid; however, no payment could make up for what you have been through."

"Roger," I growled, too weak to hate him. Lorraine laid her head on my shoulder. Talking always seemed to make her better, so I asked, "Our little boy Roger, with the traits of his Jezebel mother?"

"He should have been my son," she said. "But then, of course, he would have my traits and not hers."

"So, Gil Birla was your lover too?"

A long sigh. "Yes. Three months before we were to be married, his family sent him to Kenya to take care of a business problem. Of course, she was there, and that was that."

"But after a few years, he's back on your doorstep with the kid."

"Yes, but he was changed, caught up in another world, already very much involved in the revolution shaping in Kenya."

She sat there quietly for a while, her head still on my shoulder. The bits and pieces of her story had hooked me, and in our physical and mental state, I thought it better for both of us if she kept talking. "Okay, Lorraine, don't leave me hanging. So Gil dumped the kid on you and went back to fight the English."

"No, no, he took Roger with him. He only sent Roger to me periodically, for a rest, to fatten him up, but Roger hated being away from his father and was always anxious to return. Gil came a few times for a rest, always gaunt, war weary." She paused to groan. "Of course, I always tried to talk sense into Gil, but he was committed to revenge, revenge on the English, his English bride. You can imagine how committed, living with a child in places like Lodwar." Another groan. "Lodwar was where he met Kali, but I told you that, did I not?"

"Yes, let's see, you said that when they took Kenyatta from Lokitaung to Lodwar, Kali went with him. She was thirteen. She became Gil Birla's right-hand girl."

"Yes, that is exactly what she was." She raised her head off my shoulder to look at me. "And of course, Roger was there most of the time, only a year between them in age. They were thrown together like brother and sister, both of them acting as Gil's aides and depending on one another for the needs of children."

"And when Kenyatta was released, they both came to live with you? Why?"

"Because Gil became ill. He had a gunshot wound that didn't heal, became infected, and he was bedridden in some godforsaken place across the border in Tanzania, Roger and Kali with him." She shuddered, shaking off the thought. "Somehow, through one of his men, he made arrangements to send both of the children to me. He also transferred a great deal of money to me, and in addition he set up a life-estate for them, Kali too. In fact, Kali's estate was much larger than Roger's."

"Why? Why would he do that?"

"Kali meant a great deal to him." Her voice broke, tears on the way. "He knew Roger would inherit the bulk of the Birla empire, and Kali would only have what he gave her."

"But whatever the money arrangements, he just assumed you'd take care of them?"

She began to weep. "He died alone, far away, in a place no one had heard of. He sent me a letter just before he died, had it delivered to me by one of his men." Wiping her nose on the back of her hand, she managed to continue through her sobs. "It was only a few lines. He just said that if he had been any man at all, he would have married me and never gone to Kenya. He deemed his life a failure and a waste of time, and he was sorry he had depended on me so heavily." She had her head in her hands, crying out loud now.

I put my arm around her. The best I could say was, "You must have really loved him."

She quieted down, and in a moment she said, "It is so completely ironic that my life, so very different from Gil's . . . and now I am to die as he did, in a desolate faraway land, alone."

"Come on, Doc, we're not dead yet, and you're not alone. Lua and I are here, and we're going to make a go of it. Isn't that what you

English say, we'll make a go of it, and pip pip, something like that?" She didn't say anything else, just sniffled for a while and then crawled back into the hut, leaving me there alone, dizzy, hungry, and sick, pondering her last words.

I woke, still hunkered at the entrance. My head was swimming, pounding out of sync. I pushed the light button on my watch and struggled to make out the hands, forgetting that it didn't work. The moon was low on the horizon, the sky looked like dawn was imminent. Time was running out, and the less I had the less I seemed to care. A fish in the trap was the only thing that could save us. The trap seemed far away, but later it would surely seem much farther and less important. I got to my feet and plodded off on a wobbly course, wishing we had put the trap closer. Visibility was poor, but all I needed to do was keep the lake on the right and stay away from the reeds.

The next thing I remember was the sun, a fire blowing toward me to the sound of drums in my head. Lorraine was there, barking from under her hat, pulling on my arms. Over the drums and the wind, Lua was shouting. What was she shouting about? Something about food! I got to my hands and knees, and there she was, pulling the braided line, the trap dragging behind her. Lorraine shrieked and clapped. We would eat! I wanted to shout, too. I tried, but there was no sound. Lorraine kept shrieking, now at me. I had to get out of the sun and wind. I had to make it back to the hut. Why had I come out there alone? Jesus, I hated her barking! Lorraine was a bitch dog. Each time I tried to lie down, she was on me, snapping and yapping, yanking, growling, tugging on my limbs. I hated her all the way back to the shack, the three of us dragging ourselves and a huge Nile perch in a reed trap.

Lua cut a chunk off the fish and we passed it around, ceremonially eating from it, raw, loathing it. Lorraine's hands and mine trembled with hunger. Then Lua dumped everything out of her big leather pouch and took it down to the lake and filled it with water. When we couldn't drink anymore, she dragged the fish off to clean it and hang it to dry. It would feed us for several days, she thought, and by then we would have another one dried. Jesus, I hoped that would be true. I hated raw fish, even sushi, and God knows what kind of parasites live in ancient perch. I thought about the parasites for a while, then decided that under the circumstances, parasites were a funny thing to think about.

While Lua was working her butt off out there in the inferno taking care of our food, I rifled the contents of the pouch that she'd dumped in a pile. Maybe whatever she'd used to encircle the truck had been hiding deep in the bottom of the pouch, although if it had been a substance, she'd probably used it all. Disappointed, I found nothing new. Digging into my pocket for the ointments I'd used on the boys, I returned them to their plastic box. Reasoning that Lua couldn't see inside the aspirin tin and that she'd probably never open it, I popped a few and dumped the remains in my pocket. I held the morphine bottle up to Lorraine as a question, and she answered, "Why not?" I tapped out several, and she stuck them in her pocket, saying, "Only a precaution, mind you. I feel certain that we are going to survive . . . right, Kelly?" I gave her what I wanted to be a smile, but my goddamn banging head twisted it into something else. "Kelly, you do agree we are going to survive; I know you do!"

"Glucose!" I exclaimed, holding up the glistening clear bottle of liquid. "Jesus, shouldn't we be injecting this stuff?" She crinkled her eyes, thinking about it. I did, too, and quickly decided I wasn't capable of injecting myself, and now that Lorraine wasn't a doctor, she couldn't do it. "We could drink it," I blurted. "Sugar would be exciting in the mouth and probably do us some good, but we should probably ration it, take a little at a time, the way they drip it into your veins in the hospital."

Lorraine was still thinking, probably about the consequences of Lua's knowing we'd pilfered Kali's magic, but her eyes were starting to sparkle mischievously. Slyly, she said, "We would have to keep the bottle, hide it." Her eyes darted back and forth between the crystal bottle and me as though I were holding the stolen jewels. She was becoming excited about the prospects of the glucose, something sweet and hopeful to taste, or perhaps it was the camaraderie of doing something clandestine. Excitedly she said, "Perhaps she won't put the things back in the pouch, the pouch being the only way we have to carry water, except this other empty glucose jar, which she has not thought of . . . and neither have we." She giggled.

I already had my knife out, prying off the top, Lorraine's hands hovering. Our mental states deteriorating, we were like two children who had been punished and confined, in this case condemned to death. The glucose was something tangible, a crystal ball in which to look for hope, however make-believe. I held it in front of us. The wind gusted. Lorraine's bright eyes glowed. I put it to my lips for a short sip, then handed it to her. She took it in both hands and put it to her mouth slowly, a potion of magic, a possible cure for the incurable.

When I woke, Lua and Lorraine were sleeping. I was thirsty, very thirsty, and Lua's pouch was beside her, empty, the contents still in the pile. Struggling but able to make it to my feet, I took the pouch, braved the blast at the entrance, and nearly ran into our fish. Lua had hung it on a reed line to dry, secured by two piles of rocks on either side of the entrance. To get in or out of the hut, one had to go under the line. I assumed she had vultures in mind when she chose the location.

I pushed through the wind to our bath place and lay in the mud, ignoring the pain in my side. Protected somewhat from the wind, I drank and rinsed my face, cupping the water over my sore and swollen eyes and cheekbones. Letting the water become still, I hoped for a reflection. Just as my face was coming into focus, something moved. Eyes! Eyes coming toward me! I jumped to my feet, stumbling, falling, getting up again, running, stumbling. When I was a ways off the shore, I looked back, my heart racing. There was nothing but swirling water. The croc had disappeared completely.

Back inside the hut, I sat holding the empty pouch, waiting for Lorraine and Lua to wake, my heart still doing double time. Nothing quite like a crocodile to make one give a damn about living. In a few terrifying moments, I'd decided to start paying attention to staying alive. I remembered our frivolous bath and shivered, the brief pleasure it had given us now a chilling thought. We had used that clearing as though it were protected from more than the wind. It was Kali's bath, the bath of the witchdoctors. We'd been lucky, but maybe just some of us.

My crocodile incident seriously upset Lorraine. She lay on her side seemingly traumatized, her body curved against the reed wall, her bright eyes fixed on something in her mind. I knew she was thinking about Kali's disappearance with serious questions. Perhaps Goa had taken her things and all three camels after all. The people Lua questioned could have been wrong. Goa could have left the pouch because he wouldn't touch her magic. I'd chosen not to question Lua's theory, but now Lorraine was doing it for all of us. Lua, too, was in a heavy silence made mournful by the wind. They dragged me with them.

"Lorraine!" I exclaimed, startling both of them. "You left me hanging last night. "Roger and Kali had just been sent to live with you. How old were they then?"

There was quite a distance from my question to where Lorraine had been in her mind and it took her a minute or so to get to me. When she did, her voice was flat. "Kali was fifteen, Roger sixteen," she said, her face sour.

"So, tell me about it."

She sat up, reluctantly, and got herself into a rocking position, her arms wrapped around her knees. "They came wrapped in dirty blankets, both skinny and wild." Apparently thinking about how they looked, she stopped there. I said, "Yes?" and she went on. "I had to hire help to watch them, to keep them from wandering off, to keep them in clothes, to make them eat with utensils, to comb their hair, to take a bath." She paused, needing a few breaths. "It could not possibly have been more difficult if they had been chimpanzees." Her face had begun to crinkle, a smile in her eyes. "Every day was a new problem, another incident, behaviorally. They were wild, bright, and without social boundaries."

Talking about Kali certainly improved Lorraine's demeanor, but she was obviously growing weaker, sounding as frail as she looked. I kept her going. "But that's your field, isn't it, Doc, human behavior? Or were you doing that yet?"

"Oh yes, I was in my early forties by then, doing research for the institute I work for now. But of course I had never read, much less studied, anything the likes of what I was experiencing with Kali and Roger."

"You had no children of your own?"

"Oh my, no. I never married, never once even considered it after . . ." She scowled, crinkling everything above her shoulders.

"So Kali and Roger became . . . as your own children?"

She shook her head sadly; her words came slowly. "Kali and Roger never belonged to anyone except each other, and of course to the memory of their hero, Gil, whom they had celebrations for regularly, and huge memorials on his birthday. Their relationship was boisterous, noisy, and complete. They wanted the company of no one else, and when they had others' company, they did all that they could to end it as quickly as possible, even if it was a breach of social conduct." She sneered. "Social conduct was something they learned very slowly. To be completely frank . . ." She pause for a breath and a sigh. "I have no idea when they became lovers, but I am certain that it was long before they came to live with me."

"Really! Roger and Kali!" I thought about Roger in Lodwar, hostile, volatile, hapless, withdrawn, bolting out of Lodwar the minute we had the truck. I thought about Roger in other situations, with Kumlesh socially, when I'd done a job for him. It was difficult to imagine that even as a kid he could ever have been wild and happy.

Lorraine lay back on her side, nearly toppling over, resting her head on her arm. But in a few minutes she began again, slowly telling me that when the Birlas found out about Kali, a black girl living in the same house with Roger, they put Roger in boarding school, apparently creating even more passion for the intrepid couple, forcing them to meet secretly. Wanting to make Lorraine laugh, I told her the Birlas must have been having a cow, but she ignored me and went on talking with her eyes closed, so faintly that I could barely hear her over the wind. "It was difficult getting Kali through college. Coming from here," she said, a brief flit of her limp wrist, "directly to the Land of Oz, the United Kingdom of Oz, everything was possible, and she was easily lured away from her studies." I could imagine the difficulty, but Lorraine's weak voice sounded proud, and she went on bragging about the degree Kali finally obtained in psychology. Finally, working herself into a state of maudlin, she began to blubber.

"Lorraine, don't do that. Come on, goddamn it, sit up. I hate it when you do that." She managed to sit up again. I slapped at her knee, "Okay, when did the love affair end? Surely they didn't keep it up when Kali went into medical school?"

"No," she said flatly, "Kali did not go to medical school, and their relationship . . ."

"But Kali's a doctor, a medical doctor, surely."

"No." A satirical chuckle, and she fell again on her side. "Kali has the same doctorate that I have, and that did not come easily."

"Then what's she doing over here doling out medicine to the natives?"

"That is a very long story," she said, closing her eyes and burying her head again.

"No shit, Lorraine. This could be the longest story I've ever listened to. I feel like I've already earned an honorary degree in Kali."

Lua had gone out while we were talking and was back with water and more fish. We drank and ate and slept. The day, the wind, the heat droned on, but our lives, Lorraine's and mine, were beginning to sputter. Lua, by contrast, seemed unchanged. I'd seen enough people die slowly to know the symptoms. A few bites of fish a day wasn't enough to cure what had happened to us. The answer to Lorraine's repeated question "Can we live another week here?" was no.

That night the three of us sat in the dirt, next to the fish. The sky was brilliant with stars, but the moon wasn't up yet. At the entrance to our hut in an untracked part of deepest Africa, it was deadly quiet when Lorraine blurted out, "We are going to die here! Dear God, how could I have allowed Kali to work in this . . . prehistoric anachronism!" She startled Lua, causing her to jump up, glare at Lorraine, and wander off. I reminded Lorraine that we came here because this was where a caravan of Turkanas had seen Kali. Surely that would not be the last caravan to come this way. Sobbing, she reminded me what had happened when I'd asked the Turkanas who lived here for a ride. I thought about where I wanted to die, but I couldn't come up with any particular place that would give death significance. Where I died seemed irrelevant; it was when that disturbed me. I'd always seen my life as one picture, like the hieroglyphics on the walls of the tombs in Egypt, a continuing reel. The last part was the most important, the best, according to my grandmother.

Lorraine was still sobbing, weakly muttering something about dying. This was a woman I'd tried to kill, because I was responsible for her well-being. I supposed I still was. I had to turn her around. "Okay, Lorraine. There's something to be said for resolution, but are you ready for it? Are you ready to die?"

She looked up at the sky. "I have lost Kali. I believe I have lost my will to live."

"I don't buy that. You English are such heroes."

"Ha!" she exclaimed, choking herself. "Not heroes, not any of us. We women are steadfast, determined, but never heroes."

"Determined! Now that's the word I would use to describe you."

She coughed for a minute and went on blubbering. "And Englishmen are most certainly not heroes. They fight bloody battles in order to feed their enormous egos with ribbons and stories, much like the Turkana. They procreate to continue their lineage, their strongest instinct, much like the Turkana."

I encouraged her to keep talking, to tell me about her work, and she did a bit. She said that Kali became a major part of her research. The more she learned of the Turkana tribe through Kali, the more interested she became in the reasons primitive tribes defied evolution. I managed to plug in my theory about diet, the goddamn climate, and being slaughtered by whites, but she just nodded and went on talking about genetic cultural imprints and her own hypothesis of Kali's evolution, all of which I found almost as depressing as her lost will to live. Lua returned and went into the hut. I was looking for some finale to the evening, when Lorraine began sobbing again. "Kali has been the greatest gift of my life." I put my arm around her, and she dropped her brown, bald head on my shoulder. "I am truly sorry that you did not at least meet her," she wailed. "Everyone who meets her is captivated. Anyone who knows her personally belongs to her. I suppose she really is a witchdoctor, a very beautiful witchdoctor." That definitely sounded like a finale. I coaxed her inside, tripping over the dried fish. Lua had brought it in for the night.

When I woke, Lua was weaving sleeping pallets and looking as though she needed one. I lauded her work as well as her spirit, as best I could in my faulty Turkana, but she didn't look up. She was deep in thought, seemingly brooding, her hands a hypnotic blur. I watched, mesmerized, sitting cross-legged, listening to the changing octaves of the wind and matching the pitch just under my breath, as I had done frequently in my declining mental state. Whether it was a tic or abhorrent hut behavior, I had been taking lessons from the wind with the notion to perfect my howling, to best my grandmother. I visualized the contest, the two of us on Indian Hill, our backs straight, heads lifted. I remembered the look in her eyes, as though she were howling to something or someone far away.

Lorraine woke herself, talking in a dream. She sat up with a start and then lay back again, moaning. "I was having a nightmare. This one . . . reality." I glanced at her but wasn't ready to leave Indian Hill. "Kelly, Lua," Lorraine pleaded, gasping, "something is wrong with my breathing!" She was holding her diaphragm with the flat of her hand, her mouth hanging open.

Now she had my attention. "What, Doc? What's going on?"

Catching her breath sharply, she gasped. "The dream, waking, still in a nightmare . . . an enormous wave of depression came over me and . . ." She sucked in another quick breath. "I cannot seem to breathe normally."

"Look at me, Lorraine!" She did, her eyes blinking rapidly. "Good. Now close your eyes and take a very deep breath." She did. "Now release it." She did. "Now think about licking a strawberry ice cream cone." Flexing her scaly lips, then licking them, she began breathing normally, a slight smile creeping over her mouth. "Now, when I count to ten, you will open your eyes and count your blessings, which are Lua and me, good company, lots of fish to eat, no cooking, no beds to make."

She groaned and crossed her hands over her chest. "You are obviously feeling far better than I. I feel as though I am being hit in the stomach with hard waves of gloom."

"Warranted, considering the situation, wouldn't you say? But tonight, better dreams. Look at these sleeping pallets Lua has put together." Lua had glanced at Lorraine when she was gasping, not taking it seriously, but now she wanted my full attention. Her brooding had taken form, and she had something to say. She was up on her haunches. I wasn't at all sure that I had a translation in me. She began, slow and emphatic, her bony shoulders raising and falling with the intensity of the message. Fortunately, the message wasn't difficult to understand, although it was hard to answer. She wanted to be my assistant witchdoctor, Lorraine's too, if that was allowed.

I relayed the request to Lorraine. She said, "Why not? God knows we are desperate."

Lua was watching us anxiously, her eyes bright with hope. I couldn't think of a reason to disappoint her, but I did think of something I wanted. As well as I could, I put it to her. She could be our assistant if she would disclose the magic she used around the truck. Her reaction was quick and dramatic. She stuck her chin in the air, got up, and left the hut.

"What on earth did you say to her?" Lorraine demanded. Chagrined, I confessed. "Bloody hell! You simply must harass that poor girl until you have justification for nearly blowing us to bits!" Too weak for volume, she was clearly angry.

"I'm happy to see Lua has finally earned your concern, if not your respect," I retaliated, "but I can see you're still giving me none, not an inch!"

"Perhaps you should leave well enough alone. What if you discover that it was indeed Lua's magic that saved us?"

"Then I'm going into the goddamn witchdoctor business for real!" Struggling to my feet, I started after Lua. The wind stopped me at the entrance. I couldn't see where she'd gone, but the quivering in my knees told me I wasn't going after her. Crawling back inside, the real-ization of my physical condition came over me much as Lorraine's dream of reality had come over her. Resting my head on my knees, I covered it with my arms, relying on the wind to mute the angry fist pounding at my gut—anger, a profound symptom of the dying. Maybe this was our destiny and there was not a thing I could do about it. Even if a caravan came along and agreed to haul us out of there, we'd have to sit a camel, a donkey, or maybe a cow in the blis-tering wind and sun. I wasn't sure I could do that consciously, and being hauled like a sack of potatoes on broken ribs—well, I couldn't think about it

Lua was back. She brought fish and water, and while we nibbled, she began talking, her body exacting descriptions, her face sober and determined. Kali had given her the special magic that she'd used around the truck, the magic that kept the Ngorokos from attacking. She opened her blue bag and felt around for something, a large key. She said that there was no more magic until she returned to Lodwar, where Kali kept it in her special place. Holding up the key, signifying it was the key to the special place, she said that the magic surely wouldn't work for anyone but her and, of course, Kali. But if she could be our assistant, she would return to Lodwar and retrieve the magic. She put her head down, questioning her loyalty to Kali, I sup-posed. She was through talking. She was serious and sincere.

I announced her proposal to Lorraine. She clutched her throat and gasped. "Lodwar! Dear God, why do you torment her so? If you upset her enough to leave . . . we will die without her." The wind accented her point, and she crossed her arms defiantly. "Tell her she can be the head witch if she so desires."

"If she stays, Lorraine, it will only be to bury us, and then she'll leave. Do you care if you're buried?" Her face didn't crinkle, but she stared at me, her eyes bubbling over. I gave a concerned-looking Lua a nod, indicating that I was arguing in her favor, then studied the tears tracking over Lorraine's brown, leathered face. "I don't know where all your tears come from. Jesus, you have to be as dehydrated as I am."

She took a breath and closed her eyes, a solid brown, perfectly round, wet kiwi. "You have given up," she whispered. "You are resigned to die here. You ask that I stop crying and simply die without protest."

"Make up your mind. Last night you had lost your will to live."

"I cannot think! Not straight. My mind whirls around in circles. But if I think about dying, I cry. Is that unnatural?"

"Your mind whirls because you're dehydrated and slowly starving."

"And you? Do you believe that your mind is functioning better than mine?"

"Okay, Doc, it's fairly obvious that neither of us is in good shape. Now will you listen?" She grunted. "Lua is as strong as she ever was. She thrives on fish and foul water, and she's never known anything but heat and wind. She came here on foot in the middle of the night. She can get out of here the same way. If she can make it to the track that follows the lake south, someone will come along, maybe a government patrol. There's a chance we could be rescued."

"A chance. Turkanas are not going to rescue . . ."

"Not Turkanas! The government post at Lokitaung is manned by Kikuyu, remember? Sometimes they travel down the track by the lake to Ferguson's Gulf. Or she may be able to hitch a ride on a Turkana caravan to Ferguson's Gulf, where there will surely be someone from the government."

"So your intention is not to send her back to Lokitaung, and certainly not Lodwar?"

"No, she would need water. If she stays on the lake and travels south, she may encounter other fish camps, where she can sleep safely and she'll never be without water."

"How long will it take her to get to Ferguson's Gulf?"

"Jesus, Lorraine, it depends on all of the above. I can't see that far. Just think about it a while." I lay back on the reeds, tired of talking, my head swirling just as Lorraine had described. I thought about how far I could see, trying to visualize Lua's trek as far as Ferguson's Gulf. I saw my grandmother's eyes fixed on something far away, something she could see as clearly as I could see my own hand. Could she see the plan perking in my shriveled brain, a plan to dwell on, tread on, look to for the next minute, hour, and day, something on which to display a crystal ray of hope? I held up my hand, the wind a soprano note through quivering fingers. The wind changed keys, an alto now. I lifted my hand higher, stretching my shoulder, separating my ribs, ignoring the pain.

"Kelly, what the devil are you doing? Are you all right?"

"Never better. I think we've been spotted," I answered. She and Lua were both staring at me, Lua probably believing I was doing something magical. I asked her how much fish we had. She went to the entrance and brought it in, carrying it in front of her on outstretched arms. We talked about it, deciding that at the rate we were eating we had three days of food for the three of us. Lorraine, not sure what was going on, chipped out questions in her sharp English. I told Lua to put the fish back and give me a few minutes. I needed to convince Lorraine of a plan.

Lorraine's response was quick. "Dear God! Lua's going today, tonight? Kelly, I insist that we give this more thought."

"Okay, Lorraine, try hard to think logically!" I demanded, my voice breaking. "If Lua stays here, we have one chance of being rescued, someone stumbling on us who has livestock and is willing to haul us to safety. If Lua goes, we have two chances. For Lua, it's only a question of when she leaves. For us, it's how soon we're rescued."

She sat there looking at her frail outstretched legs, her scaly eyelids heavy, the corners of her mouth crinkling around her chin. I visualized being rescued, the helpless victim, a role I loathed to play. Finally, she looked up and asked suspiciously, "What makes you think that Lua will not just leave and forget us?"

"What was it you told me last night? Anyone who knew Kali, personally, belonged to her. Lua belongs to Kali. She wants to be Kali, she wants to be a witchdoctor and make miracles. She loves us because we're giving her that opportunity. She saved us once, and she'll do it again." I meant that to be final, a solid plan, but Lorraine kept chipping.

"Does Lua have the capability of making a government patrol

believe what she is telling them? The Kikuyu speak Swahili, do they not? Did you not tell me that Lua doesn't trust people who speak Swahili, that she considers them to be an inferior race?" I groaned, tired of her chipping, when she exclaimed, "Kelly! I have a thought. The labels to my prescription bottles, they are in my name with my address. That could help."

"Yes, yes it could!" I agreed, grateful at last for help.

From my dizzy perspective, Lorraine appeared finally to be on board, resigned to Lua's leaving, resigned to the plan. We made trips out with our plaguing diarrhea, but mostly we slept. When Lua came in to nap and rest for her journey, I moved to the entrance to accommodate my intestines. I was out of the sun, but it was at least 120 degrees. Too dehydrated for perspiration, I felt like a dried sponge, thirsty and useless. From my vantage point alongside our drying, frying fish, our bath place glistened green, a temptress of the devil, hypnotic and alluring. It was often referred to as The Jade Sea, an ancient jewel set in black lava. Scintillating, it seduced my thirst. Brilliant, it blinded my reason. I closed my eyes. It was still there, beckoning me. I was angry. I wanted a bath, wanted to be wet. Fuck the goddamn crocodiles! Barefoot, I made it onto my knees, taking off my pants and shirt. Dizziness paused me. I crawled back inside. Sitting in my underwear, I knew that I'd glimpsed insanity. I knew that Lua's leaving was our only chance.

The sun was very low when Lua woke with a smile. I envied her. I wanted to go with her, just as I had wanted to go with her when she left us at the truck. At that time, I could have made it. Now was a much later and different story. I began going over everything with her once more, showing her Lorraine's name on the prescription labels, making certain she had them tucked safely in her blue cloth bag. She looked so happy, as though leaving was funny, until I realized that she was amused because I still wasn't wearing my pants and shirt.

The sun was almost touching the horizon. Lua was ready, a stack of fish sufficient for three days in front of her. There was only one decision to make. Should she take the leather pouch or leave it? Logistics dictated that she take it. It was the only way to carry the fish. She took as much of Kali's magic as she could fit into her blue bag and left the rest with us for safekeeping. Lorraine and I helped her sort it out, keeping back the morphine and the glucose, including the empty bottle. I gave her my belt. She strutted around like Wonder Woman. I felt proud. We stood her in the center of the hut turning her around and around. It was a ceremony to give her praise and promote bravado, and to give Lorraine and me an opportunity to look at her, this woman about to risk her life once more for two pathetic white females. She smiled happily, the yellow stains on her teeth like gold. She was beautiful, a *warrioress*, her shoulders back, her chin high, her bare breasts full with courage. From the tassel of plaited hair on her crown, to the leather boots, this young woman of perhaps twenty-eight years was the bravest person I had ever known. I was reverent. I wanted to salute her, but I made it to my feet and gave her a hug. Lorraine was biting back sobs. We agreed, ceremonially, our hands piled together, that when we were all safely back in Lodwar there would be a celebration to make Lua a full-fledged witchdoctor. From the entrance to the hut, looking over the top of our fish, we watched our Lua, our heroine, disappear into the black Turkana night.

It wasn't long before Lorraine was boohooing. I tried to console her, but she was inconsolable. Standing there stargazing, battling the despair of our insignificance, our chance of survival, I remembered some words from Henry Longfellow, "a breath of more ethereal air." I reasoned something spiritual might help. Lorraine believed in a God, that of the Church of England, as I recalled. I didn't have any religious beliefs, but there were a few things that could lift my spirits to the heavens: fast horses, views from mountaintops, great symphonies, good sex, dancing, singing. Singing! "Lorraine, we can sing! I grew up singing." She ignored me. I tried a few bars of something and nearly collapsed. Singing took too much energy. The fist was back in my gut, anger. It was Lorraine's goddamn job to come up with something. "You're the shrink!" I snapped at her. "Stop blubbering and get involved in psychotherapy, or start praying. If we're rescued, we'll have to be good enough to sit a beast. Remember the donkey ride?"

Finally, Lorraine roused herself. After what seemed like a lot of thought, she said, "Role-playing. Much of what we are is what we believe." While I waited for her to think of a hero to emulate, I decided to do Lua, actually making a few attempts at walking proud and tall, but raising my chin so far off the ground made me dizzy. I asked her if she couldn't come up with something easier, like self-hypnosis or meditation. She just sat there in the dirt, her bald head draped between her legs, which brought up my anger again. "It was your goddamn idea, Lorraine! Now we're going to role-play. Let's see, you play Queen . . . Victoria. Wasn't she the bald-headed queen? Or how about Queen Elizabeth . . . the First, I think, the Virgin Queen? These parts were made for you."

That riled her. She growled like a cat. "Kelly, you are insolent to the end!"

I laughed and exclaimed, "A determined, bald-headed, virgin queen! It's your part!"

Like a queen, she stated, "Well, for your edification, I am not a virgin."

"I'm glad to hear that."

"I had Gil."

I waited, finally asking, "Only Gil?"

"Yes, I was busy, my hands full with Kali, and then it was too late."

"Too late?"

"I think it is safe to say that I am past the age of pursuing a relationship, of being courted."

"Jesus, who put the cap on that one? Is that your idea or the queen's? You're speaking like one. Are we into the role-playing?"

Quickly, she made me the subject, snapping, "I am certain that you have all the men you want."

"All I want, yes."

"I take it you mean you do not want many. Do you have any?"

"Once in a while I find one not attached to anything."

"Are they handsome—blonde, dark?

"Facades are deceiving, Doc, you know that. Take me, for instance. I look like this wholesome, homespun, redheaded country girl, but in reality I'm Sir Richard in drag."

She finally laughed, so I had to laugh also. She said, "Redheaded is the only description applicable, but you are heterosexual, are you not?"

"I think so." We were both laughing at once, choking, breathless, two dying witches.

Thirsty, we waddled off to the lake clutching each other and the empty glucose bottle. Walking was much easier without the wind, and I liked the freedom of not wearing pants. While I filled the bottle, Lorraine tossed rocks all around me, which I wasn't at all sure repelled crocodiles. Swilling like pubsters, we drank until we gagged, proud of our pluck. Our pathetic condition at some point became humorous, at least I think that was why we continued finding things to cackle about. Sipping at the glucose, we felt drunk, heads swimming, knees jelly. We collapsed early.

Just before dawn, I began waking, easing into reality, taking in courage through wispy images of hope. The sun blasted up at the same moment Lorraine's grating voice began accompanying the wind with its morning's tuning. She was quietly singing, between the keys, a kind of sea ditty. I supposed she needed something to prevent yesterday morning's breathing problem, but I was surprised she had the strength. Waiting politely for her to finish, hoping she wouldn't begin another, I asked her if she was feeling better. She gave me a half-cocky look and said, "I have to be." I certainly needed that to be true. We agreed that the pallets Lua had made helped us sleep better, and the diarrhea pills had helped. It seemed that I was stronger, too, although it may have simply been wishful.

We had our few bites of fish, which Lorraine, role-playing, insisted was eggs benedict. In our established walking positions, Lorraine's arm around my waist, mine over her shoulder, we traipsed toward the lake for water. Our faces turned from the wind, we were nearly to the lake before we saw it. A crocodile! Staggering, gasping, we stumbled backward, falling down, crawling back up to the hut.

Basking at the water's edge, the croc didn't move. We watched from just inside the hut entrance, thirsty. It was out there, all fifteen feet of it, waiting. We didn't discuss it, not a word, just watched and waited. It was several hours before it slithered into the water, into our bath place and out of sight. A few minutes later, I pushed myself back to the lake with the glucose jar. Without benefit of Lorraine supporting me, I cussed the goddamn crocodiles all the way there and back. When I handed her the jar of water, she just said, "Champagne, how lovely. It will go wonderfully with our brunch of Quiche Lorraine and mangoes." We were either better, or going insane.

The day blew on. We slept a lot. At some point, Lorraine took off her pants. Then she shed her shirt. "Lorraine!" I exclaimed. "You've pulled a stripe off your face. You've started to peel." I looked at it closely, a confetti-sized pink stripe from below her eye to her chin. "It looks healthy," I reported, "pink and clean."

She shrugged, more concerned about her sunburned chest, which she could see. It was also peeling, a colorful contrast to her frail legs, pasty white above the knees. She picked at her chest and talked about Lua for a few minutes, in awe of her bravado, wondering where she was. Worrying about Lua brought up Kiuka's fate, which caused Lorraine to become fidgety. But she turned it around. She had a game she wanted us to play, which sounded like one of those shrink games that aim to expose one's true Freudian nature. Without much effort, I diverted her, asking her how long Kali and Roger had been an item.

"After Kali received her doctorate, they were married." She beamed.

"Married! Roger and Kali married?"

"Yes, married, and are to this day."

"No fooling!"

"Oh, Kelly, I wish you could have seen how happy she was, how very beautiful!" She flopped on to her side and closed her eyes. "The wedding was small. Roger did not want a production; in fact, he did not tell his family for six months." Pausing, either to rest or remember, she lay there for a few moments. Finally, she went on, speaking slowly, her eyes still closed. "When they returned from their honeymoon, they were, well, as they had been when they first arrived from Kenya in dirty blankets, wild children without boundaries, the envy of everyone who saw them." After a reminiscent groan, she added, "Particularly me."

"Does Roger look like his father?"

"Yes. Gil was more handsome and much more flamboyant, but yes, there is a strong resemblance. But Kali, so free and beautiful." Another mournful, tired groan. "The way I wished I could have been, if I had not lost Gil." She stopped there, her eyes still closed, stuck in regret.

Finally, I said, "Okay, go on. I know that's not the end."

"They moved to France!" she blurted, opening her eyes, happy to be unstuck. "Roger's family wanted him in Kenya, and indeed he did go there occasionally, but he was never away from Kali for long."

"And then?" I was impatient for the end.

"It was Gil's birthday, the annual memorial celebration." Rolling onto her back, she stared up at the hut's ceiling. "At the last minute, I could not go to Paris. They called me during the festivities, exuberant as they always were at this time."

"Except?" I hurried her.

"Except, the next day Kali was back with me. She never saw Roger again."

"Just like that? Jesus! What happened?"

"She decided to do cultural research, here, with her own people. She was well aware of her limitations, organizational skills, and asked me to help her, be her partner."

"Lorraine! Why did Kali come back? What happened in Paris?"

Struggling onto an elbow, she ranted in a whisper, "What happened in Paris was the result of Roger's inheriting his mother's genes!"

"You're the expert, Lorraine." She was coughing, and I knew she wasn't going to tell me what happened in Paris. I gave her back a pat, adding, "And Roger sure as hell has never been a prince in my book." After she had her coughing under control, I said, "But you still haven't told me how she was able to play 'real doctor' over here with the natives."

"She went to nursing school, while I put together the program, completely. All she had to do was fill in the blanks."

"She went to nursing school? Well then, she had some qualifications for practicing medicine in Turkanaland."

"A nurse in this place God abandoned is far superior to what they have without a nurse."

I thought about those two little boys who probably would have died, bled to death, or maybe just lost their legs. And Kali was undoubtedly giving penicillin to girls whose circumcisions had become infected. She was Mother Teresa in the guise of a witch, and all the while she was filling in Lorraine's blanks, attempting to answer questions that would help determine why Turkana remain Turkana. "Jesus, Lorraine, you know, I thought *my* work was audacious!"

"Audacious, yes, and a terrible mistake!" She didn't say anything for a minute while her eyes clouded and she wrapped her arms around her knees. "Actually, Kelly, to be quite honest, the reason I came here was not to bring supplies. My intentions were to convince her to give it up." She stopped long enough to bite her lip and look about nervously. "If I had only been here sooner! If my bloody sister had . . ."

"It probably wouldn't have made a difference." I gave her a consoling smile. I thought about it a few moments, this incredible scenario. "So how did she get all that medicine in here?"

"Roger and I, between the two of us . . . that's Roger's business, importing and exporting things all over the world." She flung a slack hand. "He was agreeable—not pleased, but agreeable, as long as he did not have to see Kali." She looked at me, her wet eyes flashing anger.

"So Roger was a part of all this? He sure didn't appear to be, particularly in Lodwar."

"You can only imagine how painful Lodwar is for him, if indeed he feels pain," she sneered, her voice beginning to break. "I talked to him about Kiuka and Lua, Kali's arrangement with them, put it in a letter as well, so there would be no misunderstandings!" Tears were welling and spilling now. "After all, he is her husband!" She was sobbing. I wished I hadn't insisted she finish the story. I put my hand around her shoulder. She looked up at me pathetically and wailed. "All of those records lost, nothing to testify to her work, and she worked so very, very hard, just to come back here and die. And, dear God, how did she die?" She was bawling out loud, her back pulsing away the last of her energy. I squeezed her and tried to think of something consoling, but she quieted down and was asleep within moments. I sat looking at her, this frail woman with the ghastly head, wondering what would become of her if she did make it back to London. And what was she going to look like when the crust peeled from her face? I fell asleep looking at her round, brown head.

Voices woke me, Turkana voices! Men jabbering, several at a time! I couldn't make out a word over the wind; they were not very close. Lorraine was sleeping soundly. I touched her shoulder and she bolted to a sitting position. She heard them immediately. We didn't say anything, just crawled through the tunnel in our underwear and peered carefully around the corner at the entrance. There they were: six men, maybe seven, in two canoes about seventy-five yards offshore. Several of the men were standing, their poles in the water staying the canoes against the wind. All of them had their hands up, shielding their eyes from the sun as they talked noisily. As best I could tell, there was a good deal of speculation going on as to why there was one very good hut on an otherwise vacant beach. Since they were looking directly into the sun, I was sure they hadn't seen us, and I wasn't at all sure they should.

"What do they want?" Lorraine whispered.

"Goddamned if I know. My guess is they're trying to decide whether to investigate. If the hut is abandoned, they might want the sticks and reeds, or maybe they're our old neighbors, checking on us."

Lorraine made an adamant point. "The hut is definitely not abandoned!"

"They may be a clan looking for a new encampment or crocodiles to kill."

"Or more ostrich feathers and notches on their chests!" Lorraine was scared.

"The big question is, will they help us, can they help us? They could fit us into their canoes, maybe take us to a place farther south where the track meets the lake." The men with the poles were moving the canoes closer to shore. Lorraine began squeaking. I barked at her, "You absolutely must remain calm! How do you feel about being rescued?"

"Look at those . . . people! They are completely nude, and I cannot believe they would take us anywhere, even if we offered them our fish."

"We may not have a choice. If they decide to come up here, we can't do much to stop them."

"You know they will take our fish! They may kill us, and I am certain they do not have a word for rescue, as applicable to whites!"

"Jesus, Lorraine, how quickly you forget how we were last rescued."

"They thought that they were rescuing witchdoctors, and they did not know until after the fact that we were white." Once again, the canoes were being poled closer to the shore. Lorraine had hold of my arm, whimpering, "Kelly, do something!"

"That's what you were saying the night on the truck, when I set the hyenas on fire, and then you. I'm fresh out of bombs and ideas. Do you have any?" She just squeaked. Two of the men were in the water now, about knee deep, guiding the canoes toward the bank. It was apparent that they were going to solve the mystery of the hut. The closer they came, the more I didn't like their looks or the feel of the situation. Lorraine was right; we needed to do something. They were parking their canoes. They were definitely coming ashore. Almost any action now would not lessen our chances of survival. "Okay, Lorraine, we're going to stand in front of our hut and sing. We're going to sing 'Jingle Bells.' When I count to three . . ."

"Kelly, we are not dressed!"

"All the better! You know the words. On three, we will jump out, begin singing as loudly as possible with our arms and legs spread wide, like the witchdoctor did the other day. Got it?" She swallowed hard, her eyes glazed and fixed, her body paralyzed. The men were leaving the canoes and starting toward us. "Lorraine!" I shouted over the wind, giving her crusted face a light slap. "Lorraine! You are going to sing for your life! On three! One, two, three!"

We bobbled out of the hut looking at each other like readying cheerleaders, spreading our legs and arms. The approaching figures stopped. I blasted out the words to "Jingle Bells," Lorraine's voice in there somewhere. They stood staring at us, solid black figures, huge penises hanging, until we got to "a one-horse open sleigh." Then, without any expression of alarm, they stepped backward to the shore, bent over their canoes, bare balls gleaming, and pushed off. Within seconds, they were poling away. When they were out of sight, we collapsed onto our knees, the wind whistling through our underwear.

The episode weakened us and left us feeling vulnerable. They went away because they couldn't explain us—we might be supernatural, demons or devils—but we didn't know what they wanted. The only thing we knew for sure was that we were again sitting ducks, just as we'd been at the truck. I told Lorraine we had to move.

It was an hour past dark when we settled into our new place up near the edge of the lava. If the men came looking for us and found an empty hut, maybe they wouldn't scout the area. We put down a layer of reeds scavenged from the floor of the hut and placed our pallets on top. The fish went between, at our heads—fish pillows. Lorraine said, "We are sleeping with our heads in our plates." She'd stuffed all the pills in her pockets and set the glucose jars in a rock crevice beside us. Our move out of the hut for the night was a questionable one. Physically and emotionally, it had taken its toll. There wasn't much left of us.

From our vantage point, the moon not up yet, we could see the hut, but only as a light patch on the brown dirt. We were virtually invisible; we'd checked it. From the hut, I was unable to see Lorraine settled against the dark lava edge, even though I knew where to look. From our pallets, the lake was visible as a solid dark expanse, a black hole. We were sitting at the edge of a black hole in the universe, and it felt believable. I was thinking that I'd been reading too much Carl

Sagan, when Lorraine whispered, "Perhaps the world really is flat, and here we are at the edge."

"It feels that way, but I'm sure as hell not ready to jump." She didn't respond. "You're not either, are you, Doc?"

"Jumping does not feel like an option; rather, I feel that I am slipping over the edge, without the strength to prevent it from happening. It is a feeling very similar to a dream I often have. Kali is falling, off the world, or a bridge or mountain, and I am hanging on to her, but my strength is not sufficient and . . ." She didn't go on.

We agreed to take turns sleeping, Lorraine first, but she tossed and rolled and made noises like a kid goat. I finally told her to take the first watch, but she fidgeted around, her teeth chattering like castanets. Provoked, I ranted, "Jesus Christ, are you that scared?"

"I am simply terrified!" she whispered. "And I keep thinking of Lua out there, somewhere, all alone."

"I think we're relatively safe here. Try to relax. If they come back, we'll do 'Frosty the Snowman' in two-part harmony." She didn't respond, and the castanets continued. I took her hand. She was trembling. "Lorraine, talk to me; tell me why you're so scared."

Waving an arm, she whispered, "Because we are out here, uncovered, exposed!"

"Where no one would suspect we would be. Now get a grip, woman!" I groped for the glucose and handed it to her. After a couple of pulls, she quieted down, and we sat quietly watching the hut. I thought about her story. I'd heard all the installments. Kali had been her world for over twenty years. The love of her life, Gil Birla, had given her this gift of personal responsibility, a daughter really, and a research project. Now it was over. I remembered how concerned she'd been on the truck that I know the story, that I pass it on. I wondered how long until our story was also finished and who would pass it on. Maybe both stories were going to die right here, slip over into the black hole. In a few minutes, we were both asleep.

We bolted at the same time, sat straight up, and looked at each other. "What was that?" Lorraine whispered. I put my finger to my lips, shushing her. It was a strange sound. We stretched our necks and squinted our eyes toward the hut. The moon was up and there was more light, but there was no movement that we could see. It was dead quiet; still, we had heard something. We hadn't been sleeping long, maybe an hour, possibly two. Lorraine started to say something, but I shook my head and touched my lips again. Her teeth began their chattering.

There it was again! I knew that sound. What was that sound? Lorraine grabbed my arm and we heard it again. "Camels!" I whispered. "Camels. Don't move!" I couldn't see anything, but several more times we heard the sounds of protesting, grumbling camels, as if they were directly in front of us. Then it was quiet. They had apparently gone on by. We waited, keeping our eyes glued on the light patch made by the hut, but there was nothing. Finally, I relaxed and whispered to Lorraine that it had to have been a caravan passing by. She was pointing, her hand over her mouth. There was a shadow in front of the hut, a single shadow of a person, and then it disappeared.

We huddled there, hanging on to each other, Lorraine's teeth working overtime. Several times she wanted to say something, but I kept shushing her; we couldn't risk being spotted. There was no sound, no more movement that we could see. I played scenarios of various possibilities and decided our hut was being used for the night. Camels make the most complaints when they're getting up or getting down. The camels had probably been put to bed and whoever was in our hut was sleeping. Who and how many were the questions.

I couldn't ignore Lorraine anymore. I put my ear to her mouth. She whispered, "Could it possibly be Goa?"

"Goa?" I said, nearly aloud. Jesus, could it be Goa? We looked at each other, eyes wide enough to see the whites, hoping upon hope without speaking. Lorraine's teeth kept up the chatter as I groped around my weak brain. How the hell would we know if it was Goa? We could wake him up and ask him, maybe be accosted by a half-dozen warriors.

Lorraine had her mouth to my ear again. "If it is Goa, perhaps he found Kali! She could be with him!" I shrugged, supposing it was possible. She whispered again, "Do we know what Goa looks like?" I shook my head, remembering only something about a beard. She still had her mouth in my ear. "Do we know what his camels look like?"

I shook my head again. Camels in this country all looked the same to me: brown, skinny, and tired. But there was something about Goa's camels that Lua had been giggling about. When I'd asked her if anyone saw Goa leave, she'd said that many people saw him leave with his two camels and they were empty, nothing on them except . . .

What had she said? Some way they looked, something they wore maybe, or maybe they were a strange color. Jesus, I didn't know, except that Lua had giggled as though she knew what they were talking about. If I were to creep down there and look, perhaps I could see what she meant, what was different about them. But that was risky. The camels might grumble and awake those in the hut. If we waited until morning, we would be in broad daylight. And whoever it was, maybe Goa and Kali, might leave before daylight.

There were a few big rocks around the encampment, some fairly close to the hut. If the camels woke whoever was in the hut, I could hide there until they were quiet again. I decided it was worth a try. I put my mouth to Lorraine's ear and told her to wait there until I came back. You would have thought I'd told her I was never coming back. She became hysterical. "No, no, you cannot leave me here!" I managed to calm her down and tell her what I was going to do and that two people would make it twice as difficult to pull off. She put her head in her hands and began to weep. I rubbed dirt over my face. Giving her a pat, I crept away.

My heart might have been in my throat if I'd been strong enough for adrenaline. I crept, dragging my protesting body. It seemed to take forever. Finally, I crawled behind the rock closest to the hut. I could see the camels from there, but vaguely. It looked like there were two. I needed to be closer. On my belly like a snake, I moved nearer and nearer the camels. There were definitely two, but there was nothing on them. All of their harness was in a pile next to the hut and impossible to decipher. I wiggled closer. The camels appeared to be the usual brown and skinny. I lay there without a clue, until one of the camels groaned. It startled me so that I raised up on my hands and knees and began crawling back to the rock. The camels obviously saw me and began their protest. Peering out from my hiding place, I saw someone come out of the hut. He carried a long stick and had on a cape that draped to his knees. He spoke quietly to the camels in Turkana, then walked around looking about the area. This man was wearing pants, definitely not a warrior.

An impulse came over me. I got to my feet, dizzy, steadied myself, and then walked toward him. Timidly, I called out, "Goa!" He stood very still, watching me approach. Again I called, "Goa!"

He answered, "Kali?"

I caught my breath and yelled at Lorraine. In a moment she was there, hysterical, asking about Kali. Goa knew our names, which could only mean that he had seen Lua. When I asked him about Kali, he just shook his head and jabbered at me. It was difficult to decipher his features in the dark, which made it even more difficult to understand him. He was adamant about something, pointing at the camels, pointing his stick to the south. I tried to get him to slow down, even sit down, but he was only interested in making me understand something urgent. After a few stabs, I guessed. He wanted us to go—now! Relieved that I understood, he began readying the camels. Lorraine was beside herself. I wasn't exactly calm. What was the rush? Had he found Kali? Had something happened to Lua?

We went to our pallets to get the fish and polish off the glucose. It took a while, moving as we did, and Goa jabbered loudly the whole time. He filled his pockets with the fish, crammed as much as he could in his mouth, and then motioned impatiently for us to climb aboard. Within thirty minutes of meeting Goa, we were on our way out of the encampment. We were headed south. Lorraine and I watched behind us until the hut was a light spot fading out of our lives. She said, "Kelly, if I live through this, if I live to be a hundred, I will not forget that place, no matter how hard I try."

Lorraine was holding on to me so tight that if I hadn't been in so much pain, I could have slept without falling off. Goa stopped every couple of hours or so and made the camels get down. We would get off, eat a few bites of fish, and drink from the lake. Goa ate as though he were starved, and he probably was. I continued trying to question him, prompted by Lorraine's glimmer of hope that perhaps he'd found Kali and she and Lua had gone back to Lodwar. But Goa couldn't understand me. I don't think he wanted to understand me, and my energy to make him do so was waning. He was on a mission in a hurry. All he could do was shake his head. I hoped he was following Lua's instructions to come and rescue us. She knew we couldn't travel during the day, so perhaps he was anxious to travel as far as possible that night. Lorraine and I tried talking about it, speculating, but it was difficult to maintain a thought in our grave state of body and mind.

The sun and wind came suddenly and straight out of hell. Goa stopped and took a ragged sheet with faded purple flowers out of his saddlebag. He brought his camel round and handed it to us. His beard, salt and pepper, covered most of his face, and his eyes, only slits, were sheltered by folds of dark skin. He indicated that we needed to put the sheet over us, and under us to keep it from blowing away. We did, and once again we were in motion.

There were holes in the sheet, and I used one of them to keep track of where we were, which always looked the same: the lake on our left and black lava as far as I could see on our right. The heat was excruciating, and the wind required us to hunker and hang on, but our strength was nearly gone. Occasionally, I could feel Lorraine begin to lose her grip and slip. I gave her pep talks, called her Victoria the Determined, told her not much farther, but I was barely hanging on myself, and I had no idea what to expect, or when.

It happened as suddenly as the wind. I looked out the hole, and not more than a hundred yards away there was a vehicle. We were on the track that came from Lokitaung to the lake and continued to Ferguson's Gulf. "Holy Jesus, Lorraine, look!" Pulling the sheet away, bracing against the blast, I croaked, "Do you see what I see?"

"Dear God, Kelly! Is it true? Is it really true? Is that a vehicle?"

"Yep! It's a vehicle and it's waiting for us!"

A man in a camouflaged uniform, holding his hat against the wind with one hand and carrying a white plastic sack in the other, got out of the Rover and came toward us, speaking in Swahili. He had come from Lokitaung and was to take us back there by order of the government of Kenya. We sure didn't argue. Goa put the camels down, and exuberantly, albeit awkwardly, we unloaded what remained of our bony bodies. Lorraine tried to give Goa a clumsy hug, which he didn't understand or appreciate. She was obviously disoriented, frantic for me to ask questions in Swahili of the uniform, but unable to string an English sentence together herself. I sure as hell wasn't lucid, but I did manage to speak to him briefly. From his expression, it appeared he was fearful that we would die before he completed his mission to bring us in. Impatient and brief, he told me that a call came from headquarters in Lodwar to pick up women at this spot. As an after-thought, he held up the plastic sack he was clutching. He said that he had been instructed to give it to a black woman named Kali. Without another word, he passed the sack to Goa and hurried us to the Rover.

Confused, barely able to stand, Lorraine hadn't heard Kali's name, and I thought it just as well. The uniform helped her into the back-seat, and I made a last, feeble attempt to ask Goa about Lua, but he wasn't going to talk to me. Standing alongside his camel, peering sus-piciously into the sack, he gingerly pulled out a couple of narrow boxes with fancy wrapping. Curious, watching him fondle the boxes, I noticed for the first time what was different about his camel, why Lua had giggled. The reins were twisted with red and gold Christmas garland.

The ride to Lokitaung was probably rougher than the camel ride, but it was only happening in a dream. When I woke, we were parked, and several people were leaning in, gawking and talking. Lorraine and I tried to unfold ourselves; it wasn't graceful. I was on the ground on my hands and knees when I saw one man take Lorraine by the ankles and another by her shoulders. I managed to get vertical and shoo them off. Taking Lorraine's arm, calling her Victoria the Determined, I told her to get up, we had marching to do. We hung on to each other in our way, and a uniform seemed to be guiding us. As we neared the door to a building, a man rushed out at us and stopped abruptly. I looked in his face and saw terror. Lorraine looked in his face and said, "Roger?"

He stood there, tall and blank, his question squeezed tight and ter-rified, "Kali . . . she, she did not . . . ?" That was all he said before he walked away, barking instructions in Swahili. The uniform turned us away from the building and marched us slowly to an airplane.

The Ritual

I don't remember the flight to Nairobi. I do vaguely remember Roger checking us into the hospital. The next few days were a blur. I slept round the clock, this time taking glucose through the veins. My X rays showed two broken ribs and a fractured skull, nothing to be done with either. The mask I wore was a sickening shade of blue, green, and yellow. The nurses gave me periodic updates on Lorraine, always the same. She was sleeping.

When I was feeling strong enough to face facts, I called Roger. Emotionless, mechanically, he filled in the blanks like a wireless tapping out information. Our conversation was short. When it was over, I curled myself in a ball and wept. It was time.

The next day I'd had all the food, glucose, and sleep I could hold. The nurse unplugged me and told me that Lorraine was actually awake. I went looking for her. There she was, a zebra, her face in stripes. I told her so and she laughed, a genuine, rested sort of laugh that I'd never heard from her. She appeared to have been awake for about five minutes. Her bright eyes twinkled, glad to see me. It was clear that she hadn't spoken with Roger.

"Well? What do they say?" I asked her. "What are you going to look like unstriped?"

"A doctor just woke me a few minutes ago." She reached for a hand mirror on the bed tray. "Apparently I have slept for three days straight. I have only just seen my face . . . and this room." She flung a hand at the room and held the mirror in front of her for a quick look. "Are you ready for this, Kelly?" She was now looking at me seriously. There was a knot in my stomach. I think I shrugged before she grinned coyly and announced, "You may have given me a face-lift!"

"No, are you kidding?"

"No, not at all! That is indeed what the Doctor said, the equivalent of a face-lift. Think of it! At sixty-two, I may look twenty-two. However, I may or may not be bald. As yet, there is not a sign of hair, but I maintain great hopes that it will come in blonde." She laughed easily, pleased with her humor.

"Jesus, Lorraine, I hope not! Your hair was beautiful. But I've sort of gotten used to this bald look. Women do shave their heads, you know. I did, when I was sixteen, but I was protesting something, probably my own hair. I was big on protests at sixteen."

"All right, Kelly, that is all the good-morning small talk I can do," she announced abruptly, swinging her feet to the edge of the bed. "I am awake now." She straightened her shoulders as though to verify that she was, and then asked, "Has there been any word yet? Has anyone talked with Goa to find out if he found Kali? What do we know of Lua?" She rattled off the questions, and I crawled up on the bed beside her. She looked at me and winced, dreading what was next. "You have heard," she said warily. "I can see that you have heard." She screwed up her face, making her stripes crooked.

"Yes, I called Roger yesterday. Believe it or not, he went back to Lodwar to question Lua and Goa. Lua's fine, Goa too."

"Tell me, Kelly!"

"Kali and Goa were robbed by Ngorokos, near where Kali's bag was found. It was daylight, and very near an encampment, probably why the thieves didn't kill them. But they did take one of their three camels, the pack camel, and of course, all their belongings, food and water, too." Lorraine was biting her lip and probably already had it figured out, but I went on. "After they were robbed of everything, they had to go to the lake for water. They arrived at the fish camp on their two remaining camels, at night, much as Lua did. No one really knew how many camels or how much stuff they came with because it was dark, and during the day Goa had the camels off searching for grass.

And of course, to add to the confusion on the night they arrived, there were those two boys in critical condition. As we know, Kali spent the remainder of the night sewing them up. She was there the next day, while they built her hut, and the day after that she disappeared. Lua assumed that Kali left the encampment on one of the camels, still possessing all their belongings less the magic bag, because the people told her they saw Goa leave several days later on two empty camels."

Lorraine put her feet up on the bed and lay back on the pillow. Hands covering her face, she murmured, "I cannot bear to think of it! Our worst possible suspicions."

"Then don't think of it now. You'll have plenty of time to grieve." I removed one of her hands and peeked at her. "The rest of the story is . . . Lua ran into Goa on the track and sent him to get us; then she hitched a ride to Ferguson's Gulf and talked someone there into wiring the authorities at Lodwar. Lodwar wired Lokitaung, telling them where to meet us."

"What an incredible woman," Lorraine said softly, staring up at the ceiling glassy-eyed. "She walked off that night, that incredibly dark night, as though she were taking a walk in the park. And she managed to get safely to Ferguson's Gulf and have us rescued."

"Yep! She did it. She saved our asses twice!" We thought about it a minute, until I felt compelled to say, "And of course our dear son of Jezebel had been communicating with Lokitaung. I'm sure that when he found out Goa was alive, he assumed that Kali was too and zipped up there. He's a confused man." Lorraine's eyes welled, and she bit her lip. "I'm sorry, Lorraine. I didn't need to say that."

Her voice cracked as she said, "He sent those boxes of dried apricots for Kali. He thought . . . hoped she was with Goa."

"Those boxes the soldier gave Goa were dried apricots?"

"Yes, Kali's favorite treat." She sniffled, and I handed her a tissue. She blew her nose. "I assume that soldier thought Goa deserved them. Roger has most certainly done some incredibly deep thinking, much too late." She lay there dabbing at her eyes, while I wondered what could possibly have separated two people who had loved each other so completely for so many years. I was sure Lorraine knew.

She sat up suddenly, gallantly, asking, "So then, I assume that you and Roger have reached an understanding with the payment of your services?"

"I was paid in advance, Lorraine, always. In my business, if one isn't paid in advance, one may not be paid. I don't always bring good news. But I did talk to him about a bonus."

"Good, you are entitled to one," she said convincingly. "You could never have anticipated the grief that you were put through."

"A bonus for Lua," I said. "Our savior!"

"Lua! Of course! What a wonderful idea." She looked mischievous. "The magic she put around the truck is sufficient reason for a bonus."

"We're going to find out! I made it a condition of the bonus, our witchdoctor ritual. Roger is flying her here to Nairobi in three days."

"Of course, how absolutely marvelous! Dear God, I will bet a year of biscuits that he was extremely disgruntled at your request."

"As I've never seen Roger happy, I wouldn't know the difference."

It was mid-afternoon, and Lorraine and I were waiting at the Norfolk patio bar for Lua to arrive. Roger had promised to deliver her himself. Lua had never been out of Turkanaland. Before she went to Lodwar for medical help, where she met Kali, she lived in a tribal encampment and had never seen a white person. I wasn't at all certain we were doing the right thing by Lua, but if she was going to be a witchdoctor, she needed to see magic. We had a deluxe suite with three bedrooms waiting for her, and Lorraine had put together a ritual. We bought her a flowing African print wardrobe that we deemed appropriate for a witchdoctor, accessorized with wicked-looking jewelry of hair and bone.

Lorraine was wearing an African print she'd bought for herself, and she was trying to feel good about it. "Tell me the God's truth, Kelly, how do I look?" She was standing beside the bar, posed, her round head, now a perfect peach, set atop hanging folds of bright color. "It is much more appropriate with my bald head, more so than a real dress, do you not agree?"

"Bald matches the costume perfectly," I stated, without reservation. "I can't believe it. You look better than you looked before I torched you!"

"It is absolutely true, is it not? One would truly believe that I had a face-lift. And feel, Kelly!" She put my fingers on her face. "Is it not wonderfully soft?" She pointed to her brows. "Those are painted on. There is still not a sign of a hair on my head." Throwing up her hands as though surrendering, she said, "My new look!" Then she plopped back on her bar stool and whispered, "Every hour I find it necessary to think of some way to cheer myself. I still cannot believe I have lost Kali."

I ordered another round of ice water with a splash of quinine and gin. "You're going to be fine, Vicki." She shot me a puzzled expression, barely mussing her peachy skin. "Short for Victoria," I laughed. "I feel we're on sufficiently intimate terms for me to address the Queen of Determination by a nickname."

She filled her chest, a sort of breathing exercise. "Yes, determination, but without Kali, without . . ."

"Doc, knock it off! I've seen who you are, in the absolute worst of conditions. I'm not going to spend a minute worrying about what's going to become of you." The bartender set our drinks down. "To the next chapter!" I said, picking up my glass, a tall clear, crystal concoction, which at that moment became the jar of glucose.

Lorraine saw it, too. Cautiously, carefully, she picked up her own jar with both hands and held it to the light. "Our very own magic, Kelly." We were both a bit choked up, standing there clutching our crystal jars, finally tipping them to one another, slowly as women do. We held each other's eyes, and I thought I saw our entire trip flash before us.

"Right!" she exclaimed, slapping the bar suddenly. "And you look so lovely in a dress, Kelly!"

"Nice try, Lorraine," I quipped, looking down at my calf-length dress sagging to the ankles. "And I don't think this green matches the green on my face worth a damn, either. You turned out a lot better than I did."

"You still have all that hair, Kelly, and the rest will heal. Do you think my hair will come back? You know, my hair was always my best feature."

"Damned if I know, Doc. What did they say at the hospital?"

"What you just said, more or less."

There she was! Lua getting out of Roger's Mercedes, boots first. She was wrapped in a dirty white cotton blanket, and her blue bag wagged between her legs where the blanket separated at her knees. Goddamn Roger. He could have done better than that. Lorraine and I rushed to meet her. She looked as though she might be in shock, her eyes round above her high cheekbones, her pretty mouth gaping.

With a snap of his fingers, Roger secured a drink for himself and had us moved to a table in the back. He looked much like my fuzzy recollection of him at Lokitaung, a dark head, heavy over a tall, bent body. Before he sat down, he announced, "Lua cannot sit here. She must be smuggled to her room, scrubbed, and clothed." His voice was flat, void of expression, as though referring to a stray cat rather than a heroine and an about-to-be witchdoctor.

"It wouldn't be necessary if you had dressed her as decency and respect dictate!" I barked, bracing myself for his caustic retort.

But there wasn't one. He sat down stiffly, looked around, and said quietly, "They will make her leave." There were a few moments of awkward silence before he told Lorraine and me that we looked better than we had in Lokitaung.

"The trip was unimaginable, Roger!" Lorraine blurted. "If not for this woman," she pointed to Lua, "and this woman, too," she gave me a nod, "we would surely have perished, without question!"

Again, reflex had me waiting for Roger's normal nasty comeback, but all he said was, "I told you not to go."

I felt a need to respond for her and snapped, "Obviously, she needed to go."

His dark eyes drooped, and he looked at me pitifully, as though I had said a dumb thing. Limply, he asked me, "Why?" then took a drink from his glass and glanced around the table, shaking his head as though he were drinking with idiots.

Challenged, I answered his *why*. "Because of her unconditional love for Kali."

He flinched, a direct hit into his wound. Closing his eyes, he reached for his handkerchief and wiped his mouth and face. He was broken, grieving, and lost. If he'd been wearing Lua's dirty blanket and smelled as she did, it couldn't have been more obvious. Ignoring me, he turned to Lorraine and began discussing Kali's estate, a chore he obviously loathed. I couldn't hear them over the noisy bar crowd. What I saw was the selfless woman who had taken in a young, wild boy out of Africa, the son of the Jezebel who had stolen her love.

I put my arm around Lua's shoulders and gave her a pat. She was still peering out from her blanket, wide-eyed with wonder. With Roger sitting next to her, it was easy to think about when he and Kali were sent to Lorraine wrapped in blankets, wild and innocent, inseparable, worshiping the memory of the man who brought them together. All those years of shunning mores, loving each other passionately, finally married, ecstatically happy. Lua sat there looking much like I was sure Kali looked at the end. Roger treated her as a heathen, himself crippled with hate, unable to love or laugh, as he'd been able to do only with Kali. Jesus, what happened? How could such a fire for life and love turn to dust? I scoffed at myself. Lives and loves turned to dust every day, everywhere. Theirs was just another story.

Lorraine and Roger continued talking quietly about the settling of Kali's estate. Lua still had her arms under the blanket and nothing to drink. I handed her my water glass with ice, and she looked at it suspiciously. After I told her what it was, she timidly took out a hand and held the glass just under her chin, staring into it much as Lorraine and I had done with the jar of glucose. In my broken Turkana, I asked her how she liked flying in an airplane. It was as though I'd put a quarter in her machine. Her face came instantly to life and she began jabbering and gesturing, attracting the attention of everyone in the bar. An exuberant wave of her arm brought the blanket down, exposing a shabby piece of cloth tied over just one breast, the other bare.

"Damn you, Roger!" I blasted. The floor manager was rushing to our table, followed by the bouncer. I barked at Lorraine to distract them. She jumped in their face. I whisked Lua away, slipping quickly through the lobby and to our suite.

Lua walked around, looking at everything as though it might come to life. She did some poses for the mirror, some with her clothes on and some with them off. I got her to bounce on the bed with me a few times, my ribs in protest. She drank orange juice from the minibar, suspiciously, wanting to know if it would make her different. Eyeing her bulging, blue bag, I was more than curious, but I would wait for Lorraine. It was imperative that she be there for the unveiling of Lua's magic in order for me to take delight in watching her eat crow.

It took some persuading, but I got Lua to the shower door. To get her in, I had to go with her. I shampooed her hair, which she didn't like much, complaining something about mussing her do. We scrubbed with soap, dropping it a dozen times, playing, giggling children.

Out of the shower, wet and shiny in the mirror, black and white, Lua and I looked at ourselves and each other, bursting out laughing at the same time. I dried her off with a fluffy towel, and she dried me. She was fascinated with the body lotion, how it disappeared when I rubbed it on her. She was certain it was magic and wanted to know if she could have it to use in her new position as witchdoctor. An easy request.

Unhappy with what I'd done to her hair, she sat naked in the middle of the bed and began working it over. I brought her a disposable razor and showed her how to use it. We added it to the list of witchdoctor tools. When she was through primping, I laid out her new clothes and told her to pick something. She touched and smelled each color, several times licking the fabric with her tongue, tasting it. She wanted me to put something on first, I supposed just to make sure it was safe. She pointed to a black and white zebra print. I pulled it over my head, a long tunic affair with loose flowing sleeves, like Lorraine's. It was very exciting to her, seeing me dressed like a zebra. Quickly, she put on the orange and red frock and paraded back and forth in front of the mirror. Then she wanted to change with me. She'd decided to be the zebra.

I gave her the beaded sandals we'd bought for her, and after she examined them thoroughly, she climbed onto the bed and tossed them one at a time onto the floor, studying carefully the way they landed, a Turkana way of making decisions. The sandals went back in the box. She put on her boots.

It was time for the accessories, the hair and bone and feathers. I brought out the big bag and set it on the dresser. As I pulled out each piece, untangling it from the rest and laying it separately on the bed, I watched Lua's demeanor change to dead serious. This was the big stuff, the difference between assistant and witchdoctor. The wicked-looking jewelry was premature. Lorraine was the guru. She had to do the donning and anointing. Laboriously, I explained that to Lua. She was delighted, glowing with anticipation. Her eyes fixed on the bed, she sat down in a chair to wait.

Lorraine came, looking as though she'd been to Kali's funeral. I sat her in a chair and mixed her a drink. After a few swallows and a few breaths, she began taking notice of Lua and me, cleaned and polished, in our new threads. She quickly brightened and had us parade around in front of her until she clapped her hands and joined in, wrapping an arm around each of us, turning us in a circle in front of the mirror. "Tell her how beautiful we all are, Kelly! Dear God! Look at us here, alive! Tell her what a wonderful witchdoctor she is going to make!" I tried. Lua beamed and pointed to the jewelry laid out on the bed.

Someone knocked at the door. I let the bellhop in, who was carrying a large, tattered box tied with assorted string. He announced that it was from Mr. Birla. Lua jumped up and began chattering. She'd brought the box from Lodwar. I paid off the bellhop and began rubbing my hands together, excited, sure it was the truck magic. But within a few minutes, Lua managed to make me understand that the truck magic was in her blue bag and this box contained something different. Kali had kept the box in the special place with the magic. Lua didn't understand what was in it, but now that she was going to be a witchdoctor, Lorraine and I could teach her. Digging into her blue bag, she produced the large brass key, reminding us that it was the key to Kali's special place and anything kept there was very important.

Lorraine seemed to have a hunch. She had it open within seconds and began to shriek. In it were the infamous research records! Lua thought Lorraine's reaction was caused by something supernatural in the box, and she climbed up on the dresser. Leafing through the files, Lorraine said, "They are dated to the time she left on her last trip." She plopped in a chair and chewed on her lip. "Only those she had with her on the pack camel were lost." Looking up suspiciously at Lua squatted on the dresser, she asked me, "Why did she not give me these when we were in Lodwar searching for them?"

I asked Lua. She understood immediately, and it was simple. At that time, she didn't know that we were witchdoctors. Kali had told her that only witchdoctors and assistant witchdoctors, she and Kiuka, could enter the secret place. Crawling off the dresser onto the bed, Lua went on to say that the secret place was empty now; that is why Lorraine came, to fill it up again. She looked at Lorraine demandingly and asked when it would be filled.

When I translated Lua's concerns, Lorraine said, "I have that arranged with Roger. He is maintaining Kali's hole in the wall for Lua. I will send her first-aid supplies and aspirin and vitamin supplements, perhaps some glucose." She chuckled and got up to give Lua a hand off of the bed. "The rest will have to come from this woman's obvious inner magic." She gave Lua a kiss on the forehead, saying, "Kali had it. She was genuinely a witchdoctor, and I am certain you are as well."

The ritual went on for over an hour. Lorraine was elated over recovering Kali's records and got us into a ceremony. She said that ritual was critical for all cultures, the imprint of what we stood for, the lasting memory that kept us true. "Like marriage rituals," I quipped. She scowled her peachy face and went right on with it, placing Lua on her knees, draping her in bone, feathers, and hair. In the end, we had to drink cola from the same glass, swirling it and passing it around as we'd done beside the poor mother's hut at Lake Turkana. Lua was, at long last, a full-fledged witchdoctor. It was time for me to see her magic in the blue cloth bag.

Sitting cross-legged in the center of the bed, the bag in her lap, Lua reminded us that Kali had taught her to use this magic and it probably wouldn't work for anyone else. She opened the drawstring and pulled out a brightly colored piece of cloth held together by a rubber band. Lorraine giggled, knowing how much I'd looked forward to this moment. Lua took the band off, her long, bony fingers unwrapping the precious contents. With both hands, she presented me with a brightly colored plastic cylinder. The bold labeling said, "For Hobbies and Crafts—Made in England." Glitter! It was gold glitter!

Lorraine had her hand over her mouth trying to contain herself. I said, "You knew, didn't you? You knew all along!"

"I sent it to Kali, a crate of it. Of course, I had no idea what she wanted it for until I saw Lua out there sprinkling it on the ground."

"You saw Lua do it? You knew the entire time that it was glitter around the truck, and you still tormented me about my bombs!" It was funny, but not enough to keep me from being incensed. "Well, now that your little joke is out of the glitter bag, I want to hear something appreciative about my bombs, please!" Lua was looking at one of us and then another, waiting for a response she understood. I held the cylinder of glitter over my head as though paying homage to her magic and presented it to her as she had to me. She was delighted and wrapped it back in its pouch. "I'm waiting, Lorraine! Let's hear how losing your hair was better than the alternatives!"

"Kelly," she began with her peach cocked. "Have you given thought to how a ring of glitter might have looked to them in the moonlight from their perspective at a distance?"

"Of course not!" I snapped. "I was only just this minute apprised of what you've known all along and refused to share with me!" I scratched my head. "But considering it now, even if they had been spooked by the glitter, when the moon set the glitter was gone, and my bombs saved our asses!"

"Good grief, Kelly!" Her tone was authoritative. "They most certainly had to have known that the glitter, the magic, was still there!"

"Jesus, Lorraine, you're the most obstinate woman I've ever encountered!"

"Victoria the Determined," she quipped, breaking into a riotous laugh.

We took Lua to dinner at one of the hotels with a buffet. It had to have been the most unbelievable event of Lua's life, the ultimate magic. Attracting every eye with her strange language and body movements, she jabbered a mile a minute; all of those colors, textures, and smells were food, food to be eaten as one eats fish. It was difficult for her to resist touching everything with her fingers, but we stood on each side of her with our forks, guiding her through the process of plate loading. At last we sat down in the back of the room with a pyramid of food in front of Lua that she had designed by color. Watching her eat it, using a fork for the first time, was comedic, but not pretty.

Lua was nearly asleep when we put her to bed. Even though she knew that our rooms adjoined hers, she wanted us to stay with her. This woman, fearless in the dark Turkana night, did not want to be left alone in a hotel room. Lorraine and I poured ourselves a brandy and sat in the overstuffed chairs watching her sleep.

"There is one for your research," I said. "Lua the invincible, out of bullets before we are. She can't take this perfect weather and good food. She's been cold since she arrived."

Lorraine didn't comment, lost in thought. After a few minutes, I asked her if she felt all right. Rousing herself, she said, "I am still in shock from my meeting with Roger. He is turning Kali's estate over to me." She shook her head in disbelief. "He said that as I have maintained responsibility for her all these years, it belongs to me. He said that Gil would want me to have it. Bloody hell, I almost cannot believe it!" She was still shaking her head. "It is quite large; you know Gil left her an incredible estate, and through investments I made for her, it has grown."

"That's great, Lorraine. And you had no idea he was . . ."

"No. Roger and I have not been on good terms since Kali left Paris, when their marriage ended."

"Well, Roger has a heart, after the fact."

"Perhaps. However, he knows full well where most of it will go."

"Where? Where will it go?" I winced at my impertinence.

A very long sigh. "It is unbelievably expensive, the cost of keeping Roger's mother in the very best institution, and of course Roger and Gill hated her so, they never contributed. Until now. I suppose this is Roger's way of finally doing so."

Was I hearing her right? "You take care of Jezebel?"

"I do not take care of her personally, but of course I do look after her and keep the bills paid."

"Jesus, Lorraine, are you a saint?"

"Goodness no. I have no choice. She is my sister. She has no one but me."

When I recovered, I topped off our brandy snifters. Lorraine held her glass for me while cocking her head sideways to look at Lua's face. "Lying there so peaceful, she looks as Kali looked a thousand nights, when I would go into her room, just to make certain that she was really there, that she was really mine to love." Stretching her neck for a breath, fighting tears, she sipped her brandy. "And many nights she was not there. She was with Roger. There was absolutely no way to keep them apart."

"What the hell happened to those two, Lorraine? After all those years, such passion! Then when they have it all together, it blows."

Squinting her bright eyes, she said, "I have told you nearly the whole story. I may as well tell you the rest." She sipped again and thought about how to say what she was about to say. "That last night in Paris, Gil's birthday celebration, the one I couldn't attend. They were celebrating with champagne, and Kali must have had too much—more than two glasses was too much for her—and certainly when they called me it sounded as though she may have had more." She looked at me and grimaced, as though she had second thoughts about telling me. But she continued. "I told Kali on more than one occasion that she could under no circumstances ever tell Roger." With her eyes closed, she made a quiet sigh. "But I suppose that night, Gil's birthday, remembering him, the way she loved him, the champagne, she either told Roger or perhaps he guessed, but he knew. And then it was all over." She lay her peachy head back on the chair as though that were the end.

I said, "Well, I could guess too, but why don't you tell me."

Lifting her face, her blue eyes set on me in order not to miss my reaction, she said, "Kali was Gil's lover, too." I had guessed, and Lorraine saw that I had. She went on. "Gil had lived those many years outside society, lonely. Kali was a beautiful young girl in a wild land without rules, and she worshiped him." She looked straight at me again and said, "Do you know, she never once saw anything wrong with loving Gil as she had, in fact it made her proud. If it had been up to her, she would have told the world."

We sat there another hour, drinking brandy and rehashing our adventure. At one point she said to me, a little tipsy, "Kelly, we have done this thing that I daresay no two women have done before us, white women anyway, and here we sit, the story closed, and I know nearly nothing about you. How could that be?"

"Oh, I think you know me."

She thought a moment. "Yes, I daresay I know who you are, what one can expect of you, but I know nothing of your life, your history."

"I told you. I'm an explorer. I've always been an explorer."

Even for an explorer, Africa on Africa's terms is sometimes too tough, if not physically, philosophically. After Turkana, I nearly hung it up. I knew there were no answers to the hard questions, but I asked them anyway. The plight of the Turkana, Kali, Lua, Kiuka, that young mother with the botched circumcision, lived on in my head. Finally, it took my grandmother. She read the story, she took me to Indian Hill, we howled, and then she said, "We all have our lot. You're responsible for exploration and writing it down. Now, get back in the ball game." And so I did. Lorraine and I remained fast friends, bonded by our experience. She continued her research, determined, but never returned to Africa. Her hair came back. I was with her when she died of cancer three years ago.

ACKNOWLEDGMENTS

Eric Swenson, you are the very best friend a writer could have. Your support is my confidence.

Judy Hart, you are always there with pom-poms in your briefcase singing, "Here comes life."

Karen Waymire, you shared your home, your children, your love, and your incredible spirit.

Mary Moton and Arla Smith, you were with me in the beginning, comrades of intention.

Ellen Levine, you are my beautiful, lucky star.

Mauro DiPreta, you say everything I need to hear, perfectly.